Play, Pain and Religion

Play, Pain and Religion

Creating Gestalt through Kink Encounter

Alison Robertson

SHEFFIELD UK   BRISTOL CT

Published by Equinox Publishing Ltd.

UK: Office 415, The Workstation, 15 Paternoster Row, Sheffield, South Yorkshire S1 2BX

USA: ISD, 70 Enterprise Drive, Bristol, CT 06010

www.equinoxpub.com

First published 2021

© Alison Robertson 2021

All rights reserved. No part of this publication may be reproduced or transmitted in any form or by any means, electronic or mechanical, including photocopying, recording or any information storage or retrieval system, without prior permission in writing from the publishers.

ISBN-13 978 1 80050 028 0 (hardback)
         978 1 80050 029 7 (paperback)
         978 1 80050 030 3 (ePDF)
         978 1 80050 111 9 (ePub)

British Library Cataloguing-in-Publication Data

A catalogue record for this book is available from the British Library.

Library of Congress Cataloging-in-Publication Data

Names: Robertson, Alison, author.
Title: Play, pain and religion : creating gestalt through kink encounter / Alison Robertson.
Description: Bristol, CT : Equinox Publishing, 2021. | Includes bibliographical references and index. | Summary: 'Play, Pain and Religion is the first consideration of the practices associated with BDSM (Bondage, Domination, Submission and Masochism) in the context of Religious Studies scholarship. The focus is an exploration of BDSM experience as it emerges from the complex interactions of kink activities and relationship' – Provided by publisher.
Identifiers: LCCN 2021006849 (print) | LCCN 2021006850 (ebook) | ISBN 9781800500280 (hardback) | ISBN 9781800500297 (paperback) | ISBN 9781800500303 (epdf) | ISBN 9781800501119 (epub)
Subjects: LCSH: Sex–Religious aspects. | Spirituality. | Sadomasochism. | Bondage (Sexual behavior) | Sexual dominance and submission.
Classification: LCC BL65.S4 R53 2021 (print) | LCC BL65.S4 (ebook) | DDC 205/.66–dc23
LC record available at https://lccn.loc.gov/2021006849
LC ebook record available at https://lccn.loc.gov/2021006850

Typeset by JS Typesetting Ltd, Porthcawl, Mid Glamorgan

*For my Master, who is the safe place from where I can explore
and to whom I can always return*

Contents

	List of figures	viii
1	Introduction: Processes of religioning	1
2	Setting the scene	14
3	What it is that we do: Experiential accounts of play	32
4	The play experience (1): Making play-spaces	40
5	The play experience (2): Inside play-spaces	60
6	Subcultural identity: Kink in context and in clothes	80
7	Kinky bodies	106
8	Exploring the edge	130
9	Kink ritualising	152
10	Conclusion: Gestalt kink, gestalt religion	179
	Appendix A: A kink glossary	187
	Appendix B: Research participants	190
	References	197
	Index	205

List of figures

1	A selection of BDSM toys	15
2	Implements for corporal punishment	19
3	Fetlife profile page, with list of roles	30
4	E-stim equipment	38
5	A selection of floggers	46
6	A spanking bench	54
7	A violet wand and attachments	58
8	Jewellery with a kink 'edge'	83
9	Story of O ring	83
10	Torture Garden dress code	86
11	Bondage equipment	95
12	Examples of household 'pervertables'	99
13	Collars	103
14	A violet wand powered up and in use on skin	109
15	Canes, crops and birches	118

1

Introduction

Processes of religioning

> All [religions] claimed to be the one true way. For me they were not. Do not get me wrong, my way is not your way, and that is the way of it. How one searches for the reason they exist, the way that allows them to come close or to touch the divine is individual ... The world of, as some call it, kink, is my world. I do not consider it kink, nor off centre. I consider it the basis of the human condition that we have forgotten.
> (Master Dennis, 2010, pp. 30–31)

> I never aspired to be a 'Dominatrix' per se, but I knew from the dawn of my BDSM explorations that this calling was bigger, deeper and more powerful than any mainstream view could represent it.
> (Minax, 2010, p. 226)

As a newly qualified teacher of religious studies, the first Scheme of Work I wrote was for introducing year 7 to the study of religion at key stage 3.[1] This was to be via the topic *Religion: What and Why?* My overall key stage 3 curriculum changed over the years, but that topic always remained in place. During those lessons the students and I considered the important and complex questions of what religion might be, and why it matters sufficiently in the contemporary world to deserve study. We identified common themes across the boundaries of institutional religion, pondered how 'the religious' and 'the everyday' intersect and interact, and reflected on whether there is any single thing all religion shares.

---

1. Key stage 3 is years 7–9, pupils aged 11–14.

At much the same time a prospective partner ruled themselves out of my long-term future by declaring themselves unwilling to trespass, even temporarily and with my enthusiastic consent, upon my status and bodily integrity. This refusal (to which they were fully entitled) was loaded with judgements about the mental health of people interested in BDSM – which they understood as practices involving bondage, domination, sadism and masochism (the most common expansion of the abbreviation). In their judgement of such practices equality and the avoidance of pain were presented as not only desirable, but as absolute moral goods, with self-evident meaning and forms of expression that it would be insanity to question. I had never encountered such an absolute rejection of kink before. My own sanity did not seem to me to be in doubt, but my desire to explore pain, power and helplessness were undeniable and previous positive experiences suggested I was not unique in this. I began to ask, for the first time, why people want to play with pain and power, and why that desire felt sufficiently important that to reject *it* constituted rejecting *me*.

These two sets of questions seemed wholly separate at the time, but both stayed with me. My thoughts on each unfolded gradually over the years: through discussion in the classroom, on social networks, with friends and colleagues; through personal experiences and encounters with different forms and expressions of pain, of kink, and of religion; through academic study and a diversity of reading material. I came at last to think of these questions as being connected, as each in fact containing at least part of the answers to the other. In this book I explore that connection and offer my response to those initial questions based on my original research. The principal aim of that research was to explore BDSM experience, as it emerges from the complex interactions of activities and relationships which contribute to the making of each BDSM scene. This exploration is made in relation to a broad concept of religion as lived and living: a process that is inseparable from the material situation in which it arises and/or to which it responds, and which is intimately concerned with relationship, embodied practice, kinaesthetic experience and the personal narratives used to make sense of these. In placing BDSM experiences within the sphere of the religious my intention is to highlight the potential of these as contributors to such personal narratives, rather than to make a claim that all BDSM activity is religious in nature. I also seek to emphasise the value and significance given to BDSM practice and identity by practitioners.

Religioning

Instead of seeking to identify an essential element shared by all religions, I have chosen to follow McGuire's (2008) suggestion that to understand religion we should avoid creating images of what we think it is, or ought to be. Considering what people actually do, and how they understand it, opens the study of religion beyond the conceptual bundles of belief, practice, text, doctrine etc. endorsed by named institutions. It also enables movement away from the idea that people have '*a* religion' towards a more abstract concept of 'the religious' as an element shaped to and by individual lives – a process of religioning. My interest is in things which begin, perhaps, as simple enjoyment or relaxation, but which over time become woven into individual lives in ways which add 'something else' – whether this is acquired through created experiences, in how the activity is valued, or its place in life perceived. BDSM involves individuals who are embedded in nature and in culture; that culture contributes, not only to the weighting of the term religion in popular discourse, but to understandings of self, identity, bodies and relationships. It is in the contribution of BDSM to experiencing these things differently and to the sense of place within a complex reality that I locate my claims to BDSM as religion.

In placing BDSM within the category of the religious I am not claiming it as *a* religion but rather as a practice with the potential to contribute to a process of world-, meaning- and/or story-making that can be understood as religious. I use the term 'religious' as a category label, with an analytic purpose and I do not intend to suggest that all or most of my participants considered 'religious' as any part of their identity. It is important to be aware that the same term can be put to distinct uses, and that use in one way does not automatically constitute, or imply agreement with, use of it in another. Such conflations oversimplify the fluidity and complexity of lived experience, wherein it is entirely possible to engage in an activity categorisable as religious and simultaneously to reject any claim to that as a part of personal identity.

It is my view that the sphere of the religious is the best-fit category for understanding human activity which is valued beyond its functionality or end results, that contributes to understandings of self and other (or Other), that offers a source of meaning-, world- or story-making or that gives opportunities for profound, intense and/or transformative experience. In shaping this category and examining BDSM practice and experience within it I recognise that many of my research participants make no claim to any kind of religious identity; nonetheless I contend that understanding BDSM within this framework enriches understanding of the meaning and value the practice holds in their lives. By disposing of the determiner 'a' it is possible to recognise religion, or the religious, as an element of human existence shaped to and by individual lives. This approach allows for the use of religion as a category label without the assumed identity status which association with a named religious tradition might carry. Possibilities are thus opened up for exploring how the religious might manifest through practices which are not part of any established institutional religion.

The religious in this sense is dynamic and fluid, a constant and active process of exploration and creation which is best thought of as 'religioning' (Nye, 2000). This concept of religion as a verb rather than a noun arose against a background of debate about the nature of religion as a category and what Nye saw as the failure of the study of religion to engage with ethnography, postmodernism and theoretical discourses in related fields of study. In proposing a religioning approach Nye recognised the critique that scholarly uses of religion as sui generis made it effectively 'the basis of a modern theology' (Fitzgerald, 2000, p. 4) rather than a useful analytic category. Nye argued that religion 'is not something that does, but is instead done' (Nye, 2000, p. 456); something that can only be known through its manifestations. The switch from noun to verb signals a concern with the doing of religion, rather than with naming of religion as a thing with an essence to be talked about. Therefore, in framing the practices of BDSM as religioning I do not say 'BDSM is a religion', nor do I say to my research participants 'you are religious'. What I say instead is that kink practices can function within individual lives as other forms of religioning do, and so that concept offers an analytical lens through which the meaning and significance attached to kink by (some) kinky people can be understood. In sum, I suggest that anything that is greater, or other, than the sum of its parts (a gestalt), and of more significance to the individual than any single idea could explain, can be viewed as contributing to that individual's personal processes of religioning.

Gestalt

A discourse of religioning moves away from named religions to look at 'religious influences and religious creativities' (Nye, 2000, p. 467) as dynamic and ongoing processes. This allows practices not generally placed within the category of religion to be considered as potential contributors to personal processes of religioning. This, in turn, creates the necessity of distinguishing those occasions of a given practice where this is happening from those where it isn't: if anything *can be* religion does that mean that everything *is* religion? I offer the idea of gestalt not only as a tool to address this question but also as an inclusion in the list of taxa for a polythetic definition of religion.

Lived religions approaches argue that religion is to be found in practices which contribute to 'making the invisible visible, concretising the order of the universe, the nature of human life ... and the various dimensions and possibilities of human interiority' (Orsi, 2005, pp. 73–74), in the 'processes of experiencing things of value' (Taves and Bender, 2012, p. 2) and in all of the places where people 'share, enact, adapt, create and combine the stories out of which they live' (McGuire, 2008, p. 99). Given this, anything which makes such contributions can be part of an individual's personal processes of religioning, but there is no necessity for any particular practice to do so. The point at which a given activity, practice or experience becomes a part of religioning is the point at which emerges a sense of that thing as more than 'just' entertainment, leisure, pastime, enjoyment, gratification etc. For some a practice like BDSM is just fun, just release of tension, just sexually arousing, just an adrenaline rush – it is ordinary. But for others it may be all these things and more. It becomes gestalt – by which I mean that it is felt to be more or other than the sum of parts which went into it. The elements which go into the practice remain unchanged but the place it occupies in a person's life and self-understanding is different.

I have named this emergent sense of 'something else', this new sheen given to an otherwise ordinary thread, a sense of that thing as a gestalt. Gestalt is a German word that arrived in the English language in the 1920s, via the academic discipline of psychology. Gestalt psychology describes a theory of mind that is rooted in the basic German meaning of 'an organised whole' (Crocker, 1999; Sills et al., 2012). The term has no direct single-word English translation, and carries wider meaning and stronger connotations of significance than its closest putative equivalents (Gregory, 1987). My use of the word draws on this foundation rather than any of the detailed developments of either gestalt psychology (broadly, a theory of knowledge) or gestalt therapy (a form of psychotherapy with strongly contested links to gestalt psychology). I am not concerned with the psychological processes of perception, nor with the role of conceptual gestalts in psychotherapy, although I do share with the latter field an interest in the '"wholes" of meaning' (Sills et al., 2012, p. 46) that individuals create in their lives. While I agree with the therapeutic principle that an individual person is always a complete entity within a specific, responsive and highly idiosyncratic context, my focus is not on undoing or repairing particular cognitive gestalts or on exploring how conceptual or perceptual gestalts contribute to health and well-being. I am interested in whole and integrated experiences and the ways they are woven into personal identity, relationship, sense of self and other and processes of meaning-, world- and story-making.

As I use the term, gestalt is a felt quality associated with a specific experience or practice; thus, gestalt bondage experiences can be distinguished from bondage experiences where this quality is not perceived. It is a sense of otherness arising from the combined constituent parts that is neither perceptual nor cognitive. It is emergent, in that it arises unpredictably from an individual's whole experience of a given phenomenon as it is integrated into their world, and this creates consequences in terms of value, significance and meaning that do not result from any one part in isolation. This emergence is highly individualised. One person may engage in giving and receiving spanking with their lovers as a part of foreplay because both of them find it sexually arousing and exciting, and that may be all there is to it. For another person the concept of being a 'spanker', 'spankee' or 'spanko' might become a basis for seeking romantic partners or a part of the way in which they understand themselves and their identity. This person may then begin to seek more spanking encounters, outside the context of sexual relationships, resulting in a different kind of fulfilment and satisfaction. The behaviour becomes an end unto itself, rather than a means to an end (Newmahr, 2011b), and the things it brings to the person's life become harder to articulate in words, although they remain clearly felt. This is when the spanking becomes gestalt spanking or, in a broader sense, BDSM practices become gestalt kink; it has become more, or other, for the individual than its original parts.

This is the kind of experience and understanding that I discussed with my research participants under the title of 'meaningfulness'; behaviour is meaningful in that it is not trivial, not just any one identifiable thing. This is not meaning in a symbolic sense, nor does it involve any concept of definition or answer to a specific question. It is this ambiguity which initially led me to search for an alternative term. The concept of gestalt, in the sense of more than the sum of constituent parts, emerged in my research conversation with Griff, as we worked our way through issues of meaningfulness, religion and spirituality. No one else used this precise word, but other conversations did touch on the inadequacy of common words and the shared perception that the significance of their practice was not wholly captured in the words available to describe the experiences they shared with me. I had chosen meaningfulness as an initial descriptor for these feelings, but the perceived connection between meaning and linguistic definition proved a distraction. Describing something as meaningful seems to carry strong connotations of cognition (Ezzy, 2014), and/or a sense of deliberate purpose behind the activity so described, and I found the term increasingly less appropriate.

I do not claim that gestalt kink is ineffable, unless that term is being used to signal the existence of experiential aspects that are non-linguistic in nature by people aware of the gap between the experience they have had and their ability to describe it in a way that seems adequate to them (Blum, 2012). Regardless of whether this descriptor is employed in relation to a specific experience, the concept of ineffability neither captures the wholeness of the milieu within which that experience was attained, nor does it explain anything about the experience. Further, the association of ineffability with experiences of special or altered consciousness risks masking other factors contributing to the sense of gestalt. Gestalt offers a means of recognising that when focused on a whole, which includes but is not restricted to discrete powerful experiences, there remains something left to know when all the words have run out. With its root meaning of other than the sum of the parts, gestalt captures a quality which emerges from the whole and which can only be grasped properly from a holistic perspective. As I use it here, it describes BDSM that is contributing in multiple and multiplex ways to those processes of self-, world- and story-making that constitute lived religioning.

Religion, spirituality and gestalt

It is not my intention to offer gestalt as a single factor sufficient in itself to define all religion; I reject the possibility that such an essence exists. My interest is in the blurry areas where things which began, perhaps, as simple enjoyment or relaxation come, over time, to be woven into individual lives in ways which add 'something else'. I do not suggest that religion cannot be concerned with the practical, or must be somehow always beyond the ordinary; religion can certainly be found in the everyday, as well as in things to which people grant 'special meaning' (Taves and Bender, 2012, p. 11). But, in order to move something across or through the apparent boundary between what is religious and what is not, there must be a shift in some aspect of what it is on the not-religious side compared to what it is on the religious side. The acquisition of a kind of specialness, such as a sense of gestalt, offers one basis for such a shift.

Most among my research participants preferred the term 'spirituality' to 'religion' as a descriptor for things which hold such specialness for them. In my view this 'spiritual but not religious' distinction is analytically unhelpful and its usage in this way reflects a moral distinction being drawn between those who are free from oppressive authority and those who remain subject to it (Ammerman, 2013) that I am reluctant to reify. BDSM in general, and more particularly my pool of research participants, includes people who practice BDSM as an aspect of a named tradition that is recognised as 'a religion', people who find BDSM meaningful or transformative but do not refer to it in terms of religiosity, and people who practice explicitly labelled 'spiritual kink'. The experiences of these people could be considered to fall within different categories, especially if their preferred choice of identity label is a deciding factor in such placement. But since they speak of their experiences in comparable terms and communicate that sense of special value, regardless of where they place themselves in relation to terms such as religious or spiritual, I have chosen not to separate them according to these labels.

What the term gestalt offers is a means to distinguish practice which contributes to the process of religioning from practice which does not, regardless of where individual practitioners place themselves in relation to these complex and contested terms. It enables the recognition that a kind of specialness is a common element in the accounts of practitioners sited, in their own view, on both sides of the religious/not-religious boundary. Further, it enables that specialness to be explored wherever it is reported, understood as something which is emergent from but distinct to the whole, and which gains this lustre of the special without necessarily relying on a transcendent Other, a particular worldview or an established cultural tradition to provide it.

The research

To examine the question of whether BDSM can be understood as a form of religious practice I carried out forty-six qualitative semi-structured interviews with forty-four self-identified practitioners of kink. The sample was obtained primarily through snowballing, with the initial pool of participants consisting of people I already knew. I also posted calls for participants on the online network Fetlife.com and through real-world social communities (munches). Nineteen of my interviews resulted from these sources. My requirements for participation in the research were only that respondents had some real-world experience of doing kink, in whatever form that took for them, and that they regarded their kink as important in their lives. The concepts entailed in this latter requirement were unpacked and explored through reciprocal and dialogic research conversations covering a range of areas associated with kink and religion, including the kinds of experience they had had, what it is like to play in the ways they choose to play, what constitutes personal limits and edges, what makes a scene what it is, the nature of the spaces created by and through play, the relationships that are played out in these spaces, the importance of the kink community, kink as an aspect of lifestyle and identity and their ideas about religion and spirituality (both in general and in relation to kink). The same themes were explored in each conversation, with core questions worded in the same way but the order of these (except for the first and last questions) and the ways they were introduced was shaped by the flow of the conversation.

My reactions to and interpretations of participants thoughts and insights are inevitably affected by my own experiences with BDSM. In the transcripts are descriptions and reflections which were elicited from me by my research participants in the same way I drew these things from them, and I have used some of these in my analysis. In doing so I concur with Newmahr's (2008) assertion that such self-study is more than simple introspection; it involves an integration of subjective material and critical knowledge. While this does give the work an auto-ethnographical element it is not positioned wholly within that domain, as the focus of my analysis has been on the interview material I gathered (Bauer, 2014). Where I have used my own experiences directly I have tried to acknowledge them as such, but in places where to acknowledge particular material as my own would endanger the anonymity of others I have used an assigned name to cite the material.

To help ensure anonymity I did not collect demographic data, but I offer the following general observations about my pool of research participants: They spanned a broad age range from early twenties to mid-seventies. The number of years they had been active practitioners also varied greatly, from less than two to more than fifty years, with no clear connection between age and length of interest or involvement in their kink beyond the obvious fact that younger participants could not yet have achieved a fifty-year play history. Most participants presented as cisgendered and/or felt no need to declare themselves otherwise in the context of our conversation; there were four exceptions to this – two queer, one genderfluid and one intersex individual. Although I did not ask explicitly about personal relationships three participants described themselves explicitly as polyamorous, and eighteen referred to play relationships with multiple partners without using that term. Committed and primary relationships appeared to be heterosexual for all participants, but the complexities of different forms of kink and kink relationship means that conclusions about sexual identity or orientation should not be drawn from this. Most participants lived in the UK, although not in the same geographical area. I also spoke with people living in the US, Europe, and Asia. Not all of my research participants were British nationals, nor were all resident in their countries of origin.

Outline of chapters

The term gestalt makes best sense in relation to the whole of the phenomenon with which it is associated, but the necessity of critical analysis requires the clear identification of conceptual strands within that whole. This shapes the structure of this book, with the concept of gestalt intended to serve as spine from which the themes explored in the chapters descend. Each chapter identifies and considers a theme which arose from my research contributions and which contributes to the sense of gestalt kink through its part in the world-, meaning- and/or story-making processes of the practitioners. Each theme can be understood and explored separately in relation to BDSM, but each is also one strand among the many which contributes to the whole of the gestalt. The selected themes do not constitute an exhaustive list of all possible strands which could be woven into personal gestalt kink, but they are the themes which emerged most strongly from my research conversations.

The book begins by establishing a picture of what BDSM is and involves. Chapter 2 outlines the choice and usage of the term BDSM and its relationship to its wider context of culture, law and sex. It clarifies what constitutes the category of behaviours with which the remainder of the book is concerned and establishes some of the contextual frames within which my research participants both practice and understand their practice.

The next chapters are concerned with the consideration and analysis of the material collected during the research, and the themes explored in them feed the emergent gestalt. Chapter 3 offers, without comment, descriptions of BDSM experience. This is included to assist in addressing the question of how exactly play might progress and what happens within play-spaces, and to avoid the sense of 'yes, but what do they actually *do*?' which can be left by definitions alone.

I then devote two chapters to the experience of play. Chapter 4 introduces the concept of play as the core activity of BDSM; it is not a single thing but a process of combining many different activities into unique scenes. Beginning with participants' understandings of the imperfect term 'play', and the ideas that are communicated by it, the chapter outlines the intimate, relational and dynamic processes of play. Through the actions of the players a cycle of sensation and response is created, carving out a space that feels qualitatively different from 'ordinary' or 'everyday' spaces and is therefore experienced as distinct. The fact that the lifestyle couples among my research participants also engage in play and experience it in this qualitatively different way is significant and helps shape an understanding of play as 'an Experience' – a set of events, sensations etc. around which a line can be drawn to mark them off from the flow of everyday experiences. Play can be seen as performing aspects of the self and relationship explicitly that might at other times be suppressed, hidden or simply less overt.

Chapter 5 (the second play chapter) explores the nature and qualities of experiences which take place inside the spaces shaped by play. The limited literature which exists on 'spiritual BDSM' locates the spiritual possibilities of kink wholly within its potential to create experiences of transcendence. I certainly agree that BDSM has this potential, but my research suggests that many qualities scholars have ascribed to exceptional play events are common to any successful play, and transcendence is only one of a range of possible peaks of experience. Other important elements within the experience of play-spaces include the forging and expression of relationship and intimacy and a sense of deep connection between play partners. These, together with the sense of being immersed in another world, contribute to the sense of BDSM as gestalt.

Chapter 6 considers what constitutes a subculture and the utility of this concept in relation to the BDSM community. Kink, and all of the different strands which feed into a sense of it as gestalt, takes place within the wider context of society. That contemporary society is hypermodern, continuing the trends of modernity to what might once have been considered extremes. This chapter explores kink in this context, in relation to issues of subculture, identity, style and authenticity.

Chapter 7 considers the nature of the body and its involvement in the creation of experience. Bodies are presented as multi-sensory, with senses braided together into a synaesthetic dynamic whole rather than separate from one another. Movement/animation as the foundation of bodily experience is explored in the context of BDSM and the complexities of kink experience are drawn out. The idea of the medium as the message (McLuhan, 1964; Seligman et al., 2008) – that the meaning, purpose or point of BDSM play is to play – is introduced here, to indicate the importance of bodies in their full multi-sensory kinetic reality as part of the gestalt of BDSM.

Chapter 8 considers the role of edges and limits within BDSM play, suggesting that BDSM allows the exploration of many different kinds of edges and boundaries, including the transgression of social norms. This kind of exploration is part of what contributes to perceptions of BDSM as powerful and transformative when play is placed within its wider cultural context.

Chapter 9 then draws together the idea of the medium as the message with boundary exploration and the expression of relationship. It presents BDSM as a process of ritualising, that is a deliberate engaging in practices which contribute to processes of religioning. The ways in which a sense of gestalt is expressed all speak to this – the medium is the message; the point of play is to play. To experience the self as whole and embodied, to explore and transgress boundaries, to forge relationships and experiment with trust and reliance on another as a means of understanding the self and world in which one finds that self are elements which contribute to a sense of kink as gestalt in the same way a successful ritual becomes gestalt. It is other than the simple sum of its parts. It is not concerned with the symbolic or the abstract; rather the point of doing it is to do it, to have done it, to know that one has done it, and to retain the potential to do it again.

Chapter 10 draws these separate strands back together again to present the idea of BDSM as a gestalt, involved in a lived process of religioning. It also suggests ways gestalt might contribute further to the study of religion and religious practice.

2

Setting the scene

> I've been hunting for religion for as long as I can remember, searching for something I can do more than pretend to believe in ... On some level I crave spirituality with the same depth of longing as I had for leather from my earliest memories of desire. This is the kind of longing that wraps your heart in intricate bondage, from which there is no escape.
>
> (Lowrey, 2010, pp. 7–8)

The question 'what is BDSM?' is not a simple one to answer. This is indicated by the inclusion of a section, with some variation of this question as a title, near the beginning of most writing on the subject. Most of these refer to the idea of a compound abbreviation, or an 'overlapping abbreviation' (Tanos, 2003), that stands for some combination of bondage and discipline, Domination and submission, sadism and masochism, or sadomasochism and (possibly) slave and Master.[1] This is usually noted as a basic definition and then related, as a whole, to power-exchange, as in this example:

> The letters 'BDSM' represent an open-ended range of practices and expressions – including many forms of restraint, sensory stimulation, role-playing, and interpersonal dynamics. These activities are usually erotic at some level but may not involve genital intercourse. 'BDSM' derives from a combination of the letters 'B&D' for bondage and discipline (corporal punishment), and 'S&M' ... which typically involves pain and/or humiliation ... the letters 'D&S' in the middle can stand for Dominance and submission (D/s). Since both B&D and S&M usually involve at least temporary dominance by one person over another who submits to the former's control most people in the BDSM world these days view it as a

---

1. Capitalising 'Dom/Domme' and not 'submissive/sub' (or equivalent power-exchange roles) is a convention within the scene; likewise 'Master' and not 'slave'.

kind of three-ring circus where participants can either move around or stay focussed on just one or two rings.

(Rudel and Fairfield, 2014, pp. 1–2)

The letters derive from some of the activities in which kinky people engage, and each term can be defined further: bondage 'refers to the act of restricting the movement of a person. Bondage can be physical or symbolic and may involve many different methods' (Love, 1992, p. 67).

Bondage is arguably the simplest of any of the abbreviation's component terms; but the potential diversity of its forms is evidenced by the fact that the definition quoted above runs for 14 pages, includes 24 sub-categories, and yet still omits multiple bondage practices. The interlinking and overlapping of bondage with the other, more abstract, terms covered by the BDSM abbreviation thus amply demonstrates the challenges of arriving at a sufficient answer to the apparently simple question of what this thing called BDSM actually is.

My intention in this chapter is to examine the complexities of the concept more thoroughly. I will explain the choice and usage of the term BDSM as my key term over other possible options as well as considering the meanings it carried for my research participants and the range and scope of activities which fit beneath this umbrella. The different roles taken during BDSM play and the relationship between BDSM and power

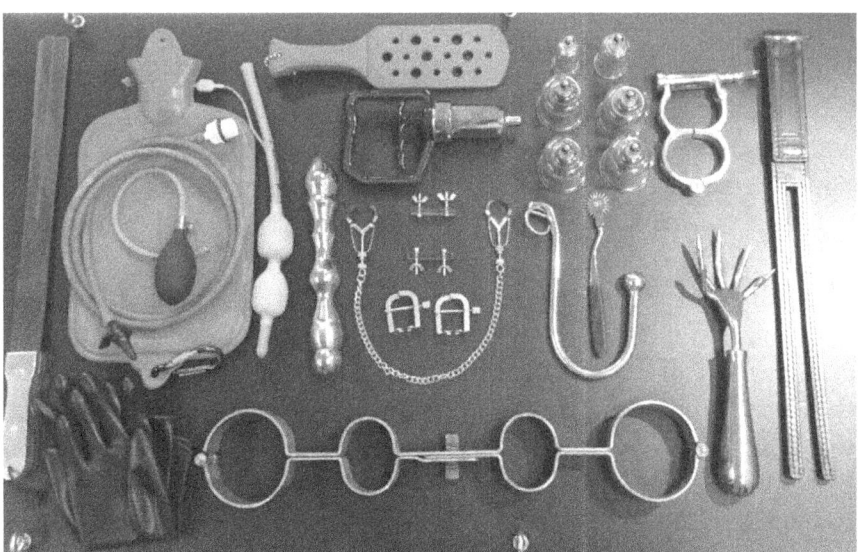

Figure 1 A selection of BDSM toys

exchange are also explored and the common assumption that BDSM is inevitably sexual in nature, with sexual gratification being its primary aim, is critiqued.

Choosing the terms

> I think BDSM ... it's come to be an accepted term ... of a whole group of activities that people dip in and out of. And I don't mind being referred to as someone who's involved in BDSM, but equally I'm not involved in all of it.
>
> (Colin)

> I think that the BDSM community, and the term BDSM, is more related to freedom, and sexual freedom, and an ability to express that in a form which befits your personality and your desires.
>
> (Friedrich)

In deciding how to describe my research to potential participants in it I chose the term BDSM. Other researchers have used this term (Kraemer, 2014; Weiss, 2011), but it is not the only possible choice. Alternatives used by other studies include: SM (sadomasochism) (Hart, 1998; Newmahr, 2011b), S/M (sadism and masochism) (Khan, 2014), consensual sadomasochism (Beckmann, 2009), SMDS (sadism, masochism, dominance and submission) (Weille, 2002), kink (Dominguez, 2004), and radical sex practice (Thompson, 1991). Looking at how the community describes itself and the types of relationship within it offers still further options – D/s (Dominance and submission), M/s (Master/Mistress and slave), DD (domestic discipline), leather/leathersex and power-exchange.

This variety may create the perception of discrete labels for different things but, when one moves from the chosen term to the specifics included under that title, no clear, essential difference between the catalogues of behaviour included under these different headings appears. The range of activities and forms of relationship practised by my participants suggests that most people who identified with the term BDSM for my research would also recognise the things that they do in the categories outlined by work which selected a different term. All such terms can therefore be understood as hypernyms, within which many combinations of kinks might be found. While the specific choice of term might well impact on who chooses to participate in research the need for flexible understanding of such terms is necessary within the community, since discussions between potential play partners would require much greater clarity as to what was and was not acceptable activity than any such over-arching term could provide.

My choice to use BDSM represents a conscious desire to encompass the broadest possible range of activities. My participants are individuals who recognised themselves in that term sufficiently to respond to my request for participants. For some it was not their chosen term to describe themselves; most preferred 'kink' as a general category label for their practices. Although it may seem that these two terms, along with the many other possibilities noted above, are thus wholly interchangeable their usage by my participants does not entirely support this. As used, kink is certainly the broader term, covering the entire array of behaviours and relationship associated with fetish, BDSM, D/s, DD etc.; it is also used as an indicator of individual placement within that larger milieu. Individuals thus speak of 'their kink(s)' – an individual portfolio of interests and associations drawn from the larger pool of all kinks and woven into self-understanding and identity. BDSM is closer to a synonym for play, as a general descriptor for the performative elements of kink or the practising into existence of one's personal kinks.

The Scene

> I know I feel more comfortable knowing that there are other people who are at least similar to me.
>
> (Barry)

> You're all in the same boat, and you all have the same kind of interests and that's where the spiritual love comes in, I suppose … you can just openly talk to a total stranger about what you're going to do to your partner.
>
> (Twisted)

Catherine Scott posits BDSM 'both as a concept and a reality, an abstract space which bodies and minds occupy in private, as well as a community publicly inhabited by a cross-section of imperfect people' (Scott, 2015, p. 8). This dual understanding is useful. My work is primarily concerned with the activity of 'doing' BDSM – usually called 'play' – which involves the private spaces occupied by bodies and minds, even when it takes place in a semi-public setting. I also needed the public community, to enable me to find these individuals and to understand what they might share with one another. Given the contested terminology which characterises both the study and the practice of BDSM it is hard to imagine how a community might come to exist, and yet it does. On the surface interests appear highly idiosyncratic and specific. Plummer (2015) has spoken of his early (unpublished) research into sadomasochism and how he despaired of finding any connection between the practices of those who responded to his call for participants. If I looked purely at what people say they enjoy doing I would experience similar frustration in trying to find a common thread between my own research participants. But they do have something in common – they all responded to a request from me asking for conversations about the experience of BDSM, in the same way that Plummer's respondents answered his call for conversations about sadomasochism. Each of them connected with that key term, even if in so doing it became important to them to explain why it was not the best term. They recognised how their practices could be placed beneath that umbrella and it is this recognition that also connects them to one another. Individuals do have preferred terminology to describe their personal tastes and practices, but most people also recognise the overlapping and contested nature of its different concepts and terminology. The Scene comes into being through the flow of debate and discussion, located in particular social, spatial and discursive milieu, and the perception of a shared core interest or group of interests (Moberg and Ramstedt, 2016).

The kink Scene is thus a single entity, comprised by diverse and overlapping sub-groups. It is a self-identifying amalgamation of people who see themselves as interested in behaviours outside the norms of bodily behaviour and interpersonal interactions espoused by 'conventional society' (Sheff and Hammers, 2011, p. 199). The community recognises itself 'through a shared, yet contested, language' (Weiss, 2011, p. vii) in which different terms may be used interchangeably or with overlapping meanings in the context of varied relationships, practices and roles. It overlaps with other Scenes which share a specific focus, such as body modification. Some people with a particular interest, such as corporal punishment (CP), might choose to separate themselves from the label of BDSM (Plante, 2006), but the kink community recognises and welcomes CP enthusiasts alongside all the other activities encompassed within it and many individuals who do connect with it practice CP, either exclusively or alongside other activities.

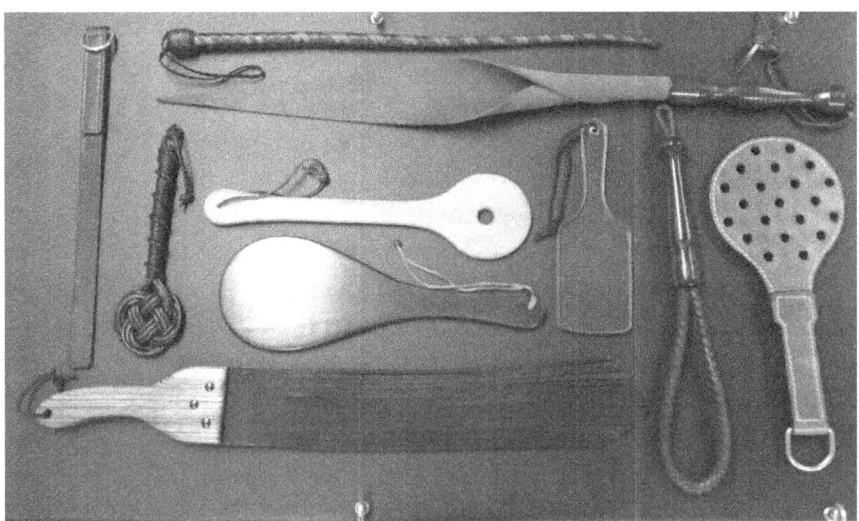

Figure 2 Implements for corporal punishment

BDSM is undoubtedly a fuzzy category, but it is one which functions practically: the community exists, people find it. They engage and identify with it, they reject it, or they create a special interest group within it. They critique it and contribute to it, construct identities around and in relation to it and find other members of it with whom they can engage in mutually satisfying play. It is a category which has meaning, even if it lacks a universally agreed name, or easily describable core element. I chose to engage with this category as it functions for the community, accepting anyone who identified with the term BDSM into my pool of research participants.

'What it is we do'

> You can't generalise. People are like 'what do you do?' and they expect 'I do CBT, nipple play'. Bollocks! ... it's not about what equipment I have. It's about me, it's about you. And you are the most important thing when you come to see me.
>
> (Cee)

'What it is we do' (WIIWD) is sometimes offered by practitioners as a definition of kink. In other words, if someone considers themselves to be doing BDSM then that is what s/he is doing. However, while it reflects the recognition of diversity of practice and honours the contested nature of other possible labels, it is not entirely helpful in clarifying (for someone wholly outside of the Scene) what kind of activities might be involved. Scott observes that the subtleties of real-life kink are strikingly absent from portrayals of it in popular media, instead what is presented feeds the 'multiple misunderstandings' relating to BDSM, which she summarises as the view that it is 'sick, freaky, deviant and wrong' (Scott, 2015, pp. 8, 12). This kind of perception leads some people to reject the term BDSM, even while recognising that their practice could be described by that term.

For many people BDSM takes place in specific intervals of time, scenes or sessions, in which people play with 'various techniques to put one partner, the submissive, in a position of helplessness and vulnerability, and the other, the dominant, in a position of command and authority' (Miller and Devon, 1995, p. 4). It is this idea which is most familiar in popular representations of kink. But my participants included a broader range : lifestyle D/s couples, whose entire relationship is structured around a power differential (at least one of these relationships did not involve any kind of play); individuals who were not interested in power-exchange at all or who enjoyed switching roles within a scene (as distinct from those who are happy in either role, but maintain it for the entirety of a specific scene); individuals who engaged in age-play with no element of physical discipline and no explicit desire for power or vulnerability; individuals who practiced their kink by themselves. Miller and Devon's understanding (self-described as representative of their own relationship) is therefore inadequate to describe the activities of my research participants.

It is this kind of complexity which led Weiss (2011) not to attempt a formalised definition of BDSM, with the implication being that we know it when we see it – an observation also sometimes made about religion (Nongbri, 2013). This may be a tempting course, but it carries the risk of misunderstandings and distortions going unchecked; what is seen may be conflated with non-consensual violence or judged according to mental health stereotypes. Familiarity with the British legal case of *R v. Brown* illustrates what is potentially at stake for individuals engaged in BDSM and why they might prefer not to rely on people recognising what they see.[2] In this case a group of men were convicted of assault amounting to actual bodily harm, and the abetting of such assault, following fully consensual and mutually pleasurable practices. None of the individuals

---

2. *R v. Brown* [1993] 2 ALL ER 75, also known as Spanner or the Spanner Case and hereafter cited as 'Brown, 1993'.

involved had complained to the police or required medical assistance. The case was brought because police officers had uncovered video of the activities and, in watching it, what they 'recognised' was criminal violence at levels sufficient to suggest lives were at risk. Weiss suggests that contemporary practitioners understand their BDSM to be 'about mutual pleasure and power-exchange' (Weiss, 2011, p. viii–ix), but in his judgement of this case Lord Justice Templeman saw 'the indulgence of cruelty by sadists and the degradation of victims' (Brown, 1993, p. 83). Lord Justice Mustill, although part of the minority in favour of overturning the conviction, observed he was thankful only a few practices were relevant to the appeal as 'whatever the outsider might feel about the subject matter of the prosecutions – perhaps horror, amazement or incomprehension, perhaps sadness – very few could read even a summary of the other activities without disgust' (Brown, 1993, p. 100). The Law Lords *did* recognise what they saw as consensual BDSM but they understood it as violence and cruelty, rather than the intimacy and shared pleasure which characterises the ways my participants describe their practice.

In contrast to Weiss most work involving BDSM does offer a definition, even as it recognises that it is probably better 'conceptualised as a set of interrelated behaviours where individuals give different emphases to particular themes' (Alison et al., 2001, p. 7). Taylor and Ussher's definition is typical, describing 'SM' as

> comprising those behaviours which are characterised by a contrived, often symbolic, unequable distribution of power involving the giving and/or receiving of physical and/or emotional stimulation. It often involves acts which would generally be considered as 'painful' and/or humiliating or subjugating, but which are consensual and for the purpose of sexual arousal, and are understood by the participants to be SM.
> (Taylor and Ussher, 2001, p. 301)

Weille describes 'SMDS' in similar terms as involving 'shared constructions of consensuality; fantasy enactment through psychodrama; and a symbolised, boundaried context … in which a dominant-submissive exchange of power occurs' (Weille, 2002, p. 134).

Newmahr has a different emphasis to most of these academic definitions, placing pleasure at the heart of her understanding. She defines 'SM' as 'the collection of activities that involve the mutually consensual and conscious use, among two or more people, of pain, power, perceptions

> **Box 1.1** A selection of kinks
>
> 24/7 – age play – anal play – asphyxiaphilia (breath-play) – bastinado (foot-beating) – birching – blindfolds – blood-play – bondage – branding – breast torture – candlewax – caning – chains – chastity – cling film – cock-and-ball torture (CBT) – caging – caning – clamps – consensual non-consent – coprophilia/scat (faecal play) – cupping – cutting – dacryphila (tears) – defilement – degradation – depilation – dildos – discipline/domestic discipline (DD) – electro-play – exhibitionism – fear-play – figging – fire-play – fisting – flogging – forced feminisation – forced orgasm – forniphilia (objectification) – hair pulling – handcuffs – humiliation – ice – incest – infantilism – klismaphilia (enemas) – knife play – latex – masochism – Master/slave (M/s) – medical play – mummification – orgasm control – pain – pegs – piercings – pinching – piggy/pony/puppy play – punching – race play – role play – rope – sadism – scarification – school – self-bondage – sensory deprivation – shibari/kinbaku (rope bondage) – spanking – strapping – suspension – tickling – trampling – transvestitism – uniforms – urolagnia (water-sports) – vacuum bed – violet wand – voyeurism – waterboarding – whips – zentai

about power, or any combination thereof, for psychological, emotional or sensory pleasure ... the objective in SM is taken to be, primarily, the experience' (Newmahr, 2011b, p. 18). This does avoid giving the impression of BDSM as only ever occurring within a defined scene and it uses the concept of power more broadly than the vulnerability/authority dichotomy suggested by some. Rather than a definition it seems to offer the beginning of the kind of polythetic taxonomy Smith (1982) sees as necessary for conceptualising religion. Newmahr's list offers the basis for a description of the kinds of practice in which my participants engaged. However, it excludes solo practitioners and implies that pain is the only sensation with which people choose to play. I have therefore added some additional qualities to better reflect the activities and relational dynamics described by my research participants:

> *BDSM: A collection of activities that involve the consensual and conscious use of pain, perceptions about pain, sensation, emotion, restraint, power, perceptions about power or any combination thereof, for psychological, emotional and/or sensory pleasure.*

This is not intended to function as an essential definition of BDSM which would cover any selection of people within any BDSM community, nor is it meant to summarise all possible qualities of BDSM activity. As a collection of qualities which may or may not be present in different combinations within any given example it offers an overview of the broad type and nature of the activities of my pool of research participants. Each individual has their own kinks and engages with them in different ways. Box 1.1 offers a list of some common kinks, from which individuals construct their own portfolio of interests and activities.

Is it sex?

> I cannot separate it like most people do. In my early days, I would feel guilty to want to cane my lover during sex. BDSM is very sexual for me, it's how I express deep love and passion.
>
> (Ms Lucy)

> It started off as something that was that cherry on the cake when it comes to sex. It started off with sex with a bit of kink in. That balance changed over time, for me ... At the moment I don't feel an obligation when I'm playing with someone, for there to be sex. But they do slot together rather marvellously.
>
> (Griff)

BDSM is commonly, one might say almost routinely, presented as necessarily involving sex. The idea that sex is at the core of what BDSM is (Langdridge, 2006) is similar to the way belief in God is commonly proposed as the essential heart of what religion is and, like that assumption, it is problematic. The routine placement of BDSM wholly within 'the paradigm of sexuality' (Newmahr, 2010, p. 317) is troublesome because it means both that the idea of sex as a core component of kink is simply not questioned (Alison et al., 2001; Sheff and Hammers, 2011; Stockwell et al., 2010) and/or that individuals who do not understand their kink in sexual terms may be explicitly excluded from consideration in research (Taylor and Ussher, 2001).

The existence of people who consider their kink as either wholly separate to sex (Newmahr, 2010) or as not necessarily including sex requires either a different category for the same activity based on practitioner understanding or a reconsideration of the essentialist definition. Nor is this the only problem with the BDSM/sex association, because the question of what sex might be is also complex (Christina, 2013) and never satisfactorily addressed by those assuming the connection. This matters because 'when two people are alone together ... one of them is naked and tied up and the other is standing over them holding whips and other torture implements, this is not the time to have a serious mismatch of expectations' (Wiseman, 1996, p. 57); if participants are approaching the matter critically then researchers should surely do likewise. The alternative to such critical reflection is to limit the ways in which kink behaviour can be discussed and understood, or to restrict the questions that can be asked about it. Either course carries the risk of further pathologising or otherwise de-legitimising the practices of people falling outside of the chosen frame.

Much of what is written by practitioners for would-be practitioners also positions BDSM as sex. Miller and Devon observe in their first paragraph that 'Oh yes, S/M is sex!' and later state as an absolute that 'sadomasochism is a form of sexuality' (Miller and Devon, 1995, pp. iii, 2). Midori goes further, advising people how to judge whether a partner is genuinely interested in BDSM or is just acting out psychological damage by asking 'does the SM or D/s they do really turn them on? Does it make them hard or wet?' (Midori, 2005, p. 66). My own experiential understanding of kink pleasure leads me to emphatically reject this as a test of either interest or enjoyment. Later she explicitly criticises how 'many of us use words, phrases and cultural references interchangeably without consideration for the actual distinction between them' (ibid., p. 123) and gives the example of two people agreeing they like kinky sex, whereupon one brings out a whip when the other one meant worshipping shoes. She observes that in this scenario neither person would have a good time. This is undoubtedly true, but it can be taken a step further to ask what would happen if both parties agreed that they enjoyed BDSM play and one assumed this meant they could sexually penetrate the other, who did not share that assumption.

Newmahr (2011b) identifies a number of clear problems with unequivocally presenting play as sex – one person is usually fully dressed, and remains so; genital play (if it happens at all) is usually one-sided (and connected with power-plays); kissing is relatively rare during play (although it may be an important part of aftercare); and people often play with individuals they do not find sexually attractive. The observations about the nature and substance of play were broadly supported by my research participants. They also observed that sex and kink can be combined and related in different ways, not just by different people but by one person in different moods and/or spaces. It is also worth noting a general feeling that play in private might well be more explicitly sexual in nature than in the semi-public settings where Newmahr's research was located. This shift does not necessarily signal a re-categorisation of play as sex within those settings, rather it is an observation that it may look and/or feel more sexual on some occasions than on others. Newmahr does not argue that BDSM is wholly asexual, but rather that the reality of BDSM play and relationship is far more complex than current narrative allows. Play is not only about physical sensation but explores intimacy with the entire person, beyond or apart from genital contact or nudity, employing sensation, emotion, risk, trust, transgression, boundaries and limits in pursuit of the experience created by the combinations of these elements. In sum, BDSM is not synonymous with sex, and play does not inevitably end up in penetrative sex, or necessarily involve genital stimulation. However, it may become sexual in these ways after the event, or a scene may involve sexual elements including penetration (more commonly with fingers, dildos or other toys than with a penis) and there may be orgasms or orgasm-like experiences for one or both participants.

In my unpacking of the concept of BDSM I have emphasised pleasure, and it would be foolish to suggest that this can never be sexual pleasure. But I would argue the opposite extreme would be similarly misleading – it is not *always* or *only* sexual pleasure. That pleasures of different kinds are tangled is clear. That one can be summarised as or reduced to the other is less so. It was common for my research participants to say sex often followed their play, less common to say that sexual stimulation of all parties was part of their play. But when asked if they considered their play to be about sex, or to be sex itself, almost all responded with a negative. By contrast Weinberg et al. (1984) identified a sexual context or shared presumption of sexual meaning as one of 5 elements involved in the definition of an activity as sadomasochism, and such a presumption continues to inform much work on BDSM. Interestingly, their research participants 'did not make SM roles a large part of their lives ... and reported more non-SM sex than SM sex' (ibid., p. 384). My research participants regarded their kink as important, and many shaped their relationships around their kink roles. This difference between two groups of research participants could simply be indicative of distinct approaches in recruitment, but it might also demonstrate the spectrum of kink behaviour which ranges from a small part of a sexual repertoire to the engagement in kink behaviour as an end itself. Newmahr conceptualised this distinction as the difference between 'doing' and 'loving':

> People who do SM engage in it as a means to a (sexual) end. People who 'love SM', by comparison, view SM as an end in and of itself. It may or may not be sexual, and it may be erotic sometimes and not others, but it is always SM.
>
> (Newmahr, 2010, p. 329)

It may be this kind of perspective that underlies the idea of BDSM as a sexuality or sexual orientation, and there are many people within the Scene who describe their kink in this way.

It has been observed that the origins of the term sadomasochism are contemporaneous with the origins of terms such as homosexuality, and this is not coincidental. As Thompson says: 'both terms were constructed out of medical discourse as a method of social control. Each term was meant to categorise and thus pathologise aspects of human sexual response' (Thompson, 1991, p. xviii). Weiss (2011) suggests that it is this connection with paraphilia and psychopathology that makes more modern terms, such as BDSM and kink, preferable for many practitioners. Nonetheless it seems that BDSM remains somehow more palatable or acceptable to talk about if it is framed in sexual terms, and it is perhaps non-sexual BDSM that is felt more likely to be pathologised. Certainly connecting it with sexuality and comparing it to homosexuality offers a framework to follow for legal campaigning and addressing equal rights issues – important concerns given that people have lost their jobs and faced other forms of social discrimination and legal action as a direct result of their BDSM activities being made public (Khan, 2014). Interestingly, the judgements in the Spanner case appear to imply that if BDSM were a wholly sexual activity the appeal might have been accepted and the convictions quashed: Lord Justice Templeman said 'there was no evidence to support the assertion that sadomasochist activities are essential to the appellants or to any other participants but the argument would be acceptable if sadomasochism were only concerned with sex' (Brown, 1993, p. 235). However, a discourse of BDSM as a sexuality repressed by the legal establishment does not necessarily constitute the resistance to power it may appear to be at first glance, since such discourse imposes conceptual limits which remain an element of social control (Foucault, 1978).

In their introduction to *Safe, Sane and Consensual*, Langdridge and Barker (2007, p. 11) state that the contributors to the volume share a 'broad' understanding of SM, one that 'includes all sexual identities and practices involving pain play, bondage, dominance and submission, and erotic power exchange', prompting the question of how they relate non-sexual kink practices to SM. Elsewhere Langdridge (2006, p. 380) has stated that 'at its core, SM, at least, appears to be about sex'. While the 'at least' reference implies that there may be kink activities which are not about sex the definition of SM he chooses makes it hard to see what these might be. Categorisation of this kind seems a general over-simplification of a complex experience; it excludes those who frame their activity otherwise and implies that they are in denial as to the 'true' motives for their play. Newmahr suggests that the sexuality paradigm is privileged because it appears to be the most common, but she also observes this appearance could be because 'SM participants who reject a sexual frame are excluded from studies' (Newmahr, 2011b, p. 67). In Taylor and Ussher's (2001) study individuals who did not both define their SM in sexual terms *and* recognise it as their preferred sexual arousal method were excluded; it is therefore unsurprising that the study found enjoyment of SM activity to be dependent on a sexual context. Alison et al. (2001, p. 3) similarly included both 'the frequency of sadomasochistic sessions and involvement with pornographic material of a similar nature' in the requirements for involvement in their study. It is also telling that Sheff and Hammers (2011), in writing about the dearth of minority group representation in extant literature on kink, have themselves implicitly excluded non-sexual players in their definition of the concept.

Some authors do note in passing that BDSM may not include sexual arousal or activity. It may also be observed, as Sheff and Hammers (2011) do, that kinky people might understand sex differently. The nature of these passing references is well illustrated by Buenting, who makes an observation in the same paper that suggests BDSM 'offers a potentially numinous schema for dealing with the sexual' (Buenting, 2003, p. 39), and that identifies 'BDSM as a system of sexual practices' and her knowledge of those practices as being drawn from 'teaching human sexuality courses' (ibid., p. 40). Having observed that it may not always be sexual, the paper goes on to describe BDSM almost wholly in connection with sex, desire and sexuality, and concludes that BDSM can function as a 'transgressive sexual ritual' (ibid., p. 48). While I do agree with this conclusion, I also consider it unnecessarily limited by absolute placement of the 'rites' of BDSM within the field of 'things sexual' (ibid., p. 48). It seems as if having observed that not everyone conceives of BDSM as sex authors are then relieved of any obligation to consider that perspective further. It is possible that people are simply more comfortable with BDSM conceived as sex, or that sex serves as a shorthand for a more complex understanding, but it is nevertheless true that the majority of my participants used words such as sex or sexual sparingly, and as a single strand among many others, in their descriptions of their kink and what it means to them.

Many among my research participants would agree with Newmahr's assertion that BDSM is 'neither a precursor to conventional sexual activity nor a replacement for it, but an end unto itself' (2011b, p. 68). This could be read as a recognition of a Foucauldian 'different economy of bodies and pleasures' (Foucault, 1978, p. 159), but she also says that, given the paucity of research on SM and particularly on the nature of play, assertions about its essential nature are 'premature' (Newmahr, 2011b, p. 67). I would go further and say that, as with the concept of religion, the quest for an essence of kink is misplaced. Any essentialist frame seems likely to exclude or silence some practitioners on the basis that the 'true' nature of their activity has been predetermined. The best answer to the question 'is it sex?' seems to me to be 'sometimes', or perhaps 'it depends'.

BDSM is arousing, exciting, intense, stimulating and intimate – all things which might spill over into conventional sex. But it is neither necessarily sexual nor necessarily asexual. There are people who hold these absolute views, but the most common lived reality seems to be that BDSM is an idiosyncratic blurring of whatever players agree sex is at that selected moment, with whatever non-sex is agreed to be. The pleasures of kink take many distinct and idiosyncratic forms, which may or may not include sexual pleasure and/or a claiming of kink as sexuality. Because it is my intention to present BDSM as described by my research participants my usage of the term is inclusive of sexual activity when they have included it and I strive to avoid an assumption of that element where they have not done so. I do not regard the question of sex/non-sex as an absolute binary, requiring resolution on one side or the other, any more than I regard spirituality/religion as two separate and distinct things. I am interested in the ways people use these terms – which is idiosyncratic and fluid – and in an analytic approach which allows for such fluidity to be recognised.

Personal labels

> You go down the high street, you see the signs and it says chemist, and it says butcher and it says bakery. And you know that there is meat in one, and bread in another and there's drugs in the other. But when you go in

you find out that one is a Boots, and it doesn't really have much medicine but gift sets. The butcher is halal so it doesn't have any pork and the bakery only sells bread but no cakes.

(Aey)

You know trying to put across what my world is on the website has been the most difficult thing in the world. Because it's just how can you get emotions, feeling, sensations in when the words are so limited and the English language is limited.

(Cee)

In addition to deciding how to describe their activities people in the Scene often make a choice of a term to indicate their preferred role in play or relationships. They are encouraged to do this by the structures of most online communities, and it is also useful when seeking potential play partners. Where an individual has a preference for any particular term that is the one I have used in reference to them, but it is also necessary to have a means of referring to aspects of BDSM play and lifestyle in more general terms.

The most common terms in popular discourse seem to be Dom/Domme or Dominant, to describe the person who appears to be in charge during play – the one who is not tied up or being hit with things – and sub or submissive, to describe the person serving the Dominant. Switch is used to describe people who are happy to take either role. However, all these terms carry an implication of power-exchange, as well as associations with particular forms of relationship which may not apply. By way of illustrating the complexity of the issue I note that Fetlife.com, which describes itself as the largest social network for kinksters, offers a list of more than 60 choices. That includes these three, along with alternatives like Master, slave and kajira (a specific understanding of slave drawn from a set of novels), vanilla and undecided.

While most of my participants offered Dom/Domme, sub or switch as their initial response to questions in this area, almost all of them then added qualifications and explanations to their choice: for example Ian specified that he would describe himself as a dom but only if it was given a lower-case 'd', as he felt this communicated something about the nature of his relationships with play partners; Rita described herself as a switch, although all her play experience was in the sub role, because she felt she was only genuinely submissive to her primary partner; Esteban described himself as a switch on the basis that he needed a label to engage with

30 • *Setting the scene*

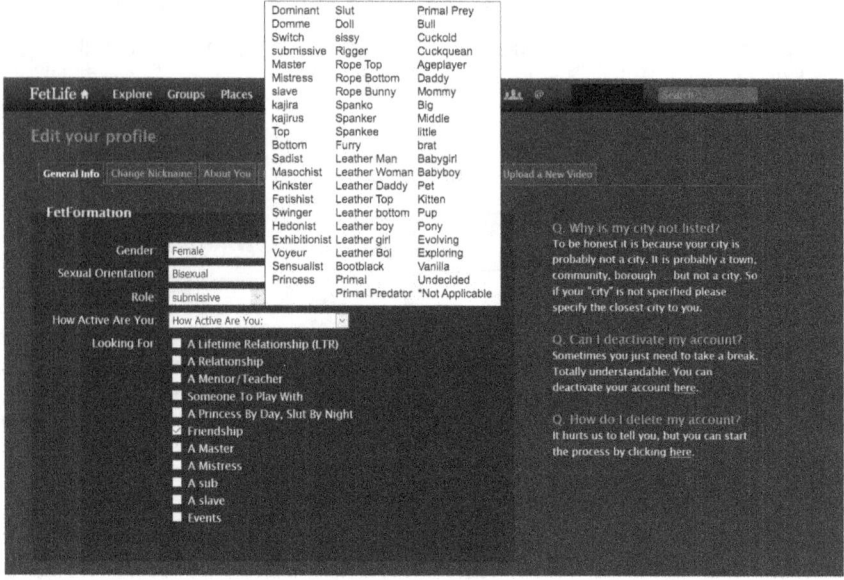

Figure 3 Fetlife profile page, with list of roles

the community and he would be happy to take either role in bondage play, however he was clear that play involving power-exchange was of no interest to him. Some of my participants chose terms which avoided any reference to a power relationship: Demon chose 'sadist' because he was more interested in playing with pain than with power; Madeleine used 'sadomasochist' as the best fit for her preferred activities although she disliked labels of all kinds; Griff used 'primal' as a way of describing his whole person, including his kink, rather than separating kink activity off from the rest of himself; Cee chose 'Fetish Practitioner' to describe herself and her play relationships in both a personal and a professional capacity, observing that she disliked most of the standard Scene terminology because of the stereotypes it carries.

Given this complexity I have chosen to refer to specific participants in my research using the terms they use for themselves. When I need to refer more generally to roles within play I have chosen to use 'top' as a description for those roles which involve the giving of sensation, pain etc., the wielding of any tools being used and the general direction of the scene and 'bottom' for the recipient. These are not unequivocal terms; 'topping-from-the-bottom' is a recognised form of play in which the person who appears to be in the bottom role is actually directing or controlling the scene. However, since none of my participants described themselves as playing in this way this blurring of apparent top and bottom roles does not prevent my use of these terms as general descriptors. Top and bottom are common terms which most of my participants felt referred more to the mechanics of a scene than to the dynamics of relationship. When discussing relationship, most of my participants chose D/s (Dominant/submissive) to characterise themselves and I have also elected to use this abbreviation and related terms when speaking generally about BDSM relationships.

3

What it is that we do

Experiential accounts of play

> I have only two arms to hold you. Let my ropes be an extension of my form, let me wrap my love around you and keep you held in my arms longer and stronger than my own limbs ever could. As I hold this length of hemp line in my hand let me lock eyes with you as it passes from my will to yours, and brings us into a shared space, a sacred space, outside of our other worries. Let us dwell in each other's presence ... In these times of pain and desperation I offer up this as a safe space to be the true you that you cannot show to the outside world.
>
> (Harrington, 2006, p. 58)

For any real sense of what BDSM is to the people who engage it to be formed there must be a recognition BDSM is something real people really do, enjoy and value. Even if it were possible to know all the possible meanings of every possible interpretation of the BDSM abbreviation such knowledge would not give a tangible grasp of what actually takes place during play. A full understanding of bondage means more than defining it; it includes the experience – the physical sensations and emotions that arise from and are shaped by the experience of being restricted or by the knowledge that one has taken so fundamental a freedom as the right and ability to move their limbs from another person. It also means recognising that not all the activities included in any list of kinks are equally enjoyable, exciting and powerful for every person who identifies with the term.

BDSM is activity; it is not one single thing but an active and responsive process of combining many different elements into unique scenes. For non-players encountering BDSM through definitions of its various components, with, perhaps, the occasional visual snapshot, it can be challenging to grasp the ways in which play progresses. This is not only because linguistic accounts of complex bodily and relational experience are necessarily limited, with aspects of such experience being wholly beyond clear description but also because knowing what a flogging involves in abstract terms is a far cry from understanding how the activity of flogging might unfold into a scene of co-constructed and mutual pleasure. To say that one person hits the other with an implement for a while is, in a literal sense, true but it is also inadequate as a description of even a simple BDSM encounter. With this in mind I offer here a selection of accounts of BDSM from various research conversations, with the intention of giving a flavour of the realities which lie behind the definitions.

These accounts have been selected to cover a range of different activities which fall within the remit of BDSM as understood by my participants. I have sought to include both more and less common kinks, beginning with corporal punishment (CP) (my own account) and bondage (Nomad and Esteban). While these activities probably form part of most people's play to some degree, CP in particular was rarely described by my participants in detail that went beyond naming an implement used. Whether this is to do with the ubiquity of the activity and therefore a presumed familiarity with it, a choice to evade the particular challenges involved in describing physical sensation or some other reason is unclear. What is clear is that although almost all of my participants referred to practising some kind of CP in at least some of their scenes the description offered below is one of only two detailed accounts I collected describing an intense CP focussed scene. Bondage is similarly widely practiced but for most people it was practical in nature and described briefly with phrases like 'I was tied in position'. The kind of elaborate shibari (rope bondage) described by Nomad is a well-known special interest within the wider kink community, while the self-bondage described by Esteban seems to be both less well known and less widely practiced. Sexual submission, like that in the account given by Friedrich, is an important part of many couples shared BDSM encounters and is one area where what is perceived as BDSM and what as mainstream pornography may blur into one another. The other four accounts – of needle-play (cate), E-stim (pussikin), fear-play (Griff) and age-play (Kaz) – may all be considered by an observer (although not necessarily by the players) to be describing forms of edge-play. This fluid term (discussed in Chapter 8) covers any form of play considered risky or extreme, either because of the physical nature of the activity being described or because it transgresses social and/or emotional taboos more strongly than other kinks are felt to do.

In sum these are personal accounts of scenes that were each focussed primarily on a single kink; I did not ask my participants to classify their narratives according to particular kinks so the identification of what is the focus of each descriptor is my own. There is probably no such thing as a typical BDSM scene and there will be people who share an interest in the kink being described but find the shape of it in these instances unappealing for some reason. Nevertheless these descriptions offer a foundation for understanding what it is that kinky people actually do with one another when they play together.

> This was to push at my pain limits, right, – I mean, that wasn't the entire point, but it had to do that if it was going to be a real correction. That's the word [he] uses for punishment when its actually about my having done something wrong, as opposed to punishment for fun ... So, he had all these different things laid out on the table. He has this huge long dining table. There were several straps, three different canes, floggers, a crop. There was definitely a belt because I'd said something to him about it being exciting to hear a belt coming off – you know when you're mid-session and it's like 'right then, time to really make an impression' – the problem is that most belts don't actually make much of an impression. Or they don't on me. And I think he was a bit miffed when I said that. Anyway, there were lots of things. Maybe fifteen, sixteen. At least that. And he told me I'm getting twenty with each thing and then a whipping with his camel whip. That wasn't on the table, it was hanging on the wall. I was just bent over the table – nothing fancy, just bent over. My bottom was bare already, we'd done some humiliation kind of stuff before this so ... yeah, twenty with each. I had to count them, but not each one. He wanted me to say when it was twenty, thank him and ask for the next set. I find it harder to keep count like that. And he gets in a sneaky extra if he's lucky while I'm saying that its twenty! And having to keep count stops me spacing. Although I'm not sure I could have spaced anyway [pause] I couldn't do that drifting into the rhythm thing or float away on a particular feeling because the sensations were all mixed up – he'd do a couple of stingy things and then a thuddy thing and then sting again. All mixed ... And he deliberately put some of them on my thighs rather than my bottom. And that's a whole different pain for me, harder to embrace somehow ... That camel whip was a whole different pain too! I'd not felt anything like that before. You know most things get less intense – you have the impact, even a really intense, stingy impact, and then it kind of spreads out a bit and gets more prickly but it's less concentrated? Well I'm here to tell you, whatever that thing is made of it doesn't do that! I've felt single-tails before that one but

honestly! Where the end of it hits it just burns and it gets hotter. More concentrated not less. It's more like being cut I think than any other sensation I have to compare it with. I've never doubted my ability to stay still and take what I'm given before but that beastie. I was practically dancing under it. But I did manage to stay in place, more or less. I'm pretty proud of that.

(Alison)

I have a friend [who] runs probably the most interesting life drawing classes that you can imagine ... So, one of the evenings she ran was a shibari evening, we did several ties and I had two models that I was working with so we'd have one tied, they'd be drawing it and we just sort of sat watching, and then we'd start to prepare if there was anything we needed to do [for the next tie]. So, I decided to do ... a pentagram harness ... The other model was tied up with her legs suspended. She had the most wonderful pair of stockings – the artists loved it because it had these intricate designs on and she had the longest legs, they were absolutely gorgeous ... suspended up in the air all tied with ropes down them ... looking superb! And so, I tied A******, because it takes a bit of time to do the pentagram harness so I tied her up first. We were stood to one side, and as I was tying her and actually it was partly the bondage and I'd tied 'round the waist as well and between the legs, and then I just held her and she just went into this [pause] state of complete and utter submission and she just submitted into my arms. What I didn't realise is that because each bit was being timed so that they could fit everything into the evening ... so everybody's finished drawing the current model and they were drawing us ... the room just disappeared for us both, we were in this different consciousness [pause] the combination of the ropes and my strength in my arms and having that connection.

(Nomad)

If I get a piece of equipment or something like that I have to plan how I'm going to use it, because I haven't got somebody there to assist me. I bought ... a leather arm binder, which is a great bit of kit but ... fucking hard to get on by yourself! So, part of the appeal of that ... is to think 'Okay, how can I get two straps over my shoulders when I've got two hands trapped inside the bag? And If I achieve that how am I going to get myself out of it as well?' So ... you try different techniques and different methodologies and when you finally manage to get it right you get a sense of satisfaction because you've worked through the problem ... [And there's] a sense of excitement that once you've ... managed to get it on then you've got that sense of excitement to realise you're actually [pause] ticked that box. And you've got that little bit of panic inside to think 'Can I get out of this? What happens if I can't get out of it?' So, you immediately get yourself out, just to reassure yourself. And then you put yourself back in it, to enjoy the experience of having your arms trapped behind your back ... [Part of] the satisfaction I get from that is if I'm bound in certain positions then you naturally would want to struggle against the bindings which means that you're [pause] ... It's a great way of locking yourself down into a situation where it's all-encompassing and you can't think about anything else because it's an uncomfortable position, so all that's on your mind is 'can I move slightly to make this slightly more comfortable?'

(Esteban)

I was with my partner and ... submission is a big thing for me and especially submission in the eyes. Pretty much everything that I do is based around [pause] they accept the fact that I'm in charge, emotionally and physically. So we were in a situation where I felt that that was achieved, and it did provoke a massive emotional response from her because she didn't think that she would ever be able to do these things that were involved. Basically I was being quite vigorous with her; I had my penis in her mouth and she was sick and she never thought she could go that far ... It was the climax in that particular moment. She absolutely submitted and she knew that she had absolutely submitted and that was what made it so intense.

(Friedrich)

He said 'I really want to give you wings', so we started doing the needles first [to hold the feathers] and [pause] I didn't space till the very end, because it was so painful and I was oohing and ouching all over the place ... I said what about a ribbon corset down the middle? So, we did that with staples ... And it was then I spaced. It was like the adrenaline got so high, the endorphins got so high and then all of a sudden I just zonked. I kind of couldn't remember anything afterwards ... [pause] I can vaguely remember a point with him saying to me 'I think we should stop'. Because I was finding it incredibly painful. And I said 'No, I want you to complete this. I want you to do this. I want you to finish this.' We were both at a point where, he could see how much pain I was in – and I was finding it for some reason incredibly painful where twice before I hadn't – it could be just because it was that day of the week, I've got no idea. But he was obviously at the point where he had had enough inflicting pain on me and he obviously felt that I had had enough of the pain. But me being me, I was going 'No please I want you ... don't stop, I want you to complete this.'

(cate)

We were well into the scene by this point, I mean I couldn't give you a blow-by-blow account but I'd been tied up in different ways and beaten with various things. But what sticks in my mind was [the] electro-play. It was only [pause] it was maybe the second or third time I'd done e-stim. And I was wired up ... insertable electrodes in my pussy and up my bum and then ... Master was using the remote control to give me shocks. Not touching me at all, he was on the other side of the room. Watching. And he was making them stronger every time ... I don't remember what I had to do, or not do to get another one – he does this thing sometimes where he wants me to recite the alphabet, or count correctly. And when I get far enough down that's really hard to do ... I think we were doing that, something like that. And if I got it wrong or hesitated I got another shock. I was pretty much broken. Crying and [pause] I couldn't even try to stop crying – that's hard for me, tears are hard. And it was at that point that he gives me the remote control and he told me to press the button myself, not for any reward, not for it all to stop or anything, just to please him. Just because he wanted me to do it to myself. It was the first time I realised how deeply I could submit, with the right person.

(pussikin)

Let me tell you about a serial-killer play scene I did with someone who wasn't expecting it. I knew she'd asked for wanting to be afraid and to be scared, but at some point in the future. So, I came in just to try out a new peg net. Like a net of clothes-pegs, like I think there was 300 ... Well, seven by twelve. That's not 300 [pause]. Anyway. So, the idea that I wanted to do is, I wanted to just see [pause] I had everything ready. I had tools ready. She was lying on the floor. Scared out of her wits. There was a moment where ... I knew that the tears were real. There is a difference between crying because of somewhere you ended up and it's nice and it's strange and you're looking for the release and crying because you're fucking petrified. They are definitely different and if you don't know the difference you haven't seen it, okay. At one point she was, she's lying on the floor not restrained in any way, ten feet away from the front door. Right. And I was, I had my back turned, I was quote in another room. I wasn't actually in another room but you know. She was convinced I was going to cut her up. She wouldn't safe-word, because she thought if I'm going to safe-word he's going to kill me. She also didn't get up and run out of the front door. She was ten feet away from the front door, literally ten feet. She didn't go anywhere ... For lack of a better description I would consider myself to be a sadist, though it isn't necessarily pain ... the physical act of causing pain that [pause] is the nail that hangs everything. Pain is useful because it is the response that I like ... but you know, doing a sort of mental game

38 • *What it is that we do*

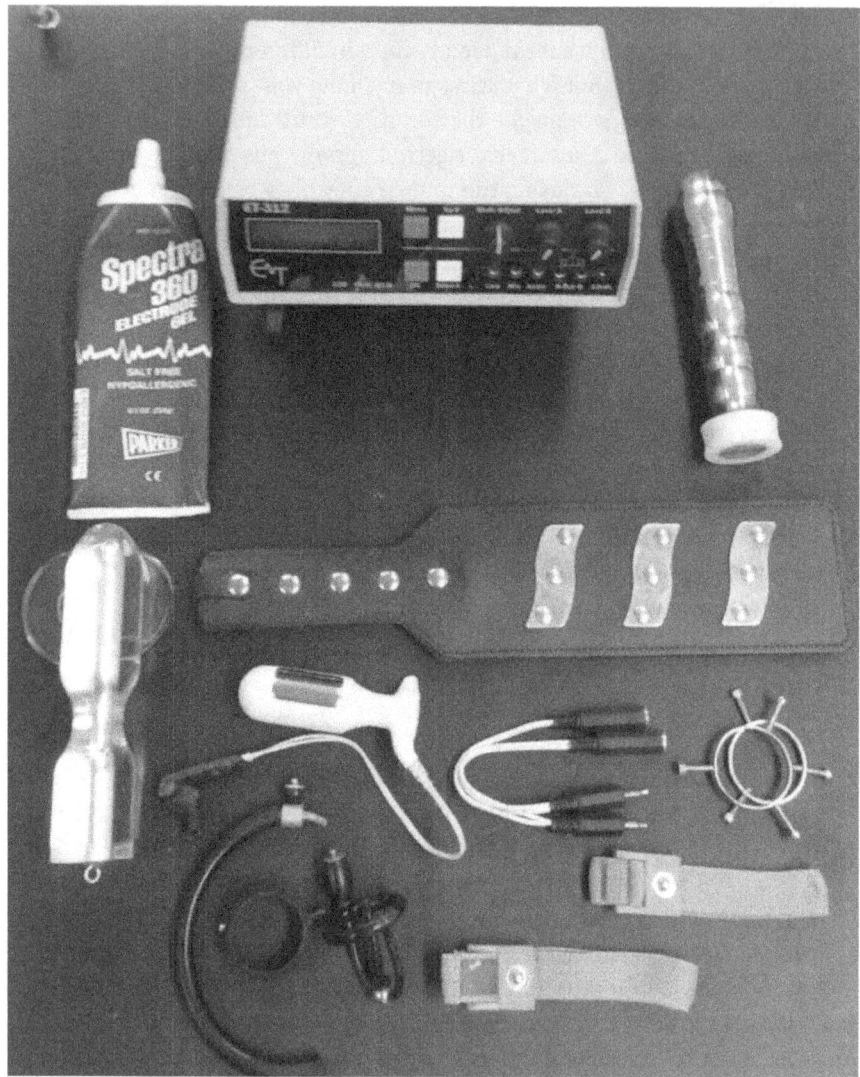

Figure 4 E-stim equipment

with someone [pause] the serial-killer thing [pause] when we started that scene, pegs notwithstanding, I didn't hurt her at all. All I did, I touched her maybe three times. It was all mental. It was all mental.

(Griff)

I started running schools maybe 15 years ago now ... With the Big School most of the people are looking for nothing but CP. But they don't want to go to a spanking party they want the whole picture, they want lessons, they want to be told off ... But then gradually I got to know people that want a school, but they don't want a big school because they don't like the discipline. So that's how the pre-prep has come about. There's lots of people that want to play an age between 3 and 7 and feel nurtured and be able to still be at school, feel like they're at school but at a pre-prep. It's not a nursery, they have to be older. Although most of them are nappy-wearers and we do wet nappy changes but it's so clinical ... There's no touching. It's purely clinical. We have a changing mat, they lay down, we take the nappy off, we clean them ... and even cleaning them, the boys don't get aroused ... I had to shout at two of the girls this weekend and the whole room just stopped because they're not used to me shouting, whereas at Big School, well! I wasn't sure I would enjoy the pre-prep. I thought ... I'll do it because these people have nowhere to go. And the thing that I get from whatever I do, whether it's mainstream BDSM or my schools, is that I'm giving something to someone else. And I can see the happiness and the calmness within those people and that's what I get out of it ... I had some people that wanted something, that had absolutely nowhere else to go with what they wanted ... what they wanted was to interact like a child would ... So, I thought I would hate it: there's not physical punishments, I can't be nasty. But actually I've found something that I actually really enjoy. I would use the word love. It gives me another element to myself.

(Kaz)

4

The play experience (1)

Making play-spaces

> From the outside it may seem that I simply kneel before her, but kneeling has become my strength and standing was always hers. Neither would hold meaning without the other, and the magic would fade to nothingness without the fuel we both provide to the fires of our spirit.
>
> (tromble, 2010, p. 20)

> Binding your lover should not be a destination to be reached, but a journey to be enjoyed and savoured ... Nothing else exists beyond the here and now. Even in a busy and noisy club all distraction drops away and I have frequently been unable to even say what music was playing, let alone answer somebody's question about what I thought of the DJ.
>
> (Argue, 2009, p. 63)

The main criteria which I used to determine eligibility to participate in my research was some experience of doing BDSM. As with other important concepts, I let my participants tell me what they considered 'doing BDSM' to be, and in this there was less variety of understanding than in other areas. BDSM can describe an entire relationship, shaped by a D/s dynamic, but when most people talked about doing BDSM they were separating it from the wider milieu of their relationship and using the word 'play' as shorthand for talking about the times when they were engaged in overt BDSM activities. My concern in this chapter is to ground the gestalt of BDSM in the practice of play. While there is a thriving online Scene of virtual kinksters who may well never practice their kink outside the virtual world for my research participants their kink is a real-world practice, involving interactions between physical bodies and tools. The processes of playing in this way create liminal spaces outside or beyond everyday reality and allows for the exploration and transgression of boundaries which would be considered inviolate by most people in their everyday lives. Such explorations can be understood as important contributors to religioning in their own right. However, it is also the case that play can create particularly unusual or immersive states of consciousness which have been considered broadly comparable to mystical states (Beckmann, 2009; Easton and Hardy, 2004; Harrington, 2009; Kaldera, 2006; Taylor and Ussher, 2001). Such states have formed the basis of most academic study connecting kink and religion to date and will be considered, as one possible form of kink experience, in the following chapter. However, while the potential to create transcendence is undoubtedly a part of the transformative potential of kink play, it is not the whole. Concentrating on these peak states implies that players give them greater significance, and perhaps even promotes the view that seeking such states is a primary motivation for play. It is my view that all successful kink play results in a degree of altered consciousness as defined by Beckmann's (2009) exploration of kink in relation to mysticism, but the transcendent peaks with which she was concerned may or may not emerge from that successful play and, for most players, most of the time, neither result is better than the other. For my research participants at least the purpose of play is simply to play and to relish whatever experience results from it. It is therefore in the process of play that an understanding of kink as a gestalt must begin.

Play has been described as the essence of humanity and the foundation of culture (Huizinga, 1950), as the 'underlying, always-there continuum of experience' from which particular realities are 'netted out' (Schechner, 1993, pp. 42, 28) and also as being involved in the origins of religion through its role in world creation, narrative construction and meaning-making (Cusack, 2013; Droogers, 2014). As Droogers defines it, play is 'the human capacity to deal simultaneously and subjunctively with two or more ways of classifying reality' (2014, p. 8), and it is the ability to play that allows for the recognition of alternatives, and experimentation with them in realities of our own devising. Through the act of playing, individuals within a culture can create personal versions of it, reject parts of it, and choose new vocabularies to express their choices in an unlimited process of meaning-making. BDSM is one among the many forms such play might take. It is more than a simple escape into fantasy since, as Kraemer observes, a person seeking BDSM play must be willing to risk social disapproval, criminal prosecution and loss of job or custody of children. She suggests that, in the absence of any obvious coercion or incapacity to understand risk and consequence, 'such nonconformist behaviour is best read as an expression of personal autonomy' (Kraemer, 2014, p. 37), and my research shows that many players do frame it in such terms. However, she also notes that it enables an 'exhilarating exploration of ... emotional and physical limits' creating 'a kind of death-rebirth experience' (ibid., pp. 92, 99) that can change and re-orient people in the way that Droogers describes. My research also shows evidence of this kind of framing. Siting play in the context of sexual experimentation, Paasonen (2018) argues that acts of play arise from a mode of playfulness which is characterised by curiosity, openness and variation and which foregrounds both pleasure and bodily intensity. While she focuses on a broader range of sexual activity including but not restricted to kink, this encapsulates the attitude of many kinksters. She goes on to observe that actualising this into real world play enables the grasping of 'sensations that have remained previously unknown, unimagined or otherwise out of reach and to expand ones ways of being, imagine and acting in doing so' (ibid., p. 3). In other words, to engage in play enables the kinds of exploration of self, world and other which constitutes a process of religioning.

Talking about it

> There isn't any other adequate name and it means that particular activity needs some sort of label. Like you hit a ball with a stick and you call it cricket. It needs a label. So, play is not adequate, but I can't think of anything adequate.
>
> (Ben)

> You need a word, because otherwise you can't talk to people ... If I were to say that play wasn't a good word your next question would be 'what word is it then?' And I wouldn't be able to give you a better alternative at all.
>
> (Griff)

Play is an imperfect term, but it remains the word of choice for most kinky people. It's meaning is certainly recognised, even when the term itself is disliked. It is widely used, as it offers a convenient means to talk in a general way about the about the activity (or activities) of doing BDSM, as distinct from the abstract concept, or the structure of BDSM relationship. Play is used to speak of the occasions when any BDSM dynamic in a relationship is overt and explicit: when a kink identity is being performed, when the toys and tools are out and in use, and/or when intense and powerful experiences are being shaped. To single out play in this way is not intended to diminish the importance to individuals of their kink identity, but rather to distinguish the times when that identity is being fully performed from the times when it is less manifest.

When people speak of play and what it means to them, it is often identified as a term which counters stereotypical ideas about BDSM. Aey says that calling it play 'brings in the lightness' which she finds in BDSM in a way other words would not; Kaz agrees that 'I never see, in anything that I do, darkness', and also feels that 'the word play implies something good … I think because we're doing what we're doing, and not conforming to what we shouldn't be doing, I think we're actually quite liberated and maybe that's what makes us feel younger or happier'. Friedrich also connects the idea of play with freedom – 'the freedom that children have in their expressions … they are free to do what they like' – while Mistress Marina observes that adults rarely play, meaning the word signals 'something you choose to do rather than something you have to do'. The rarity of adult play was also noted by pussikin, who says 'I don't think play is intrinsically trivial or pointless or whatever … If it couldn't [be powerful] why would adults be so afraid of doing it?'

Griff observes that the term play 'works on a number of levels … because play implies a certain level of communication and dance, almost'. One of the levels he identified is enjoyment; he, and other participants, expressed the view that if their kink were not enjoyable they would not continue to do it. The prominence given to this element leads Newmahr to conceptualise BDSM as a form of 'serious leisure', meaning 'a devotion to the pursuit of an activity that requires specialised skills and resources, and provides particular benefit' (Newmahr, 2011b, p. 83). This is distinct from more casual leisure pursuits where anyone can achieve a gratification that is immediate, but short-lived. Based on these definitions, most of my research participants would find categorising their kink as serious leisure unproblematic. I find myself most interested in the 'particular benefit' aspect of the practice and I suggest it is some of these particular benefits that make BDSM more than just leisure (serious or otherwise). If benefit means 'the things we get out of kink' then exploring play, and the play experience, shows among those things the creation of new worlds, and particular kinds of experience which satisfy a human need for 'bodily and collective ways of making meaning' (Grimes, 2002, p. 3); a need that has been associated with lived religion and the process of ritualising (Grimes, 2002; McGuire, 2007; Orsi, 1997). Connecting religioning with play does not make it a frivolous or trivial process; writing about video game play as religion Plate (2010) observes that games do not merely excite, they can also irritate; they can anger as well as please. Even while saying something is 'only a game', extremes of emotion can be felt and expressed: 'Choice and chance, destruction and creation, role-playing and playing ones heart, are all at the centre of the worlds that we call religion. We may live in one world, and play in another, but these are inseparable spheres of existence' (ibid., p. 228). This supports the view of play as gestalt, as more than any one of its aspects and more than the sum of them. My participants referenced this in their reflections on the choice to call it play. Kris reflected that play is a good word to use because 'it's not your everyday life, it's not your job, and you're enjoying yourself!', but noted also that 'people do thrive on it ... it helps to keep them going, it revitalises them ... It gives me a richness [to life]'. For Rosie play is the term that fits because 'it's meant to be fun ... and for peoples mutual pleasure and enjoyment. And I know there are people out there who say that it detracts from the seriousness of it but at the same time I don't feel that it's meant to be this big serious heavy thing', while at the same time observing 'it's very much a part of my identity and it's very much emotional satisfaction. It's a release. It helps me ... I don't like to say it helps me cope, it doesn't feel healthy when I say that, but it does help me cope'. Cee characterised her kink activity as 'a playground where anything is possible' and cautioned against oversimplified understandings or representations of kink because 'it's the interaction of two like-minded souls, or two souls that are wanting to experience something on mutual ground, territory ... it's not just spiritual. It's all the different layers'. Mistress Marina agreed, summarising 'there is definitely something in [play] over and above the ingredients'.

The process of play

> I've got absolutely no doubt that you can't just bend someone over and whack them, you've got to know what they want, what's in their mind, how they want something to go ... it annoys me when people say 'oh, I don't know, just do something'. I'm a great believer in listening to what somebody wants. Although maybe they don't know ...
>
> (Colin)

> I remember the first time somebody ever spanked my ass and I remember turning around and smacking his face. And it wasn't that ... I didn't want him to do that, but it triggers in me an immediate violent response. And so part of the pleasure is in fighting that and getting over it.
>
> (Madeleine)

The experience of play is complex, and the elements which go into creating a single scene are many and diverse. Any given scene might involve multiple people, the use of different toys, tools and settings, the interaction of these people and their awareness of one another. Given this complexity most 'how to' guides to BDSM emphasise that all play should begin with detailed negotiations, where potential play partners compare interests, set limits and agree parameters for play, including safe-words. This is good practice, enthusiastically endorsed by my research participants. However, most of the people with whom I conversed were engaged in committed relationships, where that kind of negotiation tends to be taken as read. Established couples do not generally embark on fresh negotiations every time they play; they are far more likely to discuss results afterwards or carry out periodic reviews of their agreed limits to reflect how their play has developed over time. This is an important indication of the nature of play – it is not a static thing, and this fluidity is true more broadly than a shifting of personal boundaries over time or a building up of tolerances to a particular sensation. The precise moments at which play begins or ends are rarely clear and, although we might speak of play in terms of 'a flogging scene' or 'a rope scene', that activity is often not the only one which the scene involved but the part that is remembered most strongly.

Even when flogging would be the best category in which to put all the physical activity which took place, it is still inadequate as a complete description. A scene is not constructed simply by one person repeatedly striking another with a flogger. Aey describes flogging as 'like a dance', involving both a range of movements and interactions with a partner:

> With a flogger you can do it close; you can do it far away. So, you move all the way around. You go over, you go under. You step forward, you step back. And it actually is like a dance. And you watch him, and the music is there, and it's very physical and it's touchy and you can do so many different things. It's like a ballet. There are pirouettes and there are kneeling parts and it's a glorious dance, right, that you do together.

There are different movements, different ways to wield a flogger and different angles to throw it from. There are different ways to combine flogging with other activities and the use of other toys – for example, the use of a violet wand with appropriate accessories results in a flogger that creates electrical sparks on contact. There are different types of flogger, varying in weight, material, length and construction and several might be used in a single scene. There are many different intentions on the part of both the top and the bottom and, while to an outsider impact play may appear to be unequivocally painful this is not necessarily so: for poppy, flogging her shoulders is 'better than an aspirin' for a headache, while Twisted compared it to 'a massage'. Sometimes the rhythm creates a trance-like state and sometimes it is about creating different kinds of physical sensation.

One expectation, supported by internet image searches and the aforementioned 'how to' guides, might be that flogging is done on the upper back and shoulders or the buttocks. These are the safe zones where beginners would be advised to flog, because the chances of doing significant and lasting harm in these places is minimal. However, different body parts create different sensations, and may be flogged if that sensation is an aim of the play. Flogging can also be used to create emotions or to disorient – for example, a flogger striking a hooded head both creates fear and distorts the perception of any background noise. Different body parts, and different floggers, also mark the skin differently, and many people enjoy marks and play in certain ways to achieve them. Chests, thighs and

Figure 5 A selection of floggers

legs, soles of the feet and genitals can all be flogged, and frequently are. Madeleine even described being 'flogged on the face, with my eyes tight shut' as 'one of the strangest, most emotionally powerful experiences I've ever had'.

Most people seem to agree with Twisted that the pain of flogging is 'a nice pain' rather than one which must be struggled through, but some people disagree. This kind of perception may also vary with the type of flogger, the body part being flogged, the temperature of the room, the play that has gone before and so on. It is also possible for it not be classified as precisely painful at all – 'for me that thud, real heavy flogging, that really deep heavy thud where you get that kind of deep bruise inside your muscles, that is my real pleasure-pain' (Molly). Flogging might also be used as a means of warming up the skin; some toys, such as canes or paddles, create less intense sensations on warmed skin, so this is one way to explore limits in relation to impact play, or to experience the stingy sensation of these toys without being pushed beyond personal limits.

In short, what is subsequently described as 'a flogging scene' might have involved different areas of the body, different implements, physical or mental bondage, and other activities entirely. The description given simply means that it was the flogging that made the strongest impression once the play is finished.

Play and lifestyle

> Our kink it stands to now. Right here in this moment, even when we're just sitting together, she's still mine ... it's just what we do as part of our everyday life.
>
> (Michael)

> It's always there. I'm always his sub, he is always my Dom ... People go 'oh what happens if you disagree about politics, do you always have to give in?'. Absolutely not! We have heated discussions about those wider things, because as he's always said him being the Dom isn't about him just silencing me and getting me to be his minion ... but it is there all the time. It may be very subtle, and certainly to outside eyes possibly even invisible, but it's there all the time.
>
> (Molly)

For those people who do not regard themselves as living a BDSM lifestyle, play clearly distinguishes times when you are engaged in BDSM from times when you are not – 'This isn't who I am *all* the time, and our relationship isn't this *all* the time. This is play' (Damien). However, for a lifestyle couple the distinction is more complex. Mistress Marina describes the relationship between herself and the sub she lives with as concerned with 'the power-exchange, the way of being. That we are … on a day-to-day basis. We live BDSM, we don't do it.' This distinction between living and doing is important to understanding play. Play need not be an integral part of any power-exchange relationship: Mistress Marina lives in a 24/7 power-exchange relationship but describes her sub as 'not really a play-sub' and they have no sexual relationship. Although she enjoys both these things, she engages in them with other partners.

Other lifestyle relationships do incorporate play. For cate, who lives as a slave in a 24/7 relationship, play describes the times when she and her Master engage in the 'bondage, and sadomasochism, and things that don't happen in the normal world'. At the start of her relationship with her Master a power-exchange was explicitly agreed and this exists regardless of what they are each doing at any given moment. This is reflected in their play by the fact that she doesn't have a safe-word she can use to stop play, but she does have a responsibility to tell him if 'there's something wrong'. It is not only that she *can* tell him, but rather 'I must tell him … Just because I can take whatever pain or whatever's happening, I might be able to take that but I've got cramp in my leg and I need him to be aware of that. Even though the cramp might go away by itself. He needs to be aware' so that he can make the appropriate decision of 'when enough is enough'. The power-exchange is always present in that he makes 'decisions for me as to what he wants me to do and when', and there are rules about how they conduct their relationship: 'I have this main rule … that I will take any problem I have to him, without drama and give him time to find a solution'. None of this is play. Their play is distinct from both their everyday interactions and the discipline to which she consented as a part of their initial power exchange. Even though discipline might seem to an outside observer to involve some of the same activities as play cate says:

> The way we conduct ourselves is different. You know punishment is very serious, and we're both in sort of serious frames of mind. There's no messing around, there's no fun … Whereas in play I can say to him 'oh, can I have the blindfold' or can we do this and can we do that. There's more fun.

Barry and poppy also both distinguished their play from the day-to-day flow of their life together. Barry feels that it is necessary to distinguish the doing of BDSM activities from the rest of a relationship, saying 'I do have a difficulty with people who say that everything that they do falls under BDSM ... It's not going to last, and it's not going to be healthy'. His relationship with poppy is a D/s lifestyle relationship because 'I am naturally dominant, and ... I end up, if you like, being Master'. Final decisions are his, except in matters relating to his health, but decisions are discussed before being made. For poppy 'the edges become a little blurred ... if Barry says something that I truly cannot agree with', but since her submission to him carries a requirement to always tell the truth she can 'say "but are you sure that that's right?" and if he still is, and I'm equally sure that I'm right, or that he's not right then ... we'll discuss it further'. She is clear that she is always submissive to Barry, it's just that sometimes they are having a row. Although, ultimately, he decides who has won their rows she is 'happy about that because I've expressed my view. And if in the future it doesn't fit or something then I can put my hand on my hip and say "well I told you so!"'. She jokes that he is always right, even when he isn't. This is living D/s, but it is not constantly doing BDSM.

For all the lifestyle individuals with whom I spoke play describes, not only a physical enacting of the power-exchange that is always present in their relationship, but is in a sense a performing the relationship itself. Molly described her play with Michael as making her 'the canvas of our D/s relationship, where together we paint, draw, whatever word you give it. It comes to life on my skin'. Play as an expression of relationship is also reflected in the effects of their play for Michael:

> When you [Molly] and I play, I do get turned on, you are aware that I get turned on, you like that I get turned on ... It doesn't happen with other people. When I play with other people it has its own stimulation and it has its own rewards that are not that and are not part of that.

Discipline, where that is an element of agreed power exchange, is always clearly distinct from play in both the intention behind it and the experience created by it, but it is similarly the performing of an aspect of the relationship.

For lifestyle couples, although they are always 'doing BDSM' in the sense that they are always performing a power exchange, they are not always playing. It is perhaps analogous to a person living in a religious order who is always 'doing religion' but is not always praying.

The power of play

I got this sort of freedom feeling. It was as if ... I actually said at the time, I did some writing on it, and I felt like, I told my ex that I would fly. And I did. I mean obviously, the suspension everybody was like 'yeah, yeah, you know you literally did'. But you know, in my mind ... in my mind it really freed me.

(cate)

It's a cathartic experience. You come out at the end different to how you went in.

(Friedrich)

The use of the term play to describe BDSM activity does not, and should not, signal that players regard their activity as in any way trivial – a concern some people express about the word. As Droogers observes in the context of religion, there is no intrinsic opposition between playfulness and seriousness; playfulness allows us to consider possibility, and to react to things as if they are so, even if we do not regard them as true, so that we 'play the game seriously, but [we] understand that [we] are playing' (Droogers, 2014, p. 23). This is also the case with BDSM; the play is serious in that participants are fully aware of the nature of the activity they are engaged in (and of any risk involved), they invest time and effort into doing it well and the experiences they create in the doing are real, not fantasy.

This last point is important; BDSM is sometimes described as role-play, but most of my participants would find this descriptor inappropriate. Their play does not require a plot-line or script and few of the people with whom I spoke regularly played in ways which involved adopting an alternate, pretend persona. The D/s relationship is real within the play-space, even for those not involved in 24/7 lifestyle relationships. It is not experienced as an invention, simulation or act. Although there are differences in personal approach and the requirements of different kinds of play, what most tops described to me about their typical session is that it begins in a desire to do a particular thing, and as they do that and the bottom reacts to it the rest of the scene begins to evolve. This is not the process of physically creating or acting out a specific fantasy, but an evolutionary process of action and reaction building upon one another. Early scenes between new partners, and experimentations by people new to the kink world, are more likely to begin with specific fantasy. Continued experimentation then depends on how well particular fantasies about sensation translate into reality. Madeleine says it is

> the most shocking thing in the world ... to top someone who thinks they are going to enjoy it, and they've fantasised about it, and they've beaten off a thousand times to the idea of me laying something across their ass and then ... it only takes one strike and you see their body go [she shrugs] ... They don't like it ... and it achieves nothing.

But for most of the people with whom I spoke, kink had been established in their lives for some time and, for them, play has become less about recreating a specific fantasy and more of a performance of the kink persona that is always present within them. Kaz was one of the few people who engaged in play which could be described as role-play, in the form of school scenes. But, although she does feel that 'I stop being Kaz, your friend. And I become Miss L, your teacher', she also reflects that Miss L 'is there. She doesn't need to be made. She is just there ... sometimes I haven't even got around to putting my gown on' – this is not a character which she puts on with a costume, but a part of herself that she draws on deliberately in some situations and which is quiescent in others. The play which takes place is not an attempt to recreate an actual school of any historical era, and the players are not pretending to be particular characters within that setting. Such a scene draws on language, images, and meanings from a specific kind of situation, but without requiring a narrative to be acted out. The interactions within the scene are felt to be 'spontaneous, pure, and authentic' (Newmahr, 2011b, p. 61), so that even a scene which is set in a fantasy scenario is experienced as an interpersonal encounter, rather than a performance piece. It is also important to be aware that the physical substance of the encounter is quite real, regardless of any possible fantasy context in which it may be enacted. A beating is a real thing, even if you stop it after the first blow you did actually feel that blow: as Madeleine puts it 'the minute that the belt hits the ass is the minute somebody finds out what they really like'.

For this reason, among others, negotiated and informed consent is the central ethic of BDSM practice. Constructing consent is an ongoing process, equally applicable to top and bottom players, through which an approval or acceptance of what may take place within a play-space is negotiated and refined. Consideration of consent begins before any given session of play, it can be withdrawn during the process of play through the use of a safe-word, and it often continues afterwards through mutual reflections and the processes of aftercare. While many kinksters would undoubtedly agree that exciting BDSM play often plays with, pushes the limits of, or purposefully obscures issues of consent (Williams et al., 2014), making it an ambiguous concept requiring explicit consideration with every new partner in every new situation, it's overall importance is never in doubt. It is the presence of consent which, for most kinksters, distinguishes what they do from abusive, criminal or psychopathological behaviours.

Although many people say, as Colin did, that 'the sub is always in charge' the experience while doing BDSM is not so clear-cut. The lifestyle submissives with whom I spoke do not live in ignorance of the law of the land; they are aware that their exchange of power exists through mutual consent and that they could withdraw this, but the exchange is based on mutual trust and fulfilment. The submissive has given the Dominant the power to decide for them, within whatever boundaries were agreed, with the corresponding assumption that they will not arbitrarily withdraw their consent to that before communicating their needs and wants fully. Trust is thus a necessity on both sides. During my conversation with Griff I observed that, for me, an off-putting thing about playing with someone new 'is having to go through that list of "I like this, I don't like this. And I don't want you to do this" because one of the things I want is to feel I am actually submitting, so I don't want to have to give someone a list of what you can and can't do' because that feels more like 'topping-from-the-bottom' than submission. But it is only possible to avoid this scripting of play once that mutual trust has been created, trust to the level poppy describes having with Barry, where if he 'said "I'm going to cut your hand off" I would actually hold my arm out. Because ... he never would do anything that left me in any danger, he just wouldn't'. Trust like this means that you can explore the things you may not feel you will like, as well as the things you know you do, so that 'playing is sort of danger with a safety net, because it's never going to be life threatening and it is never going to be more than I can take' (poppy). The submissive partner must trust that the Dominant will not abuse the power they have been given, but the Dominant must also trust the submissive not only to give them the information that they need to exercise that power well but also to remember that they gave their consent to such exercise.

This same contract of trust exists within any play-space, although where the couple is not a lifestyle couple it exists for the duration of the scene rather than the relationship. A bottom trusts a top not to violate their agreed limits and to stop if a stop signal is given. The top trusts the bottom to communicate their experience as it unfolds. In other words, it is not only failing to respect a safe-word that constitutes a betrayal of trust, failure to use one if it is needed is also a betrayal. Molly describes the safe-word she and Michael share as 'a tool of communication for both of us because it allows ... him or us together to explore my boundaries. Because he can push to those edges in the knowledge that when it becomes too far one way I am actually going to go "oooh, we're right there now".' These mutual trusts enable both parties to enter safely into a world where one has real, tangible power over the other. There is a tension between the reality of the everyday, non-kink world (with its legal endorsement and protection of equality) and the reality of the play-space, (where the bottom has voluntarily relinquished some of those rights and entitlements). Weille thus describes play as happening in 'a transitional space ... [which] represents an intermediate zone between internal and external, self and other ... [It] involves the simultaneous recognition and suspension of the norms of reality' (Weille, 2002, p. 139).

For Buenting play has a dual dynamic suggestive of the function of transformative ritual; it both reflects its cultural context and enables the creation of alternatives (Buenting, 2003). Defining ritual as 'the intentional practice of the dynamics of power' (ibid., p. 44) she notes that, if this is a useful definition, it would make the practice of BDSM a paradigmatic example of the concept. I agree that this is a useful addition to attempts to define BDSM and I also regard the concept of ritual as useful in understanding BDSM play. However, unlike Buenting, I prefer to consider ritual 'in its own right' (Handelman, 2005, p. 2). In this context that means considering what play is in relation to itself, including how it is organised within itself and how it is experienced by the players, rather than how it is 'constituted through representations of the sociocultural surround that give it life' (ibid., p. 2).

Play-spaces

> When we first play, I am aware of others, but then we're so focused on each other, it's like we are in our own little world ... regardless of our location, we get lost in each other.
>
> (Ms Lucy)

> With somebody that I have a connection with it's almost like you're in this little bubble, and it's just you and them, and what's happening between you ... There is something almost mystical about it at that point, because you can disappear to the outside, and it's just you.
>
> (Mistress Marina)

All BDSM play happens within a space that is both the physical area chosen for play and a different space, distinct from everyday reality, that is created by the play itself. Some people have dedicated play-rooms in their homes, but most among my research participants do not. Even where they do have such a room, merely entering it does not constitute the creation of a play-space, although it may mark the beginning of the process of creating such a space. At parties or BDSM clubs, play partners usually take possession of a piece of furniture, such as a St Andrews (X-shaped) cross or a spanking bench, and their play takes place on or around this, but the presence of such furniture does not make the play-space.

The space in which successful play occurs is usually described in terms like 'a different world' or 'a bubble'. This does not spring into being from the moment people decide to play together. As with ritual space it is

Figure 6 A spanking bench

'practiced into existence' (Lindquist, 2005, p. 158); the activities which take place within the space also shape it into the other-where it becomes. Being within such a bubble commonly creates experiences that are challenging to adequately describe, involving altered perceptions of the body, its perceptions and emotions and the flow of time and that create or have the potential to create new levels of awareness and self-knowledge.

Such a bubble is created through the continuing loop of the actions of the top, performed upon the bottom and the reactions of the bottom in turn feeding the actions of the top 'you build it up. It's almost like a vortex. You're building it up as you're going along' (Mistress Marina). Aey says that this 'doesn't consciously happen ... because you're so deeply focussed it tends to happen naturally' while Cee suggests that it begins as a conscious process but changes as the feedback loop is formed:

> To start off, yes, I'm very conscious of what I am, what I'm doing. But as it goes on, if you're getting really good feedback with that person and you're connecting you are actually completely oblivious to what you're wearing, what you're doing. Everything just seems to naturally flow ... what we started off last night doing, and what we ended up doing were two completely different things, because I feed on that person.

This is not a mechanical process; it is not simply the act of flogging, or spanking or bondage which creates the space. Ben illustrates this by observing:

> It's not like going to a prostitute where you get your thing done and then you get out. It's not about that ... the whole concept is, for me the whole approach is different. It's about giving joy and receiving joy. The whole phrase here is giving and receiving.

This giving and receiving is multi-directional, all players involved both give and receive in different ways, so that a scene can be understood 'very much [as] give and take. In the sense that I enjoy giving somebody something else, I enjoy what they give in return' (Damien). The bubble of the play-space is therefore co-constructed; without the contribution of all parties it cannot come into being. If the reactions are not there for the top to read, with the bottom being 'literally laid there like a plank' (Damien), then the top may well be confused as to whether the bottom has got anything from the play, and unsure about what to do next, thus breaking the loop of action and reaction on which the construction depends. Similarly ignoring or misjudging a response might break the loop. This kind of communication is not purely verbal; it takes place 'in the body' (Demon). 'It's the eye contact, it's body reaction, it's breathing. It's completely focussing on that person. And I expect them to focus on me and what I'm saying' (Cee). But neither is it just about the 'wriggling around and squeaking' (cate). Ben explains it this way:

> BDSM is a relationship. Full stop. You are in a relationship with another person. And in order to enjoy, it's a bit like paella – the prawn, the chicken, the saffron, the cloves ... each have to lose a little bit of themselves and absorb a little bit of the others and so it makes it a fantastic dish. So, if you think of a relationship as a paella or a pilaf or whatever ... not only mixing ingredients together, each ingredient willingly loses a bit of themselves and gains the other.

All participants need to understand this to make the connection that the play-space draws on. It is made 'absolutely together, unequivocally. Regardless of the roles being taken' (Griff). Mistress Marina agrees that 'the two of you need to make it together. I think if you've got someone with you that's not reading off the same page you can't go there', while pussikin said that the top and bottom form two parts of a whole 'like a hook and eye, I've got one part, and it either fits with a partner or it doesn't'. She suggests that without both parts 'you can have kinky sex but you can't have BDSM', echoing the distinction between doing and being suggested by Newmahr – 'people who do SM engage in it as a means to a (sexual) end. People who "love SM", by comparison, view SM as an end in and of itself' (Newmahr, 2010, p. 329).

A distinction between doing and being is not absolute, but most of my research participants described play without the connection between players as being mechanistic. For example, Rocks says 'I have done scenes with someone I didn't really have a connection with and I've made a reasonably competent job of it but ... it did feel quite mechanical'. Michael explained that he does sometimes play with people other than Molly, but he calls this being a 'stunt arm' as opposed to the Dom that he is with her:

> While I'm stunt-arming that loop doesn't exist ... It's far more technical. I'm still aware, I'm still connected, and I'm still paying attention. I'm still doing those things but I am removed. I am not in that moment of that situation in the same way [pause] that I am when we do our thing.

Similarly, Piers observed that if he just wants to practice his technique 'I'll use an inanimate object', because playing with the focus solely on himself is a waste that 'makes the person being struck completely meaningless, and they're not'.

Most of the people with whom I spoke had had experiences where things just did not work. The description cate gave is typical:

> I just wasn't comfortable I think … we played for a little while. Very nice person. But I just got funny vibes from it. I couldn't fully relax and so I just had to stop … [the bubble] just wasn't there for me. I was doing it because I could … I could do it if I wanted too and I was doing it because I could and I thought I would try it because I'd never actually played without the relationship before, so I thought I would try it to see what it was like and it did absolutely nothing for me, basically.

The connection is more than trust, although the importance of trust was a common observation. But for play to create this other world seems to require something 'more than just trust, it's also about bonding that occurs. When you can bond that deeply with someone … And the bonding occurs as a process. It doesn't just happen at any one point; it's something that takes place over time' (Javelin). Mistress Marina likens this play connection to sexual chemistry and the analogy is successful in that it calls to mind the idea of a hard to explain 'spark' and the impossibility of creating this spark if there is nothing to build on.

Even where the spark existed to begin with it can be broken, or the play can reach a level of intensity beyond which one of the players is not willing to go. This sort of damage can signal the end of a play relationship, although it does not have too. Aey explained how an unintentional breach of trust meant that she and her husband no longer play together:

> He has this real thing about electricity. And I had the violet wand and I was, as I do, I was threatening to touch his penis with it, right. Which I did not! But he had a tiny drop of pre-cum come down. And the little thread was there, right, and he got a shock … And that trust was gone … That was it. End of. Never wanted to do anything else.

However, with her current submissive 'there have been occasions when his trust has been betrayed but he has always known that it is unintentional' and so the bond required for successful play remains intact. Colin described the discovery, towards the end of his marriage, that his wife had explored kink as much as she ever wished to do:

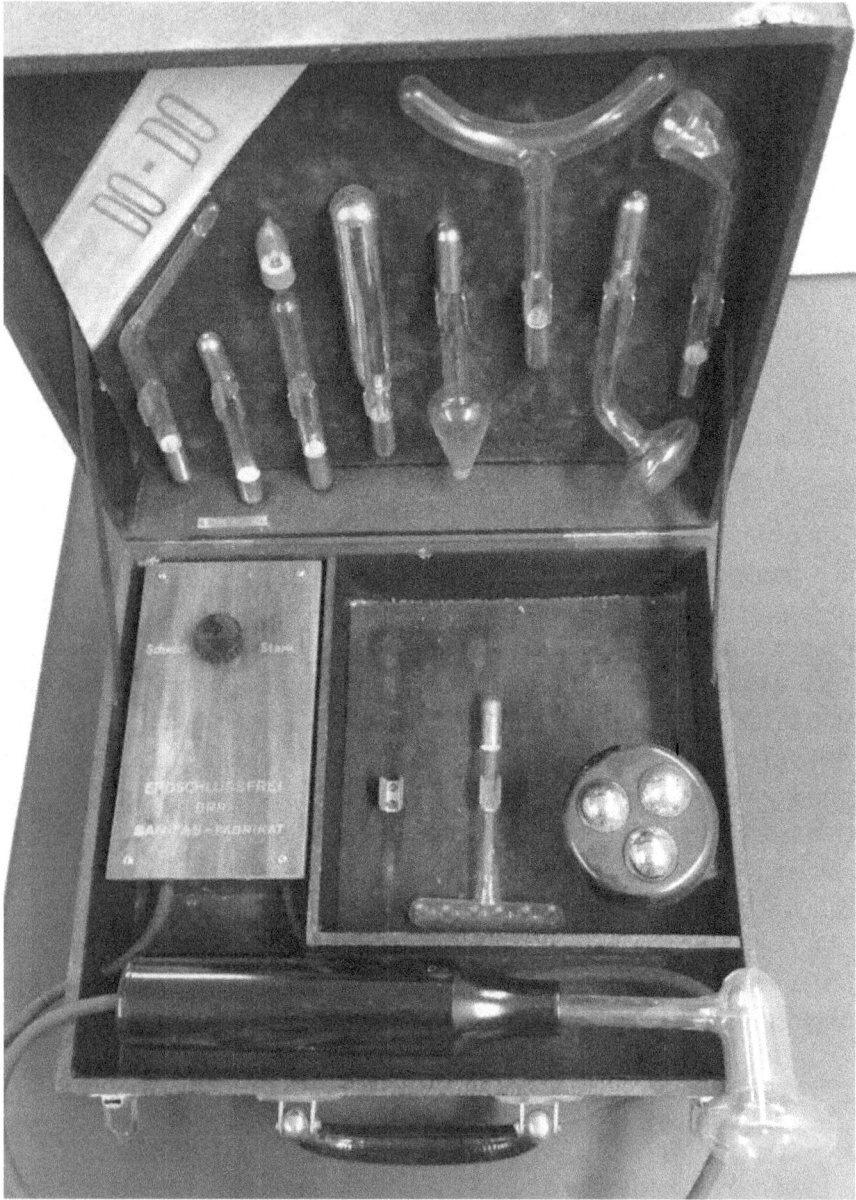

Figure 7 A violet wand and attachments

There was a night that I will never, ever forget, when she sat on the side of the bed pulling on some stockings and she said 'God, I hate doing this'. This discovery meant that 'that was it. It was finished, gone … And then there is the rest of our marriage, where I was playing more and more and more elsewhere, to find what I wanted.

Co-constructed worlds

The existence of play-space is not just about the practice, but about the relationship being enacted and performed. Play both creates and requires a bond between the players, so that as people play together more often they can also play more intensely, and enter into their shared world more completely. The space of that shared world and experiences within it are co-constructed: forming the play-space is initiated by the actions of the top performed upon the bottom; the bottom is the heart of the space; the connection and interactions of the players form and maintain the space, and the edges of it are held/defined by the top. The construction and expression of relationship, and the intimacy and trust enacted during this process are important contributors to the emergent sense of BDSM as gestalt; through these processes the world is changed, and a new space created, within which powerful experiences can occur.

5

The play experience (2)

Inside play-spaces

> What I do see in these moments are fleeting and nondescript defiantly non-verbal expressions of the spirit within the flesh. I sense the spirit riding the razor's edge of release. The silent cry for catharsis, not the clinical meaning, but the purely animalistic-human need to let something go that the rational (funny that) brain holds dearly to.
>
> (Master Dennis, 2010, p. 29)

> We are like Inana who walked willingly into the realm of Death, who was stripped of her name and her power, who was hung on a hook over the throne of the Queen of Death ... She did it because there was no other way to touch the deep wisdom she sought, no way but to stumble along dark paths to the katabasis point, and trust in all the wisdom of the Underworld that you may one day emerge triumphant.
>
> (Kaldera, 2006, p. 7)

The previous chapter's consideration of play-spaces showed how they are created through a process of action and reaction, and the concomitant forging of an interpersonal connection. As this process unfolds, it shapes an ambiguous space commensurate with that which Taves (2009, p. 159) describes as the space of 'adult ritual play', a space between 'the subjectivity of the self and the objectivity of the other'. The concern now is to consider the experiences which take place within that space which include, but are not restricted to, the peak or transcendent experiences most commonly considered by academic study to be religious or spiritual in nature.

Kink experiences do not appear fully formed out of nowhere, nor do they create themselves. They are created deliberately through the process of play. Schechner suggests that it is not the abstract concept of play which should be of greatest interest but the act of playing, as the 'ground, the matrix, birthing all experience's ... multiple realities' (Schechner, 1993, p. 28), which people simultaneously create, stand within and stand upon. Working along similar lines, Plate (2010) distinguishes open-ended and unstructured play from the playing of games. He says that 'play provides an active, potentially destabilising, disorienting, and transgressive force, while a game provides rules, and establishes order through the creation of boundaries within which play occurs' (ibid., p. 216). For Plate, religion exists in the interaction between the two. BDSM experiences are created in the same way, with the negotiation of consent and limits and the connection of trust constituting the boundaries within which the transgressive force of the play can take shape. In this framing, playing becomes religioning as the play activity becomes an intimate ritual; such ritual may be outside the formal structures of organised religion but, nonetheless, it enables a person to explore or remake themselves and to share that result with others both within and beyond the play-space (Nagy, 2005). As religioning then, play is not confined to its bubbles and dedicated spaces but emerges from them to touch and influence mundane spaces and relationships.

Experiencing play

> I think that even naming things, so like cutting or caning or needle-play, or blood-play or flogging or whatever your thing is ... the naming is somehow limiting them to this action that happens, to the event, the physical event. Unfortunately, those labels don't encompass ... the huge iceberg under the surface that's really what's at play in the experience.
>
> (Madeleine)

> I wouldn't want somebody to indulge in something, or have me do something to them, that I haven't experienced myself. Because how can I sit there and really understand what they're experiencing if I haven't experienced it myself?
>
> (Damien)

Although it is often taken for granted that experience is an inner event of total subjectivity, this perspective is a modern construction (Desjarlis, 2012), and a contentious one. We are all within a constant flow of experience, involving a vast array of elements and subject to an equally vast array of interpretation and forms of understanding. When a person designates a particular happening as 'An Experience' in everyday discourse it appears to mean an occasion when the normal flow of experiencing has been somehow disrupted, allowing a particular section of that continual, multiplex flow to be singled out from the rest, and attention focussed on its qualities. For researchers, access to such experiences is primarily through the subjective accounts of the experiencer and therefore focussed on the qualities which lead them to draw a boundary around this particular bubble of their lived reality in the first place. This then raises questions about how such accounts are structured and created.

Recognising people as bodily beings implies that experiences involving a physical practice must combine and incorporate a range of processes – sensory, organic, unconscious and cognitive. Siting bodies within contexts means examining how these processes are informed and shaped by culture, language, social context and relationship. How all this feeds into an offered description will be further affected by things such as the way in which the memory was stored, how the conversation awakens it, how many times the experience has been reflected on prior to giving that description, and so on.

As I discussed experiences of BDSM with my research participants, it became clear that a successfully constructed BDSM play-space constitutes one of the bubbles of Experience that can be picked out of the constant stream of experiencing. In talking about experience in this context I am considering what it is like to be within that bubble of a different world, created by the play, and asking whether and how that world differs from the quotidian one.

The play-space is a lived space, created by action, interaction and multi-directional communication. Lived space combines perceived space with conceived space but is more than merely the sum of the two. The perceived is physical space, 'materialised, socially produced, empirical ... directly sensible and open, within limits, to accurate measurement and description'; the conceived space is mental, and concerned with 'language, discourse, texts, *logos*' (Soja, 1996, pp. 66, 67). Lived space encompasses both but is distinct from them. It is the space of inhabitants and users, which Soja designates as Thirdspace. The space where the real (material) and the imagined (cognitive) combine in equal terms to make 'lived spaces of representation', that are 'simultaneously real and imagined and more (both and also ...) real-and-imagined (or perhaps realandimagined?) places' (ibid., pp. 68, 11). Taking a Thirdspace perspective recognises the different subjectivities of the people describing their spaces, with all the uncertainty and openness to contestation that implies, and exploring it requires the guidance of 'some form of potentially emancipatory *praxis,* the translation of knowledge into action' (ibid., p. 22) that is accomplished through the sensation-and response process of play-space construction.

Being in another world

> I stroke his face, knowing his body and mind are still humming with the vibrations. I'm glad I could do that for him. Perhaps we are not in the same 'place', but we danced the same dance together.
>
> (Aey)

> It's the eye contact, it's body reaction, breathing. It's completely focussing on that person ... And it's an energy and you can feel that energy, and you can feel it coming off someone. You can feel ... sort of like a chemical reaction in yourself. Charging up, charging up, charging up. And then you just ride on it.
>
> (Cee)

Beckmann identified a list of features as characteristic of 'transcendental states' (Beckmann, 2009, p. 200) achieved through BDSM. These features include difficulty explaining an experience in words, changes in the way the body is perceived or reacts, a loss or change to the sense of time, and a different quality of memory. She used this list to create a questionnaire about experiences she had predetermined were exceptional. By contrast my research indicates that most of these features are aspects of any successful play, although they may vary in degree, as play varies in intensity. As Friedrich summarises, the play-space is characterised by the fact that 'it feels different. It feels completely different to the normal everyday way of thinking and talking'. The specific qualities ascribed to 'there' and 'here' differed between individuals, but the generalities identified by Beckmann were commonly referenced across all my research conversations.

The most common description my participants gave for a play-space was in terms of different worlds or bubbles of different reality. This was often employed as a means of emphasising just how different (and how difficult to describe) the experience could be, as well as to share ideas about the potential transformative power of such spaces. Cee describes the play-space variously as 'another dimension', 'a magic space' and 'a completely different world', with going there likened to 'going through a keyhole'. For Ben, it is 'an environment where nothing else exists, just the Dom and you and everything else blurs out', and Damien agrees that 'the here and now sort of disappears off' and only the play-space matters. Damien uses the phrase 'the here and now' to refer to the quotidian world. In contrast Javelin uses the same phrase to explain what it is like within the alternative world of the play-space, saying 'when I'm into a scene really deep, whether Dom or sub, I'm so totally in the here and now ... I'm achieving what Buddhist monks spent years trying to achieve. I'm in the here and now, I'm focused, time tends to be gone ... I'm just in the moment.'

While accepting that the experience as a whole is challenging to capture a few people tried to give a sense of the qualities of a play-space. Damien describes it in terms of rightness, and things being as they should be:

> Think about a nice day, when it's sunny. And you're out walking, and it's just, everything is pleasant. The birds are singing. It's not too bright, not too dark. Everything just flows. And it's like that. And that's what I like about it. It's like when you're driving home from somewhere and the journey just goes, there's no traffic or anything like that. It just flows. And it's that, it's that sensation. Everything feels right .... Everything is as it should be. It just fits.

The idea of flow was also part of Oliver's description, comparing BDSM to wreck-diving. He says that he thought kink would take the place of rugby in his life, as a vent for frustrations, but instead he discovered that 'it really mellows me out':

> So, it's [more like diving] because you have to be mellow when you dive. If you panic you're dead, and pretty much everything that you do to stay alive under water is the opposite of what you would do on the surface ... And that's all about a flow state ... I get into that zone.

Marie also made a comparison with extreme sports, observing that 'the sort of endorphin rush that you get ... at some point when you're involved in spanking activities ... it has occurred to me recently that it's quite similar to the adrenaline rush that you get when you're jumping off a waterfall'. For Aey the preferred analogy is music, both the playing of it and the listening to it; while it is clear that she is the musician, her partner is sometimes the instrument that she plays and sometimes the listener absorbed and carried away in her music. She says she thinks of topping 'like playing a piano':

> Because if you're playing you pay more attention to what notes you play, whereas if you're not playing you can listen to the music and get lost in it. [When you're playing it] you can still feel it ... and you can still get involved in it. But you're doing it, so you stay [present].

Different experiences in shared space

> The best scenes are always where your personalities merge for a while. It's only you, your bottom, and the rest of the world is gone. And the really good scenes that time element disappears too. So, the better the scene, the more connected you are, the more those two personalities do merge because you're connected in a lot more ways.
> (Stoney-face)

> It feels so comfortable being in the space when you're with somebody who just knows exactly what's going on with you, [and] it doesn't scare them ...
> (Madeleine)

Beckmann (2009) concludes that the transcendental states she has identified are available primarily to bottoms and this conclusion is unsurprising, given that her research questionnaire is framed in terms more appropriate to the bottom experience than the top. The experiences are different, because the people having them are doing extremely different things, but both top and bottom are involved in the creation of the play-space and both are present in the different world so created. The experience of one is not possible without the experiences of the other. The space is centred upon, or formed around, the person taking the bottom role. As a result, the bottom is less likely to be aware of the edges of the space, or of other people trespassing into it, than the top. They are also more likely to lose their sense of self, or to experience a blurring of sensations that are normally distinct. Penny says, 'I kind of get lost in the scene', and her perceptions change so that 'I'm not always aware of how I'm feeling'. Ivy says that 'time passing especially [goes away] ... but also any kind of awareness of my image and environment and all that kind of thing, becomes very small'. Similarly, poppy also loses any awareness of her wider environment, saying that 'even when it's very noisy around us I only actually hear Barry's voice. I'll sometimes hear a buzz, but it is just a buzz, you know it could be somebody using a drill or somebody talking. I can't differentiate.' Bea described a distortion of normal perceptions, saying 'I'm a really cold person, I'm always cold. But I never feel cold when I'm there.' Sometimes this change is more dramatic than other times as she recalls 'there was one time when I was on the bed, and I grabbed hold of the duvet because I was floating away'. Up and down can also become confused for poppy:

> He took me off the [rope] spider's web, and I was convinced that the floor was actually the wall and that Barry was going to fall off it! So, I don't always know what way is up. He sat me on a chair and I immediately fell off of it.

But the bottom is aware of their top and of the connection that is being made and remade between them, as Bea puts it 'at that point he is my world. I am completely reliant on him. There is nothing in the world apart from him.'

In sum, a person who has taken the bottom role is more likely to describe an experience which fits with Beckmann's understanding of transcendental states. For the bottom to achieve this degree of immersion, the top needs to function almost as an anchor – they need 'to stay', as Aey put it, in order to keep the bottom safe, and to help them return to the quotidian world. Griff described it in exactly these terms when he told me about an intense 'serial-killer' scene he had done, saying 'I took her somewhere, and I had to carry her out but I also had to remember how to get there.' This does not mean that there is no alteration in reality for the person in the top role – Griff had to remember how to return himself as well as carry his partner back; he is not a bridge between worlds but a fellow traveller with a more stable sense of direction. His immersion is necessarily of a different kind to that of the bottom: in order to navigate this new world, the top gains a heightened awareness of the things which happen within their play-space, and of potential risks or disruptions to that bubble. Demon describes this simply as paying 'more attention to things than I would do normally'.

Michael gave a more detailed description:

> When you're topping you have to be hyper-aware of the other person. Even when you've negotiated everything with safe-words, and okay you're

gagged so you can have this thing to drop or whatever it is you're going to do. Even beyond that ... that's not enough ... it is merely one of the tools. And your awareness of what their body is doing, what their body is telling you. Even without words the body language of that is really important. So, if you're not able to empathise and be in touch and really be part of what is going on, on that really deep level, you're going to miss that and you're going to make a mistake.

Griff agrees that as a top 'you need to be aware of everything that is in the scene. And if you're in a room everything that is in the room is in the scene', resulting in a hyper-awareness of everything happening within that space. He describes this level of attention as 'black light', in the sense that 'it only shows certain things, things that are important or [pause]. Anything that moves in the room whilst I'm doing stuff, that moves without me moving it, immediately has my attention.' This is coupled with, or perhaps extended by, a similar hyper-awareness of the bottom and their reactions.

Demon explains his heightened attention with the observation that 'you have to [have it], because you're fucking around with a speed-of-sound piece of leather, aren't you?'; he is aware of inherent risks in his practice and accepts that this carries responsibility with it. As Michael explains, this responsibility means that the top cannot lose a sense of themselves or their surrounding in the same way a bottom might, 'because I have to be aware of so many things it's very difficult and maybe not good for me to lose myself completely in that moment'. Michael cannot go 'ultra-spacey' and still keep both of them safe, but this doesn't mean he remains outside the world of the play-space:

> There is this kind of being in the zone, a sort of thing that's difficult to describe. While I am in the zone, part of being in it seems to be some sort of extension of being aware. While I am kind of lost in this moment a part of being lost in this moment is being really aware of what is happening.

Damien described a similar combination of lost and heightened awareness, using a candle as an analogy:

> It's kind of ... if you stare at a candle in a dimly lit room you become aware of everything darkening down, and it's just the light of the candle. That's all, everything else will dim. And there's an essence of that, the room may disappear, background noise can fade away.

For some tops, play in a public setting is less immersive because of the need to be aware of other people who might trespass into the play-space or do something unpredictable. It is generally understood to be bad manners to get too close to someone else's play-space but, as poppy experienced, it can happen:

> We were using a cross, a St Andrews. And somebody actually leant on it. And it moved. And that was scary, because suddenly I didn't know what was happening, and I actually thought the cross was falling. And I didn't know which way was up anymore, and I actually did think it was falling down. So, I was screaming. Barry was trying to look after me and tell the chap who was causing the problem to remove himself.

However, for other tops, any other people in the room are something else that disappears. Mistress Marina says 'you're in this little bubble ... And all the other people, the periphery of a club and whatever else is going on sort of disappears into the background and it's just you.' By contrast Demon enjoys playing in public because 'I'm showing off ... I do like showing off ... So I show off to myself, I show off to them, I like to show skill.' He did feel play created a bubble, but knowing people were watching from outside it enhanced his enjoyment of being inside. Tops generally agreed that even if they might not be aware of people outside their play-space they would know if someone wandered into it.

The presence of others can be a matter of indifference to a bottom. Alternatively, it might enhance their experience: Molly describes herself as an exhibitionist, a voyeur and 'a self-voyeur ... so if there's a mirror, if I can watch myself being, well, that's a huge thing for me'. But she also says that sometimes 'if there are other people on other bits of equipment then often I will just close my eyes and shut that off because I want to be in that place, I want to be in my body and my moment'. By contrast, cate said that if she becomes aware of other people in their play-space then the space is broken, 'the headspace it just clears. It did happen last weekend; we were playing in what was supposed to be a couples' room and these single guys – the wanky-men – came in and immediately [pause] my eyes opened and I knew exactly where I was and it [pause]. We came home.' There are also people who enjoy playing with the tension between wanting and not wanting to be watched. I describe this state in myself as being 'a shy exhibitionist'. Ivy discussed a similar tension, saying she enjoys 'being watched' if she feels safe, and is confident that there is no one there 'that might have a different, a very, very different mindset'; in a setting where she can relax, being watched is 'a good thing and that, because I'm stubborn, does things like raising my pain threshold'.

Interestingly, the area where there was the greatest similarity between descriptions of top and bottom experiences of the play-space is in the relationship with time. A sense of time is, regardless of role, something that most people feel they lose completely. Damien, a top, says that 'what feels like five minutes could be an hour and vice versa, what feels like an hour could be five minutes' and Bea, a bottom, similarly says 'I have no idea of the time. It could be ten seconds; it could be ten hours. I don't care'. For poppy, temporal awareness extends to knowing that Barry always takes his time. She says that 'we can't do a quick half an hour, it's usually, you know, three or four hours', but she is not conscious of this time passing, and it takes her a while to get a sense of time back again:

> I'm never aware of it. It takes me the rest of the day, if there is any rest of the day, to work out why it is that the meal I was going to cook for tea can't happen anymore. He will say 'but there is no more time, open a tin of soup'. And I'm going 'but why?'

It may seem surprising that tops lose a sense of time, given that they become so much more aware in other ways, but it does seem to be common. Barry explicitly distinguished awareness of time and space saying that he is always 'very conscious of the space that I'm in, less conscious of time – that goes sort of into semi-suspense'. I quote Griff's description at length, as he explains how he understands the interaction of a hyper-awareness of the play-space and the loss of a sense of time passing:

> This is the thing. I think it's the difference between what actually happens and how I perceive it to be. When I'm fully focussed in [pause] in my head ... it takes hours. Absolutely hours, and I think that is because I'm fully focussed in and my brain is taking in all the information super-fast. It's just coming in coming in coming in coming in and you're not filtering, at all. Whereas if you're not as focussed or when you're moving things around or actually you're not focussed on how to make this person really, really, feel really humiliated, in fact you're thinking about 'hang on, did I have two chairs or three?' right, that thing. Then time changes again ... it's an interesting thing to think about, because I don't actually think about time. I like to take my time ... It's *my* time. Yeah, so I don't know ... it could feel like a really slow long scene and in fact it was twenty minutes whereas

there are certain things that feel like they've been, that was like just a thing, and it's actually been an hour and a half.

The difference between the space for a top and the space for a bottom is illuminated by people who are happy in either role. As a switch, Digi was able to describe both sides of his play with Twisted:

> I don't think about what she's hitting me with at all. There's just the connection between us ... I don't think 'oh she's hitting me with so-and-so now'. It's just, you're lying in the space, and what's happening is happening. And you just let it wash over you ... But if I'm topping I'm very, very conscious of what I'm doing and I'm very aware of, trying to get [hit] the whole of her back rather than just one spot.

Rocks suggests that switches have an advantage when they top, because 'how can you do something like that, particularly when it involves a pain toy, how can you use that carefully and responsibly if you don't know how it feels to be on the receiving end? ... I'd rather they said they've tried it and didn't like it than that they've never tried it at all.' But he is clear that the two experiences are different: bottoming creates 'sensation overload really, of various different sensations'; whereas, when he is topping 'I am concentrating on her and whatever part of her I am playing with at the time':

> If there's two of us it might be that I'm clawing or kneading on her bottom and someone else is maybe scratching her shoulders, but it's yes, I'm doing this here but I know about what's going on there ... all of her is the focus.

Connecting

> [It] falls back to the 'do you care about the responsibility?' If someone is going to offer you that, you've got to take care of it. Someone gives you a diamond ring you have it insured, don't you? And you don't wear it in the garden, do you? You take care of it ... it's precious. It's a precious thing.
>
> (Aey)

> I feel safe, I feel protected. I feel, no matter what he's doing, he's there, he's watching over me. I feel wanted and very much loved.
>
> (cate)

In the play-space people become aware of one another in new ways as they create, recreate and explore relationship. For Friedrich play is an opportunity for a deep and powerful connection to be forged:

> I feel like there's almost like ... I don't know how to describe it. But people, I firmly believe people have got souls ... and I believe that people, humans, are the only creatures on this planet that are truly capable of expression. And this is a form of expression between two people.

Griff uses the idea of meditation to emphasise the importance of relationship, observing:

> The thing is that with meditation, you're closing off your world. You're shutting out all the things that aren't important ... you're shutting out everything except yourself. Whereas if there is two of you shutting out everything that is not important, you're shutting out everything except you and the other person. You're almost opening yourself up to them ... So that connection becomes a lot stronger.

Connection is emphasised in the period after play has finished, which is usually seen as a period of transition back to the quotidian world. This may be the start of building meaning onto the sensations and connections that they have made. For Bea, the aftermath is a time when she feels 'a lot more closeness, a different degree of it. So, I'm a lot more huggy, and wanting to be with you [Dee] ... I just kind of cling on.' Michael described the aftermath of play in both physical and emotional terms:

> The after for me is twofold. There is a sense of release, isn't exactly the right word. Of the ache of your muscles from having used them, and the pleasure of having taken you [Molly] to a place that you've enjoyed ... and the joy of the cry-laughing, and the other things, and just the sheer pleasure and joy of it all afterwards. There's this really lovely glow. I don't know the word that quite encapsulates it; there isn't one that just wraps it all up.

For Stoney-face, both play and its aftermath relate to the exchange of energy between people. He says:

> In a scene your goal is to have your partner feel your energy, you feel your partner's energy, and your energy merges. And you play in that merged energy for a while, and do whatever you need to with it and then, after your scene ends, you sort of separate your energies again in the aftercare,

and whatever you need for aftercare and then you kind of go your separate ways ... knowing that two humans have used the energies they create and connected with in a scene to play with that back and forth, and it feels great. It's amazing.

Rocks agrees that the aftermath is a time to bask in where you have been and where you may have taken someone else:

I like the intensity of connection it brings. That's the driver for it. Yes, in the short term, when you play a scene it'll be pulling energy off your partner and giving it back in various forms, and yes I enjoy the dynamic there. But it's the cuddle afterwards, it's the connection you get as a result of that.

He also felt that the contrast between who you were while in the play-space and the person you are in the everyday world was an important part of play and reflecting on that afterwards was part of the enjoyment:

You have pushed into dark places and you have come back again and, yes, you can be this nasty person but you're not. You don't have to be. You can unleash the beast and you can put it back in the bottle again ... It's the dark side, it's the forbidden side. We're all brought up to be nice people; you aren't supposed to hit people. And here is somebody who has not merely given you explicit permission to hit them; they're getting off on it!

All of the above descriptions about being in play-spaces and connecting with others were given in relation to play which did not reach the peak state commonly known as spacing (see below). The nature of these experiences clearly suggests a degree of altering consciousness is an inherent part of creating play space, and that the kinds of meaning- and world-making processes I am framing as religioning can result even from what might be considered less intense or more ordinary play. Nevertheless, experiences similar to those which would, in a different context, be called religious experiences do take place during kink play.

Spacing

Are there actually experiences that we have as humans that are beyond our ability [to describe]? I think that sub-space is one of those, and it doesn't matter how much you describe it or the words that you use. I'm not sure you can ever give it language to make it truly understandable to somebody who hasn't experienced it in their own way.

(Molly)

When I get really deep into an intense scene there'll be times when all of a sudden I'm looking down on the scene. But I'm still also partly in my body ... I'm seeing it from a kind of floating area above the scene. And seeing it from my body too.

(Javelin)

An interest in 'religious experience', typically understood as a special kind of awareness, or 'white hot' (Taylor, 2003, p. 29) experiences of special or altered consciousness, and often presented as being fundamentally ineffable, has been an enduring area of interest for religious studies. The potential for BDSM to create forms of experience which might fit this understanding was used in Taylor and Ussher's (2001) study, providing one of the categories through which some practitioners might understand their practice. They called this category 'transcendence', defined as BDSM which is explicitly placed 'within a spiritual or mystical framework', or which is associated with experiences of a 'heightened state of consciousness, or as in some way making them more astute, more enlightened or more alive' (ibid., p. 305). The concept of mysticism, largely in Christian forms, implied in this description similarly informed Beckmann's (2009) transcendental states questionnaire.

Although most play has the elements of transcendence discussed earlier there are also white hot BDSM experiences, which stand out from the broader milieu of play in the same way a mystical encounter with divinity might be said to stand apart from prayer or religious worship. It is hard to draw a line around such an occurrence, or to say precisely where they begin and end; but it is certainly the case that, within the different worlds of play-spaces, different levels of immersion and absorption are possible. This is usually talked about in terms of greater or lesser intensity to the play, which can reach a peak that is known as 'sub-space', 'Dom-space' or just as 'spacing'. These terms are understood in different ways, but experiences which merit them are much more likely to be labelled by practitioners as altered consciousness than the more general experience of play. For this reason I believe it to be such peaks of intensity that Beckmann's research participants describe in responding to her questionnaire – in particular the questions asking about 'illusions or hallucinations during a "scene"-Experience' and feeling that 'these experience happened to you without your actual influence' (Beckmann, 2009, pp. 213, 214). This impression is reinforced by her observation that the experiences in which she is interested seem more accessible to those taking the bottom role, since sub-space is far more commonly discussed within the Scene than Dom-space. It is surprising that none of her research participants appear to have offered her either term in their descriptions; she explicitly says that there is 'a lack of words to adequately express experiences formerly unnoticed, unnamed and therefore perhaps unreflected upon' (ibid., p. 200). By contrast I found no one who was unfamiliar with the term sub-space before I mentioned it, and it frequently emerged in conversations before I raised it.

Sub-space

It's very difficult to explain ... it's like the world isn't there anymore, it's like this big cloud, and I'm in the middle of it.

(poppy)

When I'm in that state ... I don't really feel anything, to be truthful. I've got no thoughts at that point. I've gone. If I'm taken far enough everything around me is gone ... I mean I've heard people talk about this when they float above themselves. I'm not floating above myself, I am within my own body. And I'm enjoying whatever pleasures, pain that's being inflicted but I'm not aware of anything else. It's just whatever is happening to me at that time.

(Kaz)

For all its ubiquity, sub-space remains a problematic term. Some people refer to all successful play in terms of a scale of more or less 'spacey' (poppy) than other times – as poppy mused 'I think on balance if it was a ... good scene then I would have been spacey. But how spacey ... ?' – while others use it to refer only to occasional extremes. There was general agreement that the experience of it would be different for everyone, that it is hard to imagine if you have never been there, and that you would know beyond doubt if you had been.

For most people there was a significant change in the experience of sub-space compared with 'ordinary' play-space, with sub-space being a peak or extreme state. Digi described his first experience of sub-space with Twisted, saying to her:

> I'm pretty sure on that occasion you could have kept going, just hitting me harder and harder and harder. You could have drawn blood and I would have been perfectly happy ... it wasn't pain at all. It was just ... a warm massage ... It wasn't just a matter of my being in pain and my body being stretched. I was just floating.

Twisted had a similar experience of becoming unaware of pain, saying that it was 'like being drunk, but just drunk on happiness':

> It's an odd feeling, but I didn't want it to end ... I was aware enough of what he was doing to worry that clover clamps on the labia would hurt ... but no, it didn't hurt, I was drifting.

Most people would agree that pain is a largely meaningless concept once someone has spaced and that, as Barry observed, a top could 'probably get 99% of the way towards murdering' a bottom in sub-space. This is where the connection and 'the trust comes in because then you have to [trust]. There's no way that I could safe-word under those circumstances' (Ivy). Not everyone wants to make themselves this vulnerable; Colin says that while he has 'certainly taken ladies there' he has not been there himself, because 'I don't know that I want to lose control that much.'

Ideas of drifting or floating are often used in descriptions of sub-space, as is the analogy of being drunk. The latter is more commonly used to describe what a person in sub-space might look like than it is used as a descriptor of the experience itself. Rocks, who as a switch can access both observing and experiencing it, concludes that 'drunk is probably the wrong thing, slightly stoned is closer. It's that feeling that things are happening around you but not really comprehending why or what they are.' Ivy describes it as 'switching your brain off' and, along similar lines, Madeleine says it is a 'kind of semi-tonic, tonic immobility. So, you know when you hold the back of a cat's neck and it [dangles]. But it's not just doing that to your body, it's doing that to your brain.' By contrast, cate described sub-space as 'a garden', a fully realised space where 'you walk through the little door and you're there, and it has plants and a big tree and, you know, a water feature and all this sort of thing. And it's bubbling, you can hear the water bubbling.' Her descriptions of play where she did not 'space' are couched in much the same terms as others describe their sub-space experiences.

Sub-space is not the same every time, even if the people involved in making it are the same. Molly differentiates versions of sub-space by their effect on her body:

> sometimes it's like the lights are out, and it's very dark and I am very in my body. That's very calm and deep, and those are the times when I just want to get a blanket and go to sleep afterwards. I am just so relaxed. And then there are other times when it's just kind of hyper-bright. When it's still very in my body but it's almost, very energised within my body. Kind of hyper-stimulated. That ... kind of leaves me wired ... where I'm hyper almost rather than the opposite. And there's no [pause], I can't say that this makes this one and this makes that one.

For poppy, different versions of sub-space are experienced as colours:

> blues and purples are beautiful colours and I can be in a blue and purple cloud and be very happy with that ... Barry says that if I sort of got very excited and very elated, sometimes I can be in yellow then. But if he asks me where I am, if I'm sort of blues, turquoises, then he knows I'm in a happy place.

Personally, I characterise sub-space by my emotional state as I come out of it – there is a cathartic sub-space when I cry, and there is sub-space where I bask in a wonderful contentment.

Once sub-space has been reached it can take a while to return to normal even after play has stopped. People describe being very relaxed, very giggly and silly, sometimes completely non-verbal. For poppy, it is not her who has changed state, but the world around her:

> I'm still me, but everybody else has shifted actually ... It's them, they've all moved. They're slightly out of kilter ... I'm sitting in the middle of whatever it is, and the rest of it has just moved round a little bit ... I'm at sort of 12 o'clock and they're at 5 to, because ... they're just not there. They don't understand.

Rocks also described the process of coming back as feeling that you are 'not really quite being there':

> Almost as though you're walking behind yourself and watching yourself on camera, or someone is following you around with a camera ... You're not quite there, although you know you are.

He also described a state of vagueness and a lack of desire or intention, which he had to carefully think through the stages of apparently simple choices: 'I didn't know what I wanted to do … [and she said] a drink would be a good idea. But how do we get a drink? We ask for a drink … [but] I don't think I was [able to].' The lack of certainty or urgency and an absence of any particular desire to do anything are sufficiently common that some people have a routine to ground themselves while it lasts, preventing a sudden disruptive jolt back to the quotidian world. On the first occasion she achieved sub-space with her Master, cate describes how the effects of spacing meant she was unable to explain to him what she needed to prevent such a jolt, and the distress this led too:

> I was sat wrapped in my blanket, and I really wanted my chocolate, and my Master was saying to me 'no, you must have a toasty because its protein and you must have this' and he wouldn't let me have a cigarette until I could prove that I was steady. And I just completely burst into tears, I was in pieces. I just had a complete fit.

Dom-space

> When it flows … for me it's not thinking about it, it's just kind of happening. And it's not out of body. It's not me looking down upon it, or me travelling beside myself and seeing it. I'm still in charge but it's just effortless. I'm not having to put any effort into it, it's just happening.
>
> (Damien)

> I think the Buddhists will kill me if I say that it's like having nirvana, feeling of nothingness. It's feeling of nothingness. And that's also my definition of sub-space.
>
> (Ben)

Dom-space emerged in conversation less frequently and less spontaneously than sub-space. It was also subject to more diverse conceptualisation. Some people had never heard the term while others assumed that it must refer to the same qualitative state as sub-space and that it was therefore an impossibility for a responsible top. Kaz's observation of playing in the top role is one most tops would agree with – 'I definitely never zone-out. I am always fully aware of everything I'm doing and saying.' However, the idea of a peak in the top experience is problematic only if it is assumed that such a peak must always result in being less in control or aware of the self, of others and/or of ones surrounding. Rocks said that you can't achieve 'the out of body part' of sub-space when you're topping, but you can reach a peak of Dominance in that 'there's a certain point I've reached where you just say right, this is what we're doing. You are going to do it. You're going to put up with it and take what you're given.' Many tops would recognise the possibility of such a peak, without giving it a specific name. However, there were some people who used 'Dom-space' as a name for such a state, explaining how it was qualitatively different to sub-space. Stoney-face explained how a scene can peak in ways which transforms the experience of topping, calling it 'that definite top-space extension of myself thing':

> It starts out as a tool, but as the scene develops, and the energy exchange develops ... it becomes an extension. You transcend the mental process of your technique, making sure you hit them the right way and you've got proper form ... once you lose that it transcends into 'what am I doing to that one spot that's the size of a dime on her ass?' ... and it's just part of your arm at that point. I don't even see the cane anymore. It's where, that point that it's hitting. And I want to be really accurate so [pause] it transcends tool into extension of self really easily.

Javelin described Dom-space as 'the drunkenness of using someone', saying that this consists of 'enjoying the power, and enjoying being in charge ... that euphoria you feel when you pounded them good, and tortured them a bit, and made them cry'. These sorts of peaks of euphoria or a 'feeling that when things are flowing that it's ... the moment when you don't have to think any more, it just seems to occur' (Damien) were described by many tops.

A number of people characterised their Dom-space as being present in sub-space with the bottom, experiencing the other side of that space in the same way that both sides are needed to create the play-space at all. Friedrich said 'I think it is an equivalent. Kind of. I think they're like yin and yang, it's like day and night, one can't exist without the other.' Ben was unable to distinguish, because 'the only difference is how you get there':

> The Dom takes the sub, the sub follows. If you're pulling a cart, the guy who is pulling, you and the cart they all get to that space. The only difference is the cart gets pulled and you pull ... The journey is different; the space is the same.

Cee agreed:

> Sub-space is actually for the person giving as much as the person receiving ... You are just, this sort of sub-conscious state, tuned into a body part and that person's voice, and you are completely oblivious to everything else around you ... You've gone through that keyhole and you've hit the wall right at the very end.

But, however these peaks are understood, no one considered them a primary aim or a reason for engaging in play. The attitude is generally that 'if it happens, it happens' (Ivy).

Gestalt experience

While spacing appears to form the basis of existing academic work on BDSM as spiritual in nature, it is clear that no sharp line can really be drawn between different classes of experience within a play-space. What is equally important is that players do not see more intense scenes as necessarily carrying greater worth or meaning than less intense ones. Using religioning as a framework enables a move away from Christianised understanding of mysticism and removes a value weighting which is not present for most players. All play experience can then inform understanding the contributions of kink play to identity, relationship and community making, and to self- and world-understanding. A sense of meaning and worth becomes associated with kink activity in general, as the experience of play and players reflections on and uses of those experiences feed into an emergent sense of kink as a gestalt.

6

Subcultural identity

Kink in context and in clothes

> Anything that's fixed on the body for a long period of time changes your outlook on life. It changes your relationship to the body you're living in. If you put on a tight belt and wear it for 20 hours strange things will happen to you. Not just physically, but to your consciousness psychically and spiritually.
>
> (Musafar, 1989, p. 9)

> We use the conventions of roles to remove the masks of the daily roles we've allowed ourselves to become. It's a nakedness that we are not accustomed to. To be bare-faced like this is to expose all of the self: the strength, the beauty, the frightening and the frailty.
>
> (Midori, 2005, p. 16)

Practising BDSM involves many different elements: tools, both specially made and not, furniture likewise, also bodies, relationships and real-and-imagined spaces. All elements interact with one another to create the experience of doing BDSM, and all feed into and are fed by the wider context which shapes both experiences and possible understandings of them. Even though the experience of being in play-space is deeply immersive, it does not come into existence in a vacuum devoid of context, sub-text, or other bodies of various kinds. The context in which my research participants live and practice their kinks cannot be solely that of the kink Scene and so some consideration of the broader context must be relevant to understanding how kink might become a gestalt.

Scenes are actively constructed by those who site their practices within them (Moberg and Ramstedt, 2016), but this construction occurs both within and against mainstream culture; it is made from and by people who were born into a complex society, who grew, developed and discovered their kinks in the context of that society and the worlds it creates, and who were influenced by this milieu in both subtle and unsubtle ways.

The world in which my research participants live, and therefore the context of their practice and self-understanding, is a hypermodern world. Capitalism, industrialisation, rationalisation, institutions and surveillance extend to what might once have been considered extremes. In an ongoing process the values established by modernity have 'passed over into a logic of excess, to the point where no counter-power seems able to oppose their frenetic development' (Charles, 2009, p. 391). Hypermodernity is a time of hyper-individualism, constant change and rampant commercialisation. Technological and scientific developments are rapid and loaded with both threat and promise (Lipovetsky and Charles, 2005) and a culture of radical individualism renders self-fulfilment is the highest virtue (Baumeister, 1988, 1991; Varga, 2005). The relational functions of the body – emotion, sexuality, perception and so on – are denied and minimised, and the boundary role of skin potentially reinforced (Hall, 2010); individuals are understood as autonomous, unitary selves, wholly responsible for their own happiness, creators of their own identity. Within this context the human body is 'a mode of specification of individuals' (Foucault, 1978, p. 47) that exists as 'an analysed, theorised, politicised, and sensationalised entity, concurrently functioning as a medium for physical, psychological, emotional and spiritual transformation' (Winge, 2012, p. 1). Personal identity and self-understanding are thus partly expressed in the ways people choose to clothe and mark their bodies, and choices about appearance can be simultaneously considered expressions of individuality and a claiming or signalling of subcultural identity and membership. Personal style is therefore neither trivial nor frivolous, but a part of self- and world-creation and a factor in the forming of meaningful relationships. It is therefore a potential aspect of personal religioning.

Style is not restricted to clothing choice, but includes any objects necessary to enable the performance of the chosen identity (Lunning, 2013). As a contributor to personal identity construction kink style is also a contributor to the story- and meaning-making role of personal kink. Cultural and subcultural norms and values of appearance and self-expression are expressed and transgressed by kink practitioners in ways which contribute to the gestalt value practitioners ascribe to their kink. This is fashion 'in its performance as costume' (ibid., p. 1), even where that role indicated by that costume is experienced as an authentic expression of identity. The ability to dress in particular ways creates a 'space of freedom', allowing 'the flow of imagined identities' to both support identity and enrich 'the individual subject through group recognition and interplay' (ibid., p. 12). At the same time, the expressions of autonomy, free choice and difference, which are felt as an inherent part of the transgression of norms, conform to a core value of hypermodernity.

Clothing the subcultural body

> I look at the Coyote spirit in the more trickster element of playful jokes and things of that nature ... I love, inside the kink context, to be at play parties going around and making people laugh ... I run around with a see-through elephant mesh G-string with bells in it to get people to die in hysterics. And over the knee stockings, it's awesome.
>
> (Stoney-face)

> Some people [I work with] could be cross-dressing; they're then able to ... [pause] they then go into another world.
>
> (Cee)

The wearing of clothes is a powerful cultural norm, to the point where nudity in public places may well be criminalised. Clothing in a hypermodern world is not only functional protection from the elements, but an expression of values. When the concept of fashion, style and personal identity are recognised, the matter of what people wear becomes more complex still, with the ways in which people choose to present themselves visually to others potentially serving as a signal of identity, ideology, politics, morality, lifestyle and more (Haenfler, 2014; Winge, 2012). Sending visual signals about self and identity, allegiances and values, includes many different ways of marking and presenting the body. Possible body modifications range from dying hair to remodelling physical shape, from painting the skin with make-up to etching into it with needles, blades or brands. Through a selection of such means appearance can become 'body style' (Winge, 2012), a deliberate displaying of identity and affiliation. 'Objects of effectuation' (Lunning, 2013, p. 101), meaning the items used to create particular effects or aspects of identity performance, can also form a part of a chosen body style. In the context of kink, such objects would range from the obviously kinky whips, canes, crops and so on to the more subtle – choice of shoes, a *Story of O* (Réage, 1985) style ring or an '[every]day collar'.

Kink in context and in clothes • 83

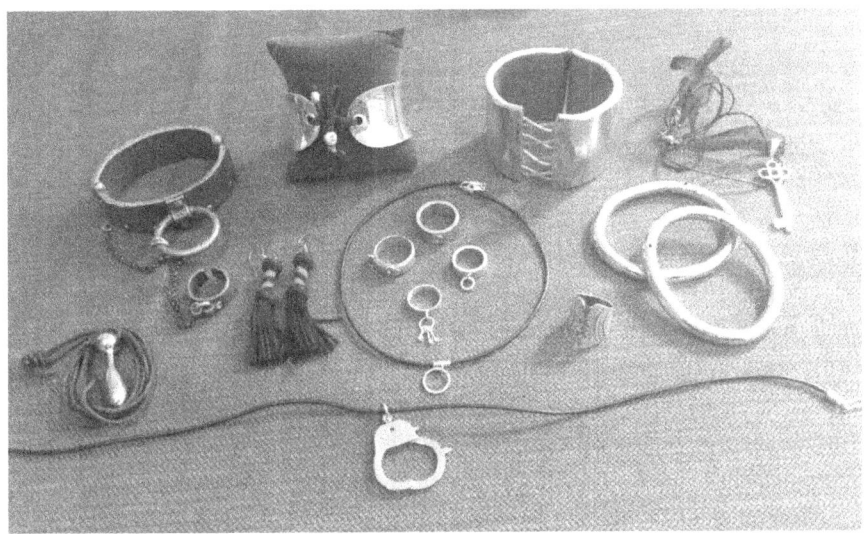

Figure 8 Jewellery with a kink 'edge'

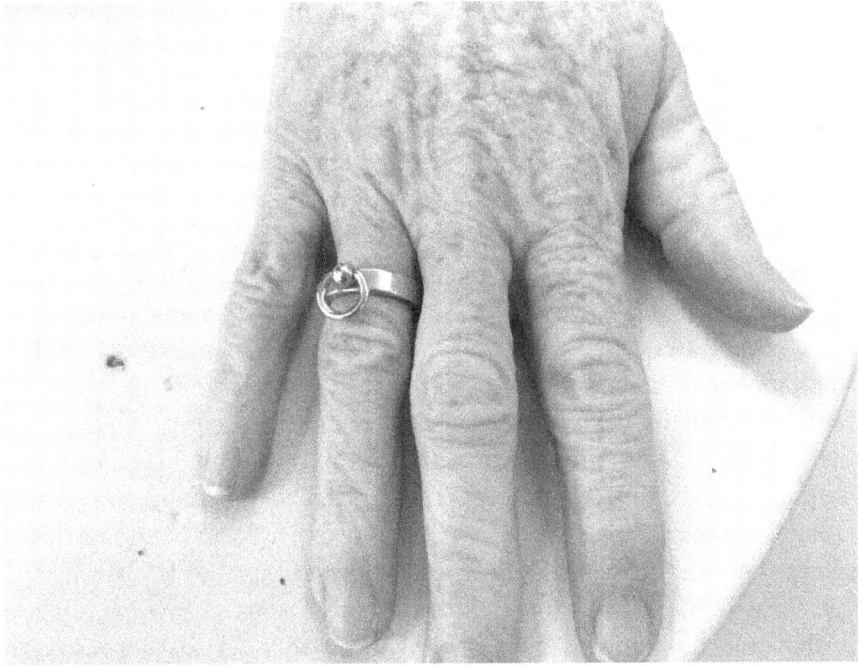

Figure 9 Story of O ring

Body style is an important tool of communication for Scenes which consciously set themselves apart from mainstream culture. Such groups build from the individual lived-body experiences of group members to create collective ideas about identity which are both shared and contested in an ongoing process, constructing an authenticity for the group (Moberg and Ramstedt, 2016). Part of this process is the establishing, and continual development, of commonly understood (although usually unwritten) guidelines or codes about authentic appearance and what is (un)acceptable within the group. Style choices for a subcultural Scene may well include elements considered non-normative by the wider society, but both style and subcultural identity are complicated by the fact that, as Winge observes, 'what is acceptable and normative is increasingly consumed from subcultural entities' (Winge, 2012, p. 48). The line between what is mainstream and what is not is increasingly blurred.

Offering a working definition of the concept of subculture, Haenfler (2014) states that the term is more a descriptor for an ongoing process of social networking. Although the boundaries of such networks are diffuse, members of subcultures have some sense of shared identity and actively create (and contest) meanings around practice, objects, ideas and values that are, to some degree, deviations from the norm. Because of this, claiming subcultural identity also conveys a degree of outsider status. As a self-identified group smaller than society as a whole, which distinguishes itself from the mainstream by and through engagement in specific activities and the associated processes of creation (and contestation) of meaning it is clear that the kink Scene can be considered a subculture.

There are a number of strong visual stereotypes associated with kink. These are used within mainstream popular culture to signal a degree of edginess and to mark dramatic depictions of kinky people (Scott, 2015). They include corsetry, gleaming latex (usually black or red), extreme high-heels and uniforms (or sexualised versions of uniforms). Collectively these looks are often referred to as fetish fashion, perhaps because these items are also common foci for paraphilias, but they are commonly worn at kink events and not everyone who does so experiences the items themselves as objects of a sexual fetish. The widespread use of these strong visuals in fashion, film and other popular culture is a matter of some concern in the kink community. This is not only because it perpetuates a stereotype many reject, but because of the resulting transfer of kink style into mainstream fashion. It is sometimes said that 'SM' has, in recent years, come to mean 'Stand and Model' (Califia, 1994; MacKendrick, 1999; Weiss,

2011), as the fashion industry and popular culture borrow dramatic looks from the kink Scene to add 'an entirely superficial sense of "edginess"' (Scott, 2015, p. 58) to their products.

A focus on clothing is not purely a matter of aesthetic choice but serves as a basis for expressing broader concerns. The worry that 'our tribal gear' (Califia, 1994, p. 42) is being appropriated by people who have no interest in actually doing kinky things, but who seek an easy route to the flavour of the exotic they feel is communicated by the look, is one such concern. It touches upon on questions about subcultural membership and authenticity, and also emphasises the importance individuals attach to their kink identity. Scott (2015) suggests that an increasingly visually orientated culture feeds the perception that looking kinky provides an indicator of who is kinkiest, which in turn implies not dressing the part means you are not 'really' kinky. Both the existence and rejection of such perceptions emerged during my conversation with Michael, who observed:

> I'm just not sure why I have to dress up to be a part of this. Why do I have to look funny, in my eyes, to do this? And yet the more ridiculous I look the more accepted I will be. If I showed up wearing a clown suit with scuba-fins and a mariachi band behind me people would go 'look how kinky this guy is!'

He says he is 'fairly resistant' to any emphasis on look, and points out the irony in having joined 'an alternative lifestyle, that is breaking the rules of mainstream society and then the first thing they do is make up more rules. You know, you can come to our fetish event if you dress in this way that everyone else will recognise as being part of the fetish world.' This is a concern with authenticity, understood as the difference between being a person who does kinky things as opposed to looking like a kinky person in order to shock or to follow a fashion.

A related area of concern is that, through adoption of a kink aesthetic, non-kinky people might be led into potentially dangerous practices they don't understand or respect (Scott, 2015; Weiss, 2011). This was referenced by my research participants, as in Damien's description of girls entering the kinky scene with an interest in the aesthetic of a corset piercing (parallel lines of rings piercing the skin, through which ribbon can be threaded), because 'they've seen pictures of corseting and that's what they want. They like the look … But they don't realise all that's involved.' As a result, they are surprised and distressed when faced with the actual process of piercing and inserting the rings.

It is true that corsets, latex and heels feature heavily in pornography, edgy music videos and dramatic depictions of kink (Scott, 2015). It is however open to question whether what is now recognised as a kinky look actually originated in an underground subculture before being appropriated by the fashion industry, or whether it has developed (and continues to develop) in a cyclical process fed by many streams (Lunning, 2013). What is certain is that BDSM clubs usually do have a dress code of some kind, which may be as simple as 'no jeans' or as detailed as the example from the Torture Garden shown in Figure 10 (from www.torturegarden.com/events1, accessed 26 February 2016).

Even where not specified by a formal dress code, all the types and forms of 'Fantasy Dress' specified above can be seen at play clubs and parties, although people playing at home are less likely to dress up unless the particular item of clothing, or material it is constructed from, is the object of a fetish for them.

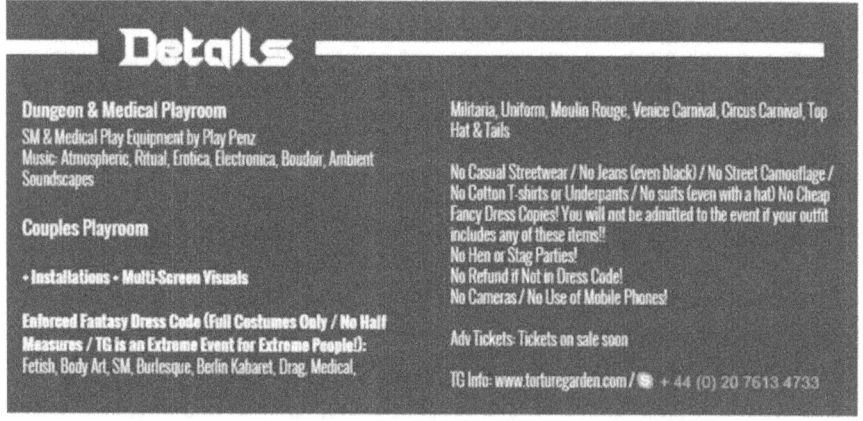

Figure 10 Torture Garden dress code

Image and experience

> I do have an aesthetic appreciation ... like looking at Effie in the mirror and admiring myself as Effie. I find that interesting, and ... sexy. Not necessarily in a highly, highly erotic kind of way. But almost a sensual way you know ... I feel great. I really do.
>
> (Simon/Effie)[1]

---

1. Effie is the name Simon adopts when dressed for play. Effie is not simply an alternate persona wholly separate from Simon, so I have chosen to use both names together to indicate that one does not/cannot exist without the other.

> I can think of two, two ladies in particular, who when they saw themselves in a mirror with an academic gown on over really nice lingerie it was 'wow, do I really look like that?' ... And I think in a way I see that as part of my mission, making people know and understand!!
>
> (Colin)

Given the strength of the BDSM aesthetic and the ubiquity of images which fit the stereotype, even within kinky social networks, I cannot help but notice how rarely clothing was mentioned as an important element of play during my research conversations. It was considered in the most depth by the two among my research participants who use cross-dressing as an integral part of their play: Colin, who is primarily interested in CP (corporal punishment) chooses a look particularly associated with that sub-genre of kink in the form of a girls' school uniform, which he wears with high-heeled shoes; and Simon/Effie, who chooses a more BDSM-typical look based on black PVC. Contra to stereotype he doesn't wear heels, to ensure he is shorter than his play-partners.

Both of them did consider the visual aesthetic of their chosen clothing, but this was not a matter of central concern. Simon/Effie said that he does 'have an appreciation. I quite like looking at Effie in the mirror and admiring myself as Effie. I find that interesting, and sexy. Not necessarily in a highly, highly erotic kind of way. But almost in a sensual way. I feel great. I really do'. It is interesting to note how the focus shifts here, from the visual looking at himself to the way that he feels. By contrast Colin finds his school uniform important to 'cover all this flab and this horrible body up' and made no mention of looking at himself when dressed. Although Simon/Effie does like to look at himself when dressed for play, he also referred to cross-dressing as a means of addressing a dislike of his body:

> What I'm doing is trying to hide my body, wherever I can, and showing the bits that I want to show ... I don't like it. I don't like it. It's not attractive. I'm too old to be, to have a beautiful body. [Being dressed as Effie] hides my bits. I've got just the right bits on display.

For both of them, cross-dressing offers an opportunity for bodily experience free from concerns about body image. This was something other people referenced as well. Mistress Marina says:

> I think one of the reasons I love being in that [play] space so much is it's one of the few times in my life when I accept my physicality. Because I do

> not like my physicality day to day. If I walk by, see myself in a shop window, that's it. I'm down for the rest of the day ... [Usually] I try to avoid myself.

In several different research conversations, I likewise observed (in conversation with Mistress Marina) that when I play looks are 'a non-issue' for me, saying that 'I feel beautiful when I play, and I look beautiful too. I mean I look in the mirror after and I see beauty, which is absolutely not what I would see if I looked right now!' An emphasis on feeling is not unusual; Colin plays in a way that requires particular clothing but he explicitly distances the visual and emphasises the felt nature of the experience of being cross-dressed, saying that 'I know I probably look a bit strange in my school uniform but I *feel* lovely in it' (his emphasis). Simon/Effie made the same distinction, even while describing a visual. Esteban distinguishes between the visual and the somatic experience even more explicitly, saying he deliberately avoids seeing himself dressed in latex, or wearing a leather harness, because 'if I look at myself if I'm in a harness or something like that, I just look at myself and think "oh, that's a bit daft. That's a bit stupid ..." It breaks the mood.' Although he appreciates the visual image of himself dressed, Simon/Effie also says that 'my body makes more sense as Effie. My physical body.'

Wearing fetish-style clothing is not purely a matter of a visual aesthetic, even in relation to an improved self-image. Subcultural styles are not simply about conforming to a pre-existing set of fashion rules but are the performance of an authentic identity. Importantly, authenticity is not felt to arise simply from the choice to wear these clothes, or even to attend the events that both require and showcase them, but from what informs or motivates those choices. The distinction is perceived as between 'being' a subcultural member and merely 'doing' aspects of the subculture (Haenfler, 2014; Newmahr, 2011b; Widdicombe and Wooffitt, 1990), and the emphasis on feeling is an important indicator of the performance of authenticity.

Even from the perspective of a purely visual aesthetic choice, clothing can be an important signal of identity – gothic 'bondage trousers' (trousers decorated with cloth straps and buckles) are not often seen in play clubs or at kink parties – perhaps because they are not up to the task of genuinely restraining someone – but a person's choice to wear them nevertheless signals something about how the wearer feels about themselves. Similarly, items of clothing that would be seen at kink venues – and probably only at kink venues, or on catwalks – signal something about the individual's kink identity. For example, a spanking (backless) skirt is unlikely to be worn by someone who exclusively tops. However, it is also clear that when considered in more depth such clothing is more than just a visual signal.

Bodies in clothes

> What I don't like about clubs is the dress code ... I feel I'm too old and I've put on too much weight to wear [fetish clothing] and that doesn't make me who I am ... I don't see why I should have to wear PVC, or rubber, or leather or a uniform to enjoy play ... But I can go to fetish club in a dress with my teacher's gown and I'm allowed in because I've got a teacher gown. But the dress underneath is who I actually am. So, when I start playing I take my gown off, and I'm just me!
>
> (Kaz)

> I don't wear heels, because if you wear heels when you're doing that you always want to tip backwards ... It's about slipping, or if you're in a place that has rubbish on the floor or wet spots or things like that ... it's just a distraction.
>
> (Aey)

The surface of the skin is always sensitive. An awareness of what is touching the skin at any given moment is always available, 'we just have to attend, and there it is' (Sheets-Johnstone, 2009b, p. 139). This includes things which are so commonplace, or so constantly in contact with the skin, that the way they feel usually lies below the surface of conscious awareness. While it is possible to choose to attend to the tactility of clothing against skin, this feeling does not force itself into our awareness every day. By contrast, clothing worn only for special occasions may do so – a person who rarely wears a tie will be conscious of its pressure on their neck and may feel short of breath or restricted in the ways they can move their head.

Iconic items of kink clothing offer examples of clothing which create an experience of wearing them that is noticeably different from wearing other clothing. Such outfits are so firmly entwined with the practice of kink in the cultural imaginary that a customer visiting a professional Dominatrix might feel entitled to complain if she is not so dressed. In addition, entry to shared social spaces may be restricted for those choosing not to conform. Yet it is also true that when play takes place in such shared spaces much of this special clothing is removed. I suggest that this has at least as much to do with the multi-sensory experience of wearing it, and the potential of that to distract from the play (in the same way that catching sight of himself in latex was a distraction for Esteban), as it has to do with a practical desire not to damage expensive consumer goods.

The spectrum of commercially available clothing ranges from adding a slightly 'edgy' element to everyday clothing to an extreme aesthetic commitment to a particular look – from a 'corset back' on a shirt perhaps, in the form of some largely decorative criss-crossed lacing, to a steel-boned waist-training corset worn twenty-four hours a day. Corset lacing, decorative straps, buckles, zips and studs constitute a fashion fetish look which overlaps with goth, punk and rock aesthetics. This kind of clothing may or may not form part of a kinky person's everyday wardrobe, but it certainly would not get someone into a club like the Torture Garden, which cautions attendees 'if your outfit wouldn't turn heads in the street – don't bother to wear it to Torture Garden' (www.torturegarden.com/about, accessed 11 March 2016). Whether or not it would constitute 'making an effort' for other clubs would be down to the individual preferences of the organisers, but if the rule were 'no street clothes' the prevalence of such garments on the high-street makes it unlikely. Wearing fetish fashion clothes is a sensory experience on a par with any other everyday outfit: the clothes are put on the same way and chosen, not solely for the aesthetic, but because they achieve that look while allowing people to get on with the things they want to do on an everyday basis. But at the other end of the spectrum of kink clothing this is no longer true.

Putting on the kink

> Corsets are a pain in the arse ... Because they take half an hour to take off ... I like the aesthetic in the street more than in a fetish club.
>
> (Demon)

> I've got a latex catsuit which I enjoy wearing [pause] I hate the smell of it ... but I do love the experience ... having a tight second skin all over ... Yeah. So, that's nice.
>
> (Esteban)

It is broadly true that, the more overtly kinky the clothing, the more the experience of wearing it differs from that of putting on and wearing everyday clothes. Putting on kink clothing is not like slipping on a jumper. It is a ritual process that involves skill, practice and relationship. Getting dressed in kink style can signal the start of passage into a kink- or play-space.

One example of iconic kink clothing which illustrates this well is the corset. Fashion corsets are typically 'boned' with plastic strips, to create a smooth outline which highlights the natural curve of the waist, rather than actually changing the shape of the wearer. In a kink context, corsets are more likely to have metal bones and be intended to reshape the waist to some degree. The experience of wearing this kind of corset begins from the moment of deciding to put it on, because it is likely that help will be required to get properly into it. A 'proper' or 'real' corset, with steel bones, should be a minimum of two inches smaller than the uncorseted waist and so putting it on requires loosening the laces to a sufficient extent to get the garment around the body for fastening; the more inches one desires to trim from the waist measurement the harder this will be to achieve, and the more likely it is that assistance will be needed to hold the edges together while simultaneously working the fastenings. The most common front fastening is a busk – two flat strips of metal which run up each of the front edges. One side has a line of short pegs and the other has flat metal eyelets with a keyhole shape; the peg needs to be inserted through the round part of the eyelet and is then pulled sideways so the upright of the peg is gripped tightly in the narrower part and cannot slip back out. The inflexibility of the busk means that the entire row needs to be fastened in one movement – a surprisingly difficult manoeuvre, even with an empty corset. But when the garment is under tension, as it is when being pulled together against the resistance of the natural body shape, fastening a busk can become a deeply frustrating exercise, in which the middle peg in particular resists alignment. Even corsets that fasten in other ways will benefit from the presence of additional hands; a corset that is open only at the back needs unlacing completely and then re-lacing around the body while being held in place and any front-fastening corset is likely to require holding together at both the top and the bottom to do up those fastenings. It is only once the garment is basically on and fastened that the process of tightening the laces can begin. It is hard to tighten laces located at the centre of the back fully and evenly by oneself, but it is necessary that they be adjusted if the corset is to fit properly. Ideally, tightening is done from the centre of the vertical line of lacing, working both upwards and downwards to achieve as even a gap along the length of the corset as possible.

After about half an hour of wear laces should be tightened again as the corset warms and moulds more to the shape of the body.

The result of all this is a torso encased in fabric and metal from hips to armpits. At a minimum a corset has metal bones along the full length of each seam, as well as at each side of any front fastening and on either side of the eyelets for the lacing. The garment shapes the body beneath it; it holds the spine straight and pulls the shoulders back. Bending and twisting are, at best, severely restricted, and some kinds of movement are impossible – it is a good idea to fasten your shoes before you put on a corset! The feel of posture and movement is also changed, not only those movements which clearly involve the back and stomach – like bending forward – but also walking, and even arm movements, as the flesh of the waist is displaced upwards. It is possible to sit down while wearing a corset, although getting into a low or soft chair is challenging and getting up from it again may require help. Seated posture and position in the seat will be changed though, and slouching or lounging are likely to be uncomfortable; an upright chair becomes a preferable option to a sofa. The kinaesthetic experience of the body is changed, not only in the ways limbs can move, but in the movements of the flesh itself; for example, breasts are likely to be pushed upwards, which is visually pleasing to many, but is a vastly different kinaesthetic experience to the wearing of a brassiere. All of this means corset wearing is far from being purely about the visual presented to others but is an experience in its own right.

Latex is also more of a sensory experience than the simple creation of a visual look; Esteban told me that he loves wearing his latex catsuit but 'I'm not fond of the smell of it', he also dislikes the way it looks. However, for him the experience overall is strong enough to overcome multiple unpleasant sensory elements. Latex is a well-known fetish item, so 'rubberists' form a shared interest group beneath the kink umbrella. Esteban however did not appear to regard himself as having a fetish for latex, and indeed his dislike of the smell and look would argue against that being the case. For him the tactile experience is more akin to an experience of bondage, which is his primary play interest.

Latex is versatile enough to be made into any style of garment, but it is most commonly used for items like catsuits, which are skin-tight over at least part of the body. In its most extreme form a latex catsuit covers the entire surface of the body leaving apertures for eyes, nostril and lips (and maybe not even all these). Because it stretches a great deal some latex garments have no fastening at all; instead, an opening like the neck band must be stretched sufficiently to insert limbs and the garment is then worked across the skin to cover the parts it is shaped to cover. It is possible to make a whole body catsuit with no fastening (thus ensuring the smoothest possible outline) but many are zipped in various locations which may or may not be accessible to the wearer.

Tight latex is challenging to put on. Although it stretches with varying degrees of ease (depending on the thickness of the rubber), once it touches skin it clings. It also induces sweat which exacerbates the clinging over time and makes the latex more likely to stick to itself when removed. This means it is impossible to pull latex straight on (as would be the case with other fabrics) and once it is on it is challenging to adjust. A sensible first step is to coat the inside of the garment with talcum powder or a specially made lubricant, so that it can be eased over the body. With a garment like a catsuit this easing process begins at the feet, as the area most distant from the opening. The latex needs to fit smoothly and comfortably there before it is drawn further up the legs. Other garments are worked on in the same way, by choosing a starting point and siting it correctly before working on the next part. Once latex is covering a patch of skin adjustment requires sliding a hand in between the skin and the latex to break the seal. If the entire garment is on, and an unwanted crease is spotted by the ankle, the easiest thing to do is to peel the garment off to that point and start again from there. How much help is required in this process will vary with the size and fit of the garment and with the wearer's level of experience in putting it on, but it is certainly a process which must be learned. Ensuring that it is sitting correctly on the body, that the seams run where they should and that any zips are properly fastened, are all points at which assistance is helpful.

Once it is on the garment is likely to need polishing; not everyone likes to wear their latex polished to the high shine which tends to feature in fetish photography, but the use of talc or lubricant is likely to mark the outside of the garment. Polishing the garment removes these, and any finger marks, as well as brightening the colour. This stage of the process almost certainly requires third party assistance to make sure the whole garment is attended to. The process of getting dressed is thus not only a tactile experience, but a relational one, as the garment is firmly rubbed over the flesh. Latex itself, and the different options available to aid putting it on and shining it up, all have distinctive scents, which will change as the latex warms to body temperature.

Wearing latex is physically restrictive, although in a different way to the rigidity of a corset. It has a degree of stretch, but the resistance is palpable and becomes more so as the stretch is increased. Worn skin-tight there is a subtle but constant squeeze of pressure, and this can be felt loosening and re-grasping as the body moves within the garment. Because skin under latex cannot breathe, sweat cannot evaporate; instead the latex lies over a sheen of moisture. This not only makes it difficult to remove but means that, when it is finally off, there is a sudden temperature change as the wet skin is exposed to the air. This combines with a sense of the skin releasing itself from the folds and creases it has been moulded into while the latex was being worn. All these different elements contribute to the fetishisation of latex, and the common recognition of latex as a fetish object means that wearing it is more likely to be recognised as an experience in its own right than the wearing of corsets. It may also be more likely to be indulged in simply for that experience than for the visual image it creates.

It is interesting to note, given the emphasis on intimacy and relationship inherent in successful play, that both these popular modes of kink dress entail relationship and touch in the creation of the look, while the physical experience of wearing them is one of constriction and holding in. Lunning argues that a desire for constriction is rooted in a desire for boundaries which can 'expand into a series of inner and outer, psychic and physical markers that contain, confine and define' (Lunning, 2013, p. 81) within the different world of the play-space. Westerfelhaus observes that 'many of the costumes and rituals employed by BDSM ... such as hoods, bondage and suspension, which promote sensory deprivation ... coupled with or followed by activities producing sensory overload' are designed and intended to 'disrupt ordinary consciousness' (Westerfelhaus, 2007, p. 270). In this he is correct, but his association of 'costumes' with those items intended to create sensory deprivation is overly narrow. The processes of putting on kink clothing can be a part of the ritual of play, by creating anticipation (Ezzy, 2011) and signalling the beginnings of liminality (Ezzy et al., 2009). In addition, the sensations involved in wearing these items, in moving in them, and in having them removed again, are fully multi-sensory and relational kink experiences. Far from being a peripheral part of the event, clothing can contribute to creating the spaces for play, to the desired sensory overload (or sensory deprivation) and to the return to the everyday world. Such clothing can also distract from or muffle other sensations; if the desire is to experience these fully clothing is likely to be removed, however such muffling or reduction of intensity might also be used to aid in the exploration of limits.

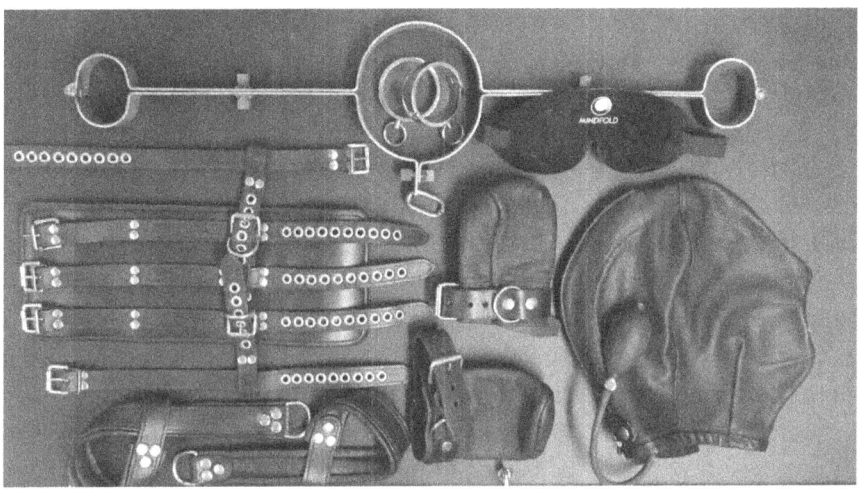

Figure 11 Bondage equipment

Community of consumption

> My biggest disappointment with the whole thing is that even these supposedly liberal minded people ... there are still snobs. There are still people who think their way is the best way and nobody else can match it; or 'you're not using the right sort of implement', or 'you didn't buy your whip from such and such a place'. And that was my biggest disappointment with the whole thing.
>
> (Damien)

> I think you grow up when you come into the Scene. When you're first in it it's like being a kid in a toyshop ... and you go there and you buy that, and that, and that ... and you want to play with everybody and everything. And then after a while you start thinking 'Oh, I don't really fancy those things. I only really like those sweets.' And you tend to be a bit more choosey about who and what you do. So, you don't get as much of it but what you do get is a better quality.
>
> (Mistress Marina)

Given the dress requirements of many kink events, and the powerful cultural associations between kink and clothing style, it is interesting to realise that to actually engage in play frequently requires a degree of undressing again, at least on the part of the bottom. This may be partly because these outfits are expensive, and strenuous play might cause them damage. Fetish garments require a degree of specialist skill in their manufacture that means even 'off the peg' versions are likely to be costly, and many people choose to buy bespoke garments, both for better fit and to have something unique. A good quality latex dress or bespoke corset can hundreds of pounds, and a reluctance to risk splits, tears, stains or other damage is therefore understandable. This is probably not the sole reason as it is also true that, while the bottom is fully clothed, the possibility for creating sensation is limited and the intensity potentially dulled; the restrictive nature of much fetish clothing also impacts on the positions that can be adopted and held by the bottom and the free movement of the top. Nevertheless, the potential costs associated with BDSM, at least in the contexts of the Scene and public play, have been remarked upon by a number of commentators (Newmahr, 2011b; Weiss, 2011) and used to argue that in a hypermodern, commercialised world 'individualism and choice are not equally available across the social landscape' (Weiss, 2011, p. 172).

Weiss has thoroughly explored BDSM as 'community of consumption' and she argues that the purchase of BDSM equipment and clothing contributes to the 'production of identity, community and attendant social relations' (Weiss, 2011, p. 111) for kinky people, just as it does in other parts of society, including subcultures (Haenfler, 2014). This observation is in accord with concerns that 'the ability to purchase SM paraphernalia so easily, and have these purchases signify one's SM identity or community belonging, will destroy the spiritual centre, heart, or something else *authentic* about SM relationality' (Weiss, 2011, p. 126). The removal of clothing for play can be seen as an attempt to cut through the idea of a purchased or surface image to expose or get at the 'real' player beneath the exciting outfit.

The removal of costume, and the resulting potential for nakedness, is mentioned by Weiss only in passing. For example, in her descriptions of a 'slave auction' she describes 'slaves' voluntarily stripping, being stripped by their 'vendor' or, in one case, stripping off layer after layer of clothing and underclothing so that they never actually become naked. She describes this young woman as having the last laugh and notes that she identified as a top, although being auctioned as a bottom. I see this as indicative of the meanings the Scene places on the wearing and removal of clothing, but Weiss does not explore it in greater depth; a surprising omission in an exploration of BDSM as a circuit which 'works when connections are created between realms that are imagined as isolated and opposed' (Weiss, 2011, p. 7). That the BDSM Scene creates such circuits I have little doubt, but I find it likely that the use of both dress and public nudity within the Scene contribute to these, as a part of the performative production of subjects.

While the focus of my research is the experience of play, and the emergence of meaning from such experience, the issues of capitalism and consumerism are part of the hypermodern context in which BDSM occurs and so cannot be entirely ignored. Kink consumer goods extend beyond clothing to the toys and tools which are arguably a more fundamental part of play than costume. Weiss observes that, although people insist it is entirely possible to practice BDSM without spending any money at all, she failed to find anyone who did so. Instead she suggests that a varied toy-bag, filled with a range of expensive items designed to create specific sensations, comes to be read as a signal of the skills and experience of the top. Bottoms may purchase items which create the sensations they wish to feel used on them. More expensive, well-made toys may also have an intrinsic artistic value, and a sense of enhanced utility that comes with quality. For Weiss, this aesthetic element can only be appreciated as an enhancement to play if the person buying the item has some knowledge of how it is used, and therefore why this particular one would be worth paying more for. She sees this as a process of consumer knowledge that allows people to 'construct themselves as active subjects through differentiated consumption' (Weiss, 2011, p. 113). While BDSM has been presented as a site of resistance to capitalist commodity exchange (Carrette, 2005), Weiss disagrees, because BDSM is 'productive of more than love' (Weiss, 2011, p. 136), and so its pleasures cannot be directly opposed to commodity exchange. She argues instead for understanding the different forms of exchange involved in BDSM as operating together, 'producing forms of identity, subjectivity, pleasure, relationality and community' (ibid., p. 137).

That commodities and services proliferate around the kink Scene is undeniable; toys and equipment cost money whether they are purchased from a high-street sex shop or from a specialist producer of kink goods. Attendance at kink events likewise costs money, for entry fees and travel at the very least. In this, BDSM is no different to many other leisure activities that are more accessible to practitioners with disposable income and, as Newmahr's conceptualisation of kink as serious leisure indicates, such commitment of capital has become a partial measure of how highly people value their chosen leisure activity. Serious leisure is distinguished both from more casual leisure and from purely sexual activity in its involvement of public spaces, the 'appreciable learning curve, financial expenditures and ... social network' (Newmahr, 2010, p. 314). People committed to a given activity as serious leisure choose to put time, effort and resources into the development of their skills and the continuation of their practice. Some people spend their money on sky-diving, some people spend it on attending sports events and some people spend it on their kink. They make this commitment because of what they get from the activity, which may well include a sense of resistance to social norms but which also involves 'intense concentration, intense sensation, and intense psychological and emotional stimulation [resulting in] an immersive and re-energising experience' (ibid., p. 324).

Weiss suggests a perception that status and skill level are often inferred from a person's toy collection and the brand names it includes (Weiss, 2011); my participants did not communicate this idea and I speculate that kink brands are perhaps less pervasive in the UK Scene of which most of my participants are part. Although some did speak of the pleasure to be had in using well-made and aesthetically pleasing tools where they offered examples of these they had generally been acquired from craftspeople at various UK 'alternative markets' and descriptions of them did not include an idea of brand or label. The importance of these artisan made tools was in the feel of their use (for both top and bottom) and in a more general delight in good craftsmanship. In the latter context, several people named a craftsman who makes one-of-a-kind floggers from hand-turned wood, and this was the closest to a brand-name anyone came during our conversations. On the occasions when I have shown one of this individual's floggers to an academic audience it has produced the same kinds of response in terms of aesthetic appreciation for the beauty of the item and the skill which went into making it as can be seen in the kinky people clustering around his stall at a fetish market. The only observable difference seems to be that academics apparently feel no need to ask someone to bend over so they can try it out.

My research participants are undoubtedly aware of the interactions between consumer culture and kink, and some of these circuits may be of concern to them. Outlay on expensive custom-made tools and costumes is not an explicit requirement of any club or group of which I am aware but may be felt by some to be necessary as a part of the unspoken guidelines that inform subcultural style or belonging. What is also true is that many people find great satisfaction in exploring 'pervertables' – Oliver described this as 'making stuff out of ordinary household stuff'. This does potentially reduce the costs of stocking a toy bag, but again the satisfaction described is less that of thrift than it is of 'creating the means to an end ... to create the experience' (Esteban). The list of 'ordinary household stuff' that can be used for kink purposes is only limited by the imagination of the user, but more obvious items would include: elastic bands, clothes pegs, wooden spoons/spatulas, rulers, meat tenderisers, slippers, plimsolls, candles, hairbrushes, cable ties, shoe horns, ice, root ginger, cling-film, ties, belts and scarves. There is also the human body itself, which can interact with other bodies in many ways. Speaking of tools for delivering a beating, Oliver says that 'the best thing is your hand, [because] I like the closeness that comes with that'. Mistress Marina agrees, 'I very rarely use a lot of equipment because I tend to think "I've got my nails, I've got my teeth. I don't need anything." I've usually managed to do what I need to do with those.' This is not simply an issue of saving money but of the intimacy and connection which are so fundamental to the play experience.

The existence of consumption in kink can be argued as an indication of a subculture, defined by the consumption of items which contribute to a prefabricated image. But this is over-simplistic. In the context of hyper-modernity, consumption is an element of any lifestyle. But a focus on this

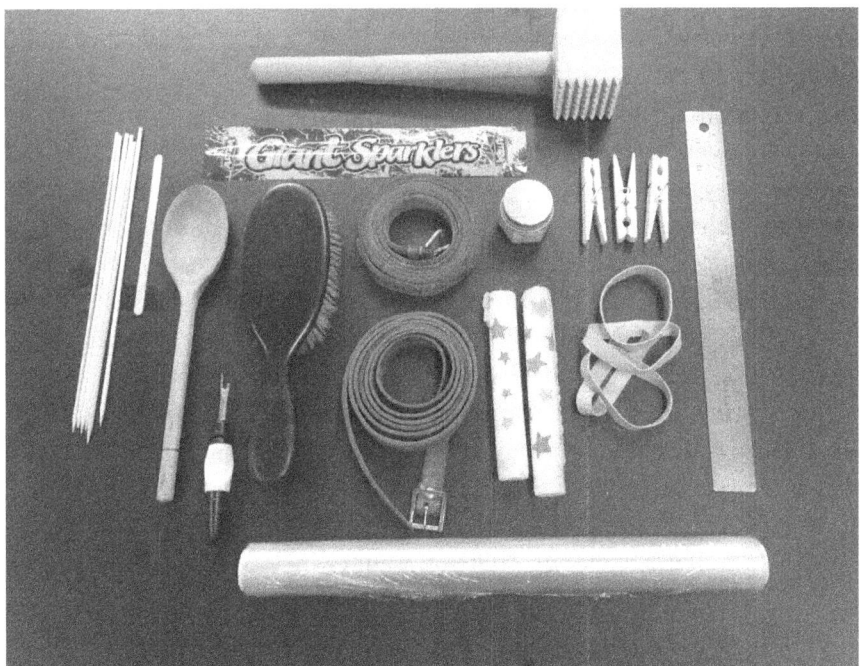

Figure 12 Examples of household 'pervertables'

element risks missing the different kinds of value ascribed to BDSM identity and its associated activities. Certainly, the ownership or lack of ownership of specific items did not seem to be significant in the accounts of experience my research participants shared with me, or in how they constructed their own kink identities.

Naked bodies

> I take my clothes off at a club, but I don't want to go to a nudist beach ... well I did once, and Barry made me keep my clothes on ... I don't want to be with a load of [va]'nilla people without any clothes on. That wouldn't work.
> (poppy)

> My Master sometimes says, when I am naked and I just have my collar on – because it needs a key, which I don't have, so I always have my collar on – he says that I am properly dressed then.
> (pussikin)

It is true that fetish clothing is expensive, and that play might expose it to damage. But when the experience of play is the centre of consideration it seems likely that more than concern about this is involved in the removal of clothing for play. The fact that being naked can only have meaning in a dialectic with the state of being clothed is often overlooked (Barcan, 2004), but it is nevertheless true; to know that you are naked, whatever that statement means to you, is dependent on your knowledge of being clothed as an alternate state. Nakedness in the context of kink often draws on this interrelationship and the complex feelings that it can be used to create.

The gradual removal of clothing, such as baring the buttocks for CP, can be an extremely emotional and/or powerful experience. The exposure is important, but it is not necessarily sufficient to create the sense and atmosphere desired. Colin feels that 'you've got to have this ritualisation of things. I hate these [videos] where ... the speed with which they want to get people naked ... The pleasure is lifting the skirt; the pleasure is ... that gradual build-up.' For Colin, this 'ritualisation' is a way of ensuring 'you include all the elements that you want to include' so that the desired play-space can be brought into existence.

Being naked with another person, or people, who are fully clothed can create many different emotions, from shame at being stripped to an illicit sense of joy in violating a norm so fundamental to contemporary society that its presence is barely recognised. To be naked is also to be vulnerable, not only in terms of exposure to the gaze of others, but a physical vulnerability – the feeling of attention focussed on breasts protected by clothing is substantially different to the feeling of attention focussed on an exposed nipple, by a top with clamps or pegs in easy reach. There is also a powerful taboo against public nakedness, and some clubs do not allow total nudity. However, the clubs at which most of my research participants described playing have no such restriction. It is interesting to note here that these clubs, Playspace and Sweet Torments, also have the reputation of being 'play clubs'; the point of going to them is to participate in or watch public play. This is seen as a contrast to clubs felt to have a fashion focus, which may have space and equipment for play, but where those in attendance are considered less likely to be interested in using it. The distinction is also implied in the dress code for Playspace: 'The Dress Code is Fetish, but a minimum of Smart Black – no jeans or trainers … Our aim is for it to be a comfortable play environment. Therefore, your apparel is what makes you happy within these minimum standards' (http://kinkyplayspace.com/welcome, accessed 19 March 2016). Playspace also includes in its guidelines for etiquette in a public play environment the need to remember that 'nakedness and play can make people feel vulnerable', so leering and commenting on someone's body is not appropriate behaviour.

The intimacy and vulnerability of nudity is such that some people, like cate, 'don't do naked in public'. By contrast poppy says 'I'll happily take all my clothes off in a club, as long as Barry is there … I'll do it happily. Because nobody cares. They'll still just chat to me, because I'm just me.' The fact that it is important to her that Barry is present is not insignificant; nudity in a play setting is an expression of relationship in that space. In public play-spaces tops rarely remove any of their own clothing, and what is removed is a matter of practicality – the shoes which might interfere with balance, or the removal of a jacket to cool down. Given the ways in which nudity has been used as metaphorical vehicle for categorising human beings into civilised/savage, sane/insane, normal/deviant (Barcan, 2004) it is unsurprising that being naked in the presence of a fully clothed other can create a sense of hierarchy, functioning as a literal playing out of the power-exchange taking place. Even within a private space relative amounts of clothing may still offer a marker of position and relationship within the scene, together with the wearing of items such as collars and cuffs. Nakedness or partial nakedness serves to emphasise the other ways in which the body is marked.

Marked bodies

> You [Michael] put that [mark] on me because you wanted to, because you can, because I wanted you to and there it is.
>
> (Molly)

> There's this beautiful moment that ... there's this tight line and then the blood that's coming out of the cut and they're not even, so there's like curls, curls, little curls of blood along the cut. And you're like 'oh, that's so fucking pretty!' It is hot, it's fucking hot.
>
> (Madeleine)

Many BDSM activities have the clear potential to leave marks on the skin. This is discussed with regard to the intimacy and relationship communicated and shaped by these marks in the next chapter, but it also bears discussion here since marks on the body, whether temporary or permanent, claim some of their meaning from their connection to subcultural identity. It is also interesting to note in this context that marks are, broadly speaking, what creates criminality in the context of BDSM, the requirement being the creation of injuries which are more than transient or trifling.[2]

Bruises are the most common, but impression marks from ropes, raised welts and cuts are all possible; marks are unlikely to be displayed outside the context of play-spaces or play-relationships, although they are often referenced in wider conversation between Scene members. Temporary brands can be created with violet wands, but the BDSM world sometimes overlaps the body modification subculture with permanent brands, scarification and tattoos being created during play and/or used to signal identity and relationship. It is not uncommon for Dominants to mark their submissives in some way, either as a complement too or instead of a collar. Less common, but not unknown, is for a Dominant to mark themselves as the owner of a submissive. Lifestyle couples may have matched or complementary markings: Molly and Michael have their hands tattooed – Molly has a lock and Michael a key, placed so that the tattoos touch when they hold hands. These kinds of mark are more likely to be visible outside of Scene contexts, rendering them potentially important markers of affiliation and identity even if their precise meaning is hidden from the 'vanilla'

---

2. The requirement for an injury to constitute ABH under the Offences Against the Person Act; first set out in *R v. Donovan* [1934] 2 KB 498 and cited as support for the convictions in the Spanner case.

observer. Marks created by a top during play are distinguished from tattoos in legal terms for reasons which are not entirely clear (*R v. Wilson*, Cr App Rep. Court of Appeal, 1996).

Relationship is also expressed through wearable items that mark and identify the body in a kink context. The clearest example is collars. Lifestyle submissives are often referred to as 'collared' and the process of play may entail for them a changing from their 'day' collar to a 'play' collar. For example, poppy wears a silver torc on a day-to-day basis which Barry removes for her when they play and replaces with a buckled leather collar. Stoney-face showed me both his everyday chain-mail collar (which he was wearing but had permission to remove so he could show me clearly) and a wide leather one he described as his 'full collar', which had been made specially for him. When I met Molly she was wearing a wide black leather collar with everyday summer clothing. By contrast cate's 'collar' took the form of a lockable metal anklet.

In contrast to the kind of kink outfits that involve latex or corsetry, collars are worn during private play as well, and putting one on or changing it over can be an important signal of the opening of a play-space. There may be ritual elements attached to this – the submissive kneeling before the Dominant, or kissing the removed collar and/or its replacement. A

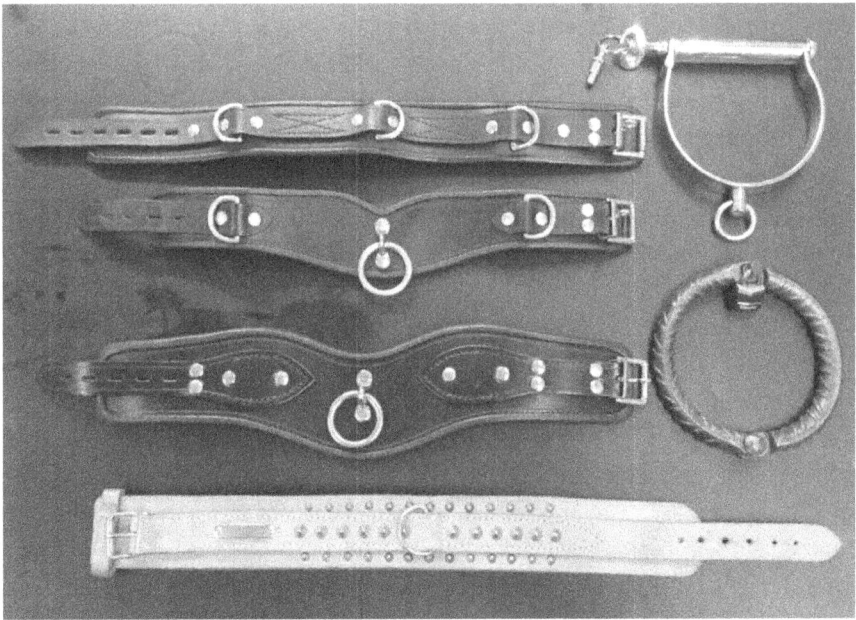

Figure 13 Collars

submissive may not be allowed to remove their own collar or may be physically unable to do so if it locks in some way. Describing an occasion of play at home, poppy remembered that 'it was a lovely day so I just put a dressing gown on and we went out in the garden with a cup of tea and one of the builders turned up! And I still had my collar, and the proper cuffs and the ankle cuffs.' The significance of wearing the collar is amply illustrated by the fact that she 'couldn't go and change because I'd still got my collar on and Barry hadn't given me consent to take it off. So, I hid indoors for a while.' Putting on everyday clothing while wearing her play collar was unthinkable to poppy, as the protocols through which she and Barry express the D/s aspects of their relationship forbade it. The likelihood that someone who was 'doing' kink rather than 'being' kinky would have rushed inside to change speaks to the meaning ascribed to collaring and the wearing of a collar for D/s couples.

Kink style, kink identity

Kink style can function as both a stereotype and a signal of kink identity; it can be an aspect of the performance of authenticity within this subculture and it can be evidence that a person is not 'really' kinky or is trying to express a kink persona that is not an expression of authentic identity. It is through such contestations of meaning in relation to mainstream culture and within the 'outsider' group that subcultures are constructed. The subcultural nature of the kink scene, including expression through clothing choice, is one strand which can contribute to the sense of kink as gestalt for an individual or within their life. Personal identity and the freedom to choose it are of supreme importance in the hypermodern world, and yet at the same time people often want to feel accepted and part of something. Many people consider their personal style to be a means of expressing their identity; this might be described in terms which minimise its importance but nevertheless people who feel their 'look' expressed who they are may feel a degree of anger, or persecution when not permitted to wear something which they consider an important marker, or a degree of insult, trespass or even violation when someone wears the same thing as if it is meaningless. Most kinksters who participated in my research would describe their kink identity as being far more than the visual aesthetic they choose to adopt, and many explicitly reject an overtly kink aesthetic in their everyday lives but style and clothing choice, whether in play-spaces or in the everyday world, are a significant strand in the process of self-, world- and story-making to which kink contributes. As a subcultural affiliation, identifying oneself with the wider kink Scene could be said to offer a ready-made solution to the problem of being both an individual and a member of a tribe. Involvement in the Scene comes with overt and shared transgression of identified norms, expression of new values, active engagement/contestation with boundaries and potential for personal meaning-making can be found within all of these. However, attendance at a kink party is no more a guarantee of finding one's place or realising the gestalt nature of kink in one's life than purchasing a pair of leather trousers would be. Kink identity can only be considered ready-made if we overlook the personal work involved in establishing the 'being' kinky rather than the 'doing' of kinky things.

7

Kinky bodies

God could not resist becoming flesh and experiencing such sensuality directly ... For flesh needs no striving or fixing to be worthy of love, but is merely and easily holy itself.

(Elizabeth aka Blessed_Harlot, 2011, p. 81)

I began to understand that I could shift my perception about whatever was taking place. This was a major realisation. I recognised that I could stop the running of a scary story in my mind by not following the rising of my first thought. Instead of engaging in a mental story I allowed my body to relax, open and surrender to the whip. I allowed myself to feel my Master's energy move into and through me via the whip. Thoughts are terribly seductive but you don't have to identify with them.

(slave Rick, 2009, p. 128)

Even if the being/doing distinction drawn by many kinky people between the authentic kinkster and the tourist is accepted, the importance of the doing as an aspect of the being cannot be ignored. BDSM engaged in as 'an end unto itself' may create a perceived authenticity, but it is authenticity found in and through 'experience, rather than ... [in] presentation to others' (Newmahr, 2011b, pp. 68, 72). This experience, which is somatic, multi-sensory and intimately relational, is the focus of this chapter.

Bodies involved in kink are an issue of importance partly because the body in hypermodernity can be seen as the 'last remaining seat of the individual's control over one's own self' (Varga, 2005, p. 229), but also because much of the perceived authenticity of a chosen subcultural identity is built around 'perceptions of embodied competencies in particular practices' (Driver, 2011, p. 980). The term bodies is not used in support of a distinction between body and mind, but rather a descriptor of a whole, living person. These are first-person bodies 'that we know directly in the context or process of being alive ... that we cannot take apart and put back together again ... that are the centre and origin of our being in the world, [bodies] whose biological reality is neither separable from, nor a third person dimension of its lived and living presence' (Sheets-Johnstone, 2009b, p. 20). These bodies are the medium for BDSM play, and so are intimately connected with the potential gestalt nature of BDSM.

McLuhan's (1964) observation that 'the medium is the message' is generally considered a reference to modern communications but a broader understanding of medium, as anything from which change emerges, is possible (Federman, 2004). The message of a news broadcast is not the content of the stories, but the changes those stories create in public attitudes. BDSM play is 'a *substance* for the transmission of force, power and energy' (MacDonald, 2006, p. 509) and this dynamic medium constitutes messages beyond the simple observation that some people enjoy inflicting and/or receiving pain. These experiences produce changes that are founded in relationship; enacted with, between and through real, fleshy, multi-sensory, kinetic bodies. The experience of doing BDSM, competence in its practices, subcultural authenticity and the changes which result from this multi-faceted involvement are experienced and internalised by these real bodies. The result is an emergent sense of the whole, its shape, place and value for the individual: a gestalt. This sense is not a single thing that '"exist"[s] in discourse as symbolic phenomena' but is constantly brought into being 'in the embodied practices of participants as they connect their own lived histories to the present' (Driver, 2011, p. 988).

This chapter therefore seeks to explore not what BDSM '*means,* but rather how it *feels*' (ibid., p. 987), as the emergent gestalt braids together the space itself, the experiences created within it, the embodied knowledge of kink that is both deployed and created there and the 'mysterious possibilities' (Sheets-Johnstone, 2009b, p. 21) for novelty which arise when the living body is awakened in an ongoing and embodied 'process of becoming' (Driver, 2011, p. 984).

Multi-sensory play experience

> When somebody's afraid their blood tastes different ... If I cut his penis, the blood there is different because it's like engorged blood as opposed to flowing blood. It's been held there for a while. So, there is a difference in that, it's thicker. But I don't really notice a difference in the taste. But ... when he's really afraid there's almost like a pepperiness.
>
> (Mistress Marina)

> Senses become heightened. So, your awareness of your own body becomes heightened and knowing what you're about to do to your body ... There is no eerier feeling than laying there having someone put their hands on you for the first time, gloved up, about to mark where they going to put hooks, because all of a sudden that's the only area of your body that you feel.
>
> (Stoney-face)

Giving attention to bodies engaged in only the most stereotypical forms of BDSM play reveals a range of clear tactile sensations being created and used – from the sting of nerves struck suddenly with a hard object to the intimate stroke of skin on skin; from the pressure of rope, leather or metal around a limb to the resistance of pulling against confinement. Diverse forms of play offer many other possibilities: the sharp double-punch of a needle as it first penetrates, and then emerges from a pinch of skin; the cold clean edge of a blade pressing tender flesh or the sudden flash of sensation when it slices skin; the involuntary spasm of an electrified muscle; the weight of a swinging flogger resisting the air, and the bone-deep vibration of impact; the tension of unprotected and anticipating flesh.

Other senses also contribute. Sounds include whimpers and screams; the echoes and cracks of impacts; the buzzing electricity in a violet wand; white noise pumped through headphones; snapped commands, delighted laughter, the sudden echoing of respectful silence, or the utterance of safe-words. Then there are the smells and tastes created both by bodies and by the materials of toys and clothing – leather, or rubber, or metal; subtle scents like the hot smell of a candle-flame dripping wax onto undefended skin, or the whiff of ozone from a violet wand; the tang of disinfectant, or antiseptic; the salt and musk of sweat, or blood; the metallic taste of adrenaline. Senses might be restricted or manipulated with blindfolds, hoods, or tight-wrappings while suspension or partial suspension plays with balance and spatial awareness. There is the kinaesthetic sense: in the swing of an arm as it throws a flogger, or the precise measuring of pinched skin to insert a needle; in the tug of muscle against bindings and the protest of joints prevented from shifting a long-held position. Movement also feeds the responses of one body to another: in the driving forward of a bottom struck by a cane and the mute pushing back again for another stroke; in the sense of personal limits as distant, approaching and tested.

Viewed from outside a scene, whether as an observer or recalling memories, it is possible to think through specific activities and identify some individual sensory elements. But in the experience of play they are

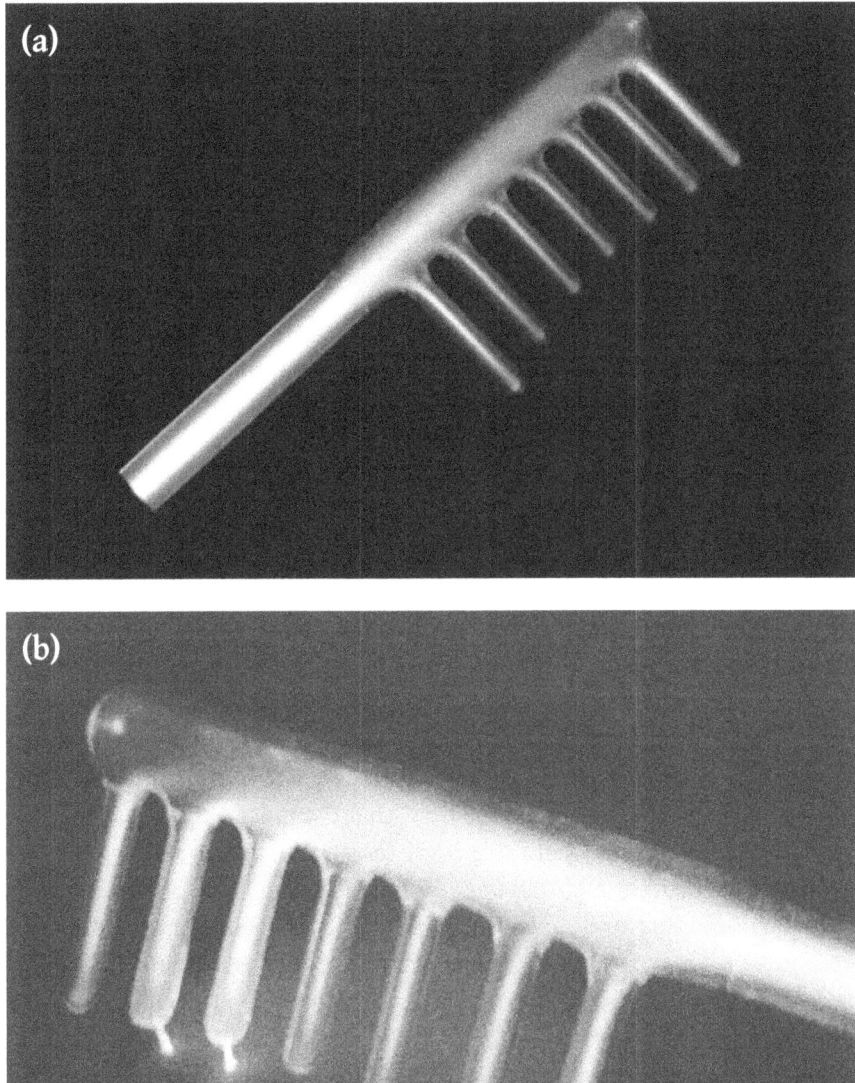

Figure 14 A violet wand (a) powered up and (b) in use on skin

inextricably braided together, with each sense informing and influenced by others. As the individuals become more immersed in the new world they are creating the diverse sensory inputs become a more synaesthetic whole. The different ways the many elements combine creates the possibility for different qualities of experience within a single activity, so that poppy can describe bondage both as comforting, 'like somebody wrapping you up in a big warm duvet and a blanket and snuggling you all in', and as something against which 'I've fought and struggled and cried'.

Sensory input can break as well as shape the play-space if it occurs in the 'wrong' way. If bondage is intended to hold a person still to receive other sensations, then a stressful position or an ill-placed knot will interfere with their receptivity. By contrast, if the aim is to leave the bottom to endure predicament bondage then discomfort is an intended part of the whole. Even a slight sensation mistimed or placed wrongly can disrupt immersion into the play-space; there are times when a hair tickling the nose can be of greater concern than a cane striking the skin. Within the privacy of play at home, intrusive sensations are most likely to be of this kind, while play in the semi-public space of a club or party involves entering a space where the layout and content of the space is beyond the control of the top, and so carries the risk of different intrusive sensations. For example, Molly observed that she found it difficult to play in one particular club because 'that room is really echoey and I do find myself being jarred out by noise there'. Aey also finds that the noise of public spaces can be distracting, especially the constant foot-traffic 'if a play-space is put right by the loo door'. But there are other distractions too: 'at some venues they put spotlights, and that's just ... absolutely hideous. First because you become like a spectator attraction, and second because it's just so glaring' (Aey). These can be addressed, to a degree, for her play partner with 'a blindfold and white noise ... to help him not be distracted'. Other distracting sensations may be harder to counter – if the entire room is cold for example, or the design of the provided play equipment doesn't match the size and shape of the body being attached to it. Nevertheless, control over or restriction of the senses offers another tool for creating play-space, leaving the bottom with only the sensations the top chooses to allow. In its most extreme forms (such as mummification – being entirely wrapped tightly in cling-film or similar – or immersion in a vacuum bed) a person is brought as close as possible to total immobility and sensory deprivation, although the materials being used to achieve this simultaneously constitute their own kind of sensory experience.

If it all works, a play-space is successfully created and the players immerse themselves into it. They are able not only to fully experience themselves as multi-sensory, kinaesthetic relational beings, but to be aware of their bodily existence in a way that is often inhibited or interrupted in the everyday world. The experience is a first-person encounter with the mysterious which, 'though implicitly known, is neither predictable ... [nor] controllable' (Sheets-Johnstone, 2009b, p. 22).

Sensory-kinetic bodies

> But I often say ... when I'm talking and people are saying 'well, what do you want to do?' I don't necessarily know what I want to do, I know how I want to feel.
>
> (Ivy)

> It is very sensual, but that's not the same thing [as sex]. Unfortunately, as screwed up as our society is, people confuse the two ... It can be extremely sensual ... Sensual is exploring things through the senses that we have, including an awareness of energy.
>
> (Kyndyl)

Embodiment is commonly used to indicate recognition that minds and bodies are not separate entities, but connected and interdependent. Sheets-Johnstone argues this term communicates a mechanical body, formed of component parts which is known to be alive through the tests and measurements to which it can be subjected. She contrasts this biological entity to the living body 'whose aliveness is something of which we are qualitatively aware' (Sheets-Johnstone, 2009b, p. 26); aliveness is not a state or condition the body is in but the sole mode of being a body has.

The concept of the mechanical body arises from a perspective which bases thinking on the idea of matter that is real and that makes up objects which really exist, enabling the idea that 'my body is a thing I call mine' (LaMothe, 2015, p. 17). In such an epistemology, matter is accessible to bodily senses and obeys material laws. It is accessible to the human mind in that it can be measured, added to, taken apart, polluted and so on. Movement thus comes to be understood as the thing which happens to matter when some sort of force acts upon it – the location of the matter changes but the substance of the thing so moved does not. Placing the idea of embodiment within this paradigm creates a 'motorology'

(Sheets-Johnstone, 2009a, p. 394), viewing the body as a mechanical sensorimotor system with the capacity to respond to stimuli in a range of different, measurable ways.

LaMothe proposes instead a new paradigm of movement. She observes that the materialist paradigm effectively undermines itself as 'if matter is that which 'resists change' then 'change' is the norm. Change is changing, and matter changes change by resisting it. Matter exists as a variation of movement' (LaMothe, 2015, p. 22); in other words movement is the defining characteristic of matter. Sheets-Johnstone similarly views animation as the foundational aspect of life. Everything that is alive moves, and not just in the macro sense, but at the cellular level. It makes sense therefore to consider bodies in relation to lived-through experiences that 'are dynamic through and through and whose dynamics resonate in bodily-felt spatio-temporal-energic experiences' (Sheets-Johnstone, 2009a, p. 397).

That BDSM utilises movement in the macro sense is clear; an implement cannot be used by an immobile body. But movement extends beyond the deliberate, controlled exercise of muscles; every sense is enabled by tiny movements within the body, down to the microscopic level, so that movement is the foundation to all perception and all experience (LaMothe, 2015; Sheets-Johnstone, 2009a). If this perspective of bodily movement as the 'source, medium and telos of all matter and reality' (LaMothe, 2015, p. 34) is adopted, then movement becomes more than a response to stimuli (as in wincing reflexively from the stroke of a cane) and becomes instead the way new things are known and learned. The sensory awareness of the body creates, responds to and engages in 'co-ordinated pattern[s] of moving into the world, being moved by whatever one's movements enable, moving in relation to what appears, and in the process becoming 'one' who has moved and been moved in this way' (ibid., p. 32). BDSM play is a process of laying down such kinetic patterns of sensation and response: patterns which combine to create a new world; patterns which create, shape and enhance relationship and intimacy; patterns which illuminate the complexity and ambiguity of physical sensation; patterns which feed the making of self and inform knowing, thinking, feeling and doing; patterns which contribute to religioning processes and to the emergence of gestalt.

These patterns are kinetic in their very nature; they are not visual, fixed or static but exist only within 'the multidimensional sensory space of a bodily self as a potential to move' (ibid., p. 4). Once such potential is realised and a particular movement made, the person becomes a person who 'has made that movement, who can make that movement, who knows she has made and can make that movement' (LaMothe, 2008, p. 583), and who can then use it to find a range of sensory experience and expression that otherwise would have remained unknown. While LaMothe's interest is dance, any movement has the potential to form a part of this bodily becoming if the sensory awareness created by the movement is used as a guide to create and become patterns of sensation and response. Practices which enable this process, as BDSM does, can be a 'life-enabling source of human thinking, feeling and acting ... [with] the power to generate new experiences and ideas about what it means to be human' (ibid., p. 584).

Body knowledge

> It's never going to work [trying to recreate a scene]. I could never even try because it's down to how I'm feeling on the day. How I'm feeling about my body, my mind, my emotions. How that person is. To get that combination, of 30 or 40 different strands ... it's just impossible ... How could you get that? You'd be going against the flow.
>
> (Cee)

As the process of play unfolds, the multi-sensory experiences it creates are internalised and stored as patterns of sensation and response, which feed future play. This 'body knowledge' is not simply mentally filed in cognitive drawers labelled 'How Bodies Work', 'What You Can Make Them Do', or 'How Sensation Y Affects Person X'. The tops with whom I spoke were in general agreement that planning (in a cognitive structured sense) is only the foundation of a good scene, with the rest being a process where 'everyone's got to be flowing together' (Cee). That process is built on many things: connection between the participants, past experience, and physical, mental and emotional states. All these can change, not just from scene to scene but from moment to moment:

> As much as you may discuss something in advance, when you actually get to it ... either your mood or the subs mood has changed slightly. It doesn't need to change much ... Within seconds [during play] people can and do ... their physical sensitivities can change in either direction. And what is acceptable now can be totally unacceptable in less than a minute's time. And on other occasions sub-space makes the opposite true, where you have to be conscious that what's acceptable now is very pleasant but that doesn't mean to say you've got a licence to do it another time.
>
> (Barry)

Patterns of sensation and response are created through practice, allowing the patterns to be internalised and new forms to emerge. A novice is therefore more likely than an experienced player to regard the activity in which they are engaged as a progression of 'distinctive, successive steps'. The aim of their practising is to achieve instead 'an arc of embodied techniques' (O'Connor, 2007, pp. 129, 130), so that the participants connect fully with one another and the play can flow intuitively.

Successful BDSM play combines such well-practiced physical skills with knowledge both about the body in general and of the specific bodies involved. But, again, this is only part of the story; a cane feels different to a flogger, but this observation is not an adequate basis to determine which you might like better, nor does knowing it to be so communicate anything of the lived experience of being struck by either implement or the enriched knowledge of the body which may result from that. It is not simply that objectively different implements must feel different to the recipient because they are different shapes and made from different materials; two different leather floggers can also create distinct sensations. A single implement might even feel different to the same person on different days, or at different points within a scene. Physical sensation is affected by factors like: state of mind; what (if any) play has preceded using that implement; expectations of the scene; skill and personal technique of the top; how comfortable the top is using the implement; the angle at which they approach the bottom; the position the bottom is in; whether the bottom can move and whether they actually do; whether there are other sensations to distract or compete with the impact; whether anyone else is present and whether the players know they are there; the time of day; temperature; the part of the body being struck; the frequency of the blows; whether either party has spaced. Many things with the potential to affect experience either cannot be known in advance or depend on the unfolding play experience, so that successful play is not just a matter of prior knowledge and reflective practice, but continual two-way communication and connection as the scene is played out.

The challenge of languaging such experience is considerable. A play experience is dynamic and fluid, and in such a context 'everyday language is clumsy and inadequate' (Sheets-Johnstone, 2009b, p. 363), giving precedence to what is stable and reifiable (LaMothe, 2015; Sheets-Johnstone, 2009b). Attempting to describe a qualitative whole requires more than accounting for each individual element, with the casual assumption that the meaning of each label is clearly fixed and defined; it must also signal a recognition of the 'multiple qualities of movement combined – tensional, linear, areal and projectional qualities, all in one complex whole' (Sheets-Johnstone, 2009b, p. 366). This recognition requires more than the simple equation of physical perception plus cognition (in relation to particular stimuli). A description given in words must recognise the experiential elements beyond or outside the words. Such a description is not the experience itself, it cannot recreate it for an audience, and it may not utilise words everyone will find equally valid and relatable. Instead, a description intended to do justice to the complexity and ambiguity of a lived experience, seeks to use words in ways which attempt to communicate with the store of non-linguistic knowledge and somatic memory in the audience, enabling them to add the dimensions which words cannot capture in ways which resonate within their own experience of the world. The process of crafting such a description can also contribute to personal reflection on and understanding of the experience it depicts: almost a third of my research participants spoke of writing about their play experiences as a means of grasping what had happened.

In the space of living experience 'everything comes together ... subjectivity and objectivity, the abstract and the concrete, the real and the imagined, the knowable and the unimaginable, the repetitive and the differential, structure and agency, mind and body, consciousness and the unconscious' (Soja, 1996, p. 57). This Thirdspace brings together the realities of the perceived (physical), conceived (mental) and lived (social) with the recognition of space, and experience in it, as 'simultaneously real and imagined and more' (ibid., p.11). The simplest movement of a dynamic living body is, from a Thirdspace perspective, not an act but 'a quite particular rippling-through-the-body kinetic dynamic' (Sheets-Johnstone, 2012, p. 395).

Different approaches to experience make possible distinct descriptions of the same event. By way of illustration I will describe a single example of play activity in two ways. The first utilises the equation of perception-plus-cognition, seeking to give a detached, reifiable account. The second draws on the Thirdspace perspective in an attempt to communicate a sense of the event which goes beyond a set of propositional statements.

Caning as perception-plus-cognition

A cane is a long flexible stick, usually made from rattan, that is most commonly used across the buttocks. It requires some skill to wield effectively and without causing damage, since the furthest end travels much faster than the end being gripped. When it strikes it compresses the narrow strip of flesh immediately underneath it, with a corresponding upwards push of the flesh on either side. This is visible in the classic 'tramline' marks of a cane-stroke: the stretching of the skin on either side of the impact creates a double line of bruising with a narrow, less-marked strip of flesh in between. The nerves compressed by the blow send signals to the brain, but almost immediately the cane rebounds off the flesh again. The compressed flesh decompresses and the nerves in it also respond to that. The physical sensation is thus twofold: first the impact and then the decompression, milliseconds apart. The latter sensation is more diffused and likely to last longer, as the restoration of normal blood flow is less immediate than its interruption. This sensation may make someone want to rub their skin as it stings or prickles. A caner wanting to create a peak of sensation may try to time the next stroke to the mid-point of this prickling. Each stroke is ideally delivered in a slightly different place. This reduces the risk of breaking the skin but is also desirable because repeated hits on one spot will ultimately become less rather than more intense for the recipient. Once the blood can flow again it flows faster in the attempt to create swelling, and so minimise further injury. As the caning progresses the skin becomes hard in patches and feels differently textured. The receiver may cry out, twitch, stand up or make other physical responses. The top will need to decide when to end the caning, which may also be the end of the scene. It is possible that the sensations build up to a point of crescendo, providing a natural end to the process that, to an observer, may look like an orgasm being experienced by the caned person (Easton and Hardy, 2004; Moser, 1998). However, not every scene goes this way; it might end with tears from the caned person, they might reach sub-space or the caner may simply decide the time is right for a different activity.

All of this is knowledge *about* the body, combined with the kind of knowledge *of* the body that cognition about perception can give. But it has little to say about the felt experience – as either pleasant or painful – and nothing at all about how the participants incorporate the experience into their embodied processes of religioning. It is this experience of 'bodies-in-process' (Driver, 2011, p. 985) that builds into what LaMothe calls a 'rhythm of bodily becoming', the laying down of patterns of sensation and response that allow a person to 'express and unfold through these movements their own individual human bodily potential for creating and becoming themselves and their worlds' (2008, p. 583).

To approach this element of creating and becoming in relation to the experience of caning it is necessary to focus on a single person's experience. The intention here is not to provide a generalisable description of caning, but to illustrate how an individual might engage with the whole experience. To do this in sufficient depth I offer an account drawn from my personal writing:

Caning as real-and-imagined

> The cane hits my skin. That first impact is absorbed easily and gone, I'm not sure I even register it consciously, although I know it must be there. But it leaves a trail. The sting remains, and each stroke adds to it. Building, not outwards towards dissipation and vanishing, but inwards. It sinks and spreads into my body, singing its way into my blood and my bones and beyond. This is pain and not-pain, delight and fear. Some strokes now take my breath, trapping it in my throat for an instant with the purity of the pain and the rush of joy and the fizzing of it through nerve after nerve after nerve. It is pain, it hurts. But it is not-pain because it is good-hurting. This pleasure-pain swirls through me, bubbling, dancing. It doesn't disperse, but trembles there on the edge of being gone, waiting for the next stroke to join it. Singing a new note in the harmony, a new beat to the dance. As each stroke arrives and joins the rest the trembling grows stronger, not just inside now but running through my muscles. I quiver. It is still fragile, it could be gone – a wrapped stroke would break it, although not irreparably.[1] A loss of balance would shatter it. But if it lasts, if it builds stroke on stroke, in the end all those trembling notes will explode back outwards, turning me inside out, exploding me through my own skin and out into the universe.

This is not simply knowledge *of* my body, or knowledge *about* my body. Or even a combination of the two. It is knowledge that I am body, body is me. In those few moments of that final explosion the subjective self is shattered by 'a context in which delight and pain are not readily distinguishable' (MacKendrick, 1999, p. 146). The immediate aftermath is a gradual collecting together, putting what is 'meant' to be on the inside back on the inside. This takes a while: perceptions are skewed, language is

---

1. Where the end of the cane extends too far and flicks the hip bone.

a nonsense, moving my body (mine again, not me) is something requiring thought, conscious thought. But I find my body beautiful in this process. It is not beauty in the sense of being aesthetically pleasing but a beauty that comes from knowing in my flesh what it is that I am. Through this subject-shattering experience I learn that my 'flesh may surpass ... subjectivity' (ibid., p. 108). The 'I' in my brain is not all that there is, and 'my' perspective from 'in there' is not all that I can know. My physical being is not a burden to be borne or an unruly thing to be tamed, trained, shaped and used. In the real-and-imagined space created by those cane strokes, I am body and body is me; I have become a person who has been beyond the subjective self, and who knows that I have done that and that I can do that.

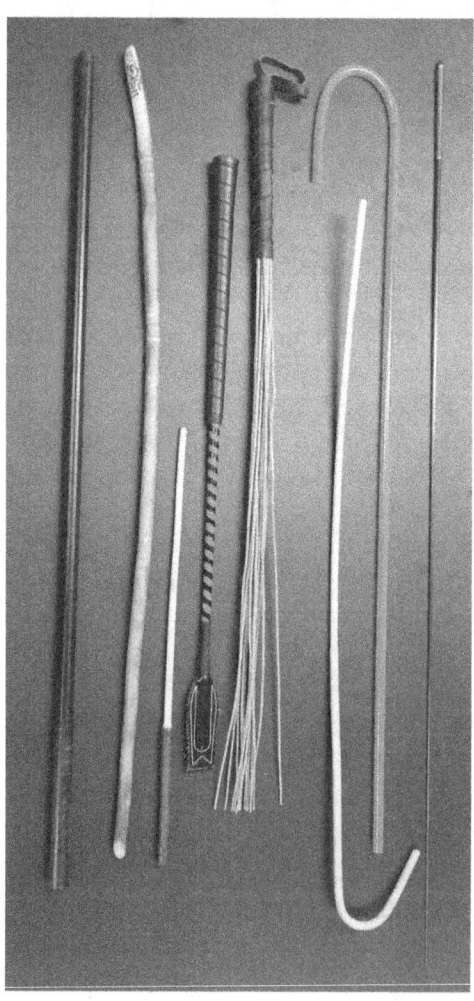

Figure 15 Canes, crops and birches

As Sheets-Johnstone (2009a, p. 390) observes, 'each experience is what it is', and that is not language. The body in play is thinking in and through movement, not words. It is not symbol-making, or seeking to mediate the world through language. It is an 'existentially resonant body ... [which] creates a particular dynamic world with no intermediaries' (Sheets-Johnstone, 2009b, p. 35). Although the powerful reality of that can only be partially captured in words it remains a felt truth which contributes to the value of kink and its potential to become a gestalt.

Bodies in pain?

> Flogging my shoulders will cure a bad headache, better than an aspirin ... So, if I get a really bad headache ... and if we're not rushed for time I'll say 'is there any chance of a quick flogging please?' And it's superb, and that [headache] will go.
>
> (poppy)

> I like the thought of pain. [But] not always. Depending on my mood depends on how much pain I can actually take or want. So for instance [one time] I were, not quite bleeding, but I were definitely hurt, a lot. And I were like 'fucking carry on! Nyer-nyer-ny-nyer-nyer!' ... And I were black and blue with stripes ... And then on other days it's like somebody even strokes me, and I'll be 'Grrr ... let's just put the rope on and pretend'.
>
> (Rita)

The assumption that BDSM must involve the deliberate creation of physical pain is sufficiently entrenched that people use 'sadomasochism' (SM) or 'sadism and masochism' (S&M) to stand as an indicator for the entire Scene, and all practices within it. That this is an over-simplification should by this point be clear. However, the idea of pain offers an opportunity to delve more deeply into the broader engagement with sensation that occurs during play.

The International Association for the Study of Pain's (1976–77) influential definition of pain as an 'unpleasant sensory and emotional experience associated with or resembling that associated with actual or potential tissue damage' locates it firmly within the realm of the physical body (Bourke, 2014). It also tells us that the essential experience of pain is unpleasant, that one can only be in pain if one is aware of it as pain, and that pain is a function of the nervous system. Bourke observes that as contemporary research perfects the technology to see the brain as responds to noxious stimuli medical perspectives of pain become more reductive, identifying 'a millisecond of brain activity as pain' (ibid., p. 10). It should also be noted here that cultural discourses about pain shape the moral context of experiencing it: if pain is wholly a noxious experience then the act of choosing it, or the desire to give it, can justifiably be considered pathological. This perception is something of which most kinky people are acutely aware.

To approach a kink-relevant understanding the idea that pain has a 'definite ontological presence' must be rejected. Pain can instead be regarded as a type of event, a specific form of 'one of those recurring occurrences that we regularly experience and witness that participates in the constitution of our sense of self and other' (ibid., p. 5). This allows for pain to be less a matter of the intrinsic nature of raw sensations and more the way in which those sensations are experienced. Pain is invented as it is encountered, in a process which involves the entirety of our lived experiences: physiological senses, emotional states, cognitive structures, cultural and social expectations and values and so on. It is never simply the response of nerves to noxious stimuli but a contextualised quality of an experience (Robertson and Wildcroft, 2016).

The complexity of pain experiences in kink is reflected in my conversation with Molly, quoted here at length:

Molly: [Masochism is] interesting. That's a word that I have struggled with. I don't identify with it as a label and yet I do know that that is something that I can be. So ... the thing for me that I really get off on is not necessarily the pain in the moment, it's the marks afterwards; ... it's what's left behind; it's the marks on my skin. So, I know that I will really grit my teeth and bear pain beyond pleasure-pain to get the marks that I will get off on. I currently have got the remains of a belt mark here on my thigh and that's ... I will [pause] I'm not keen on the word endure because that makes it sound like something I don't really want to do, but I will certainly kind of grit my teeth and say 'go on do it' ... because I want that mark afterwards. I want it.
Alison: So some kinds of pain are pleasurable?
Molly: Yes.
Alison: And then there are other kinds of pain which you definitely experience as pain but ...?
Molly: There's a reward.
Alison: And you ... I don't want to say struggle with, because it doesn't sound like a struggle ...

Molly: I'll psych myself up for it.
Alison: You grapple with it?
Molly: Yes
Alison: And you kind of ride it, because you get something else out of it?
Molly: Yes. Yeah. I think that's a fairly good way to say it. But there certainly is pleasurable pain. For me that is thud. Deep, deep thud ... [This paddle] delivers this thud inside me. For me that thud, real heavy flogging, that really deep heavy thud where you get that kind of deep bruise inside your muscles, that is my real pleasure-pain. Although I will say that the vampirey gloves,[2] kind of spikey things, also give me pleasure-pain. The pain which I will ride and endure, for want of a better word, because I know it will get me marks, is stingy stuff. Really stingy pain for me is pain. I can't find the pleasure place in that pain. But thud is the pain for me. Although ... I don't even think of it as painful. Also knife play, which we will do so that it leaves real welts and even so it will nick the skin, that's not pain for me. That's pleasure.

As this fragment of conversation indicates, pain can be felt and understood in different ways. Digging below the labels of 'sadist' or 'masochist' is something many people in the kink Scene do, as they seek to reconcile the medicalised language and its negative connotations with the complexity and joy of their experiences. Pain sensations are most likely to be experienced by the bottom partner during play and, since 'service topping' (where the top acts on the instructions of the bottom) was not represented among my research participants, people who bottom or switch were the more likely to have reflected on the direct experience of pain, and its relationship to the experience of pleasure. Each individual who plays with pain is actively engaged with their experience, challenging the assumption that pain is only a cause of action and positioning it instead as a kind of action in itself (Asad, 2000). Not all bottoms identify with the term masochist and, even among those that do, their experience is rarely understood as simply as enjoying the pain. Instead they engage in what Asad describes as a 'process of structuring' (ibid., p. 41). Asad's example draws on the use of metaphoric descriptions of pain as musical notes or numerical values, which he argues is not necessarily making the experience 'meaningful' but is contributing to the process of 'living painful relations' (ibid., p. 43). My research participants rarely used such direct metaphors in relation to their experiences, but they nonetheless engage in processes of structuring pain, in a range of different ways:

---

2. Leather gloves studded with sharp pins.

There are people who speak of surrendering to pain, feeling it as it is, without judgement. As pussikin describes:

> If you give in to that sensation, stop thinking 'god that hurts' and start actually feeling it ... then all of you is really there, you know what I mean – you're not thinking about what it feels like, you're actually feeling what it feels like and you don't need to analyse it or question it, there's just ... everything that you are, right there.

Or they speak of struggling with pain, striving to hold it and wrestling with its power to overwhelm, seeking the triumph of not being destroyed by it:

> I don't get off on pain itself but I get off on the emotions that surround it. I get off on being able to push myself, on being able to push my body to do something it's never done before, to go further than it's ever gone before.
> (Rosie)

> I work on the basis that I don't like being caned but I like *having been* caned ... I like the feeling of knowing that I've taken whatever has been given to me ... so there's a pride element to it.
> (Will)

Or they speak of submitting to pain that is given to them, as an expression of service, commitment or love:

> I can take an awful lot of pain and its ... all to do with my headspace though. I mean he can dish out ... as much as he can dish out to me and I will continue to take it. It's because in my head ... the pain brings pleasure. But knowing that it's pleasing him to see me taking this is more pleasure for me.
> (cate)

Madeleine describes this kind of processing of the pain as like 'transubstantiation'; even though 'I try very hard not to use Catholic language', the term fits the experience because during play 'you're turning this very quotidian physical pain into – or humiliation or tears –but you're turning it into something ... as an offering. So, who are you offering it to? I have no idea. The minute that I could answer that I would be a happier person!' She has considered this from the sadist's perspective too and suggests their involvement in this process is twofold: 'one is that you're enabling or bringing about this transition but number two – you're sacrificing your humanity to do it'.

Or they speak of embracing pain, delighting in it because the sensations are, or can become, pleasurable. Madeleine says:

> I hate the cane and I love the cane. But for me pleasure is mental. So the physical sensation is pure pain … I'm not a pain slut. But the submission to the pain is intensely pleasurable, mentally, to the point where I may be feeling pain but I get incredibly sexually excited at the same time.

Rosie describes pain and pleasure as a spectrum, saying 'actually they can be the same thing … If you compare it to sexuality, one side is straight, one side is gay, middle is bisexual. So, a bit of pain, a bit of pleasure … equally there's varying severities of pain and varying intensities of pleasure.'

Or they speak of enduring pain, of holding it within them or weathering it as it flows over and through them, accepting it as the state in which they exist for those moments, or even of experiencing it as terrible but delighting in it after the event. Ivy says 'some of the things that I do I get pleasure out of having done them rather than out of doing them at the time'. Endurance of pain might also create something else that is important or desirable, as when Molly says she will accept pain that is not directly enjoyable to achieve the marks which are. Colin describes using the structured pain of kink to bring about the cessation of unsought pain from an arthritic knee: 'Before I had my … knee done I was walking bone on bone, and it was hell. I had an absolutely superb thrashing and I was pain-free for six hours. Absolutely pain-free.' The context and nature of the space also contributes to the experience of sensation, as Stoney-face describes:

> I do not like pain … [but] I've kind of, sort of parked myself in the kink Scene really by doing hook suspensions, especially [as it's] three now … Because tell anybody you don't like something in kink and they go 'but you do hook suspensions!'

He explains the difference is that during play 'I'm not getting the endorphin rush that masochists feel':

> My brain shuts it off. But in hook suspensions I get that rush, I get that masochistic rush of endorphins … Because I'm approaching it from a ritualistic aspect and because this particular hook suspension tradition for

> myself is Sundance related. And the Sundance was my flesh sacrifice for the rest of the tribe.

All these are processes of structuring pain into lived experience, some of which transform pain into something else, and some of which give meaning to the pain. But all support the view that pain is a field of experience largely constituted in the interplay of sensation and context. It arises and is lived differently according to the background and immediate history of the sensation, whether mundane life or peak experiences. Marie speaks for many so-called masochists when she observes:

> I stubbed my toe the other day, and it was horrible, and I was swearing. And I was thinking 'how is this that just one knock gets me swearing and yet I can bend over and have someone beat me repeatedly and love it?'

I suggest the answer to this commonly pondered question is because there is no pain without the crucible of context (Robertson and Wildcroft, 2016). Pain is a powerful sensation which cannot but 'break the order of things' (Glucklich, 2001, p. 76). However, when it is deliberately met and engaged with it can constitute not just the unmaking of worlds (Scarry, 1985), but their remaking in the knowledge of ourselves as people who have encountered pain and not been destroyed by it. Glucklich suggests that the 'efficacy of pain' deliberately chosen derives from its bridging of '"raw" sensation with our highest qualities as human beings in a community of other humans' (Glucklich, 2001, p. 44), and in BDSM play the process of somatic and relational meaning-making inherent in the process of creating and experiencing sensations including pain constitutes such a bridge. In sum, the active engagement with pain that occurs in BDSM play allows for the transformation both of the pain and of relationship with it. The sensation is cast into the crucible of experience and personal and spiritual rewards can thus be distilled (Robertson and Wildcroft, 2016).

Intimately marked bodies

> It's like the best thing in the world is to bear a decent bruise ... there's pride, genuine pride.
>
> (Rita)

> Marks are important. I like nothing better than looking at them the next day. Absolutely marks are important. But I don't want things that will inhibit me for future play.
>
> (Colin)

These different engagements with pain lead me to return briefly to the issue of marked bodies. Here the issue is of marks inscribed into the flesh itself by the performance of relationship that occurs during play. There is an overlap; mention was made of tattoos as markers of identity and/or subcultural belonging, and body art or body modification can fuzzy the boundaries of play and not-play, kink and not-kink. Griff explained to me that he does a lot of cuttings and brandings, only some of which take place in a play setting. He is interested in the visual aesthetic of the work because 'I want to make a pretty picture', but also in the physical process of creating:

> I want to see how it heals ... I design things with the process in mind. It's not *just* a pretty picture, it is the fact that I am either branding this in skin or cutting this in skin. But if I'm doing that, which is great, I don't want someone to end up, if it scars, I don't want them to end up with a nasty looking thing going 'look at this, man, it's like I've been attacked by a tiny bear!'

While the cutting or brand is never just a pretty picture the experience of creating it is different in play and non-play settings. When carrying out this sort of body art for people with whom he does not want to play, he says, 'I'm not sure how to describe it better than the words, or the term, "intellectual hard-on". I get off on that in a very ... almost a rational way where I sit there and I go "this is awesome!"' By contrast, if he is in a play context, 'I like playing with it [blood] ... Yeah, give it a nice smack when you're done. Then you grab the paint-brushes and you make a picture right, that's what you do!' This kind of play is intimate, and Griff recognises that 'there's lots of people that want cuttings and there's not a lot of people that I want to be doing that play with'; performing cuttings and brandings as a form of body modification for people within the kink world allows him to 'just sort of explore that fascination' that breaking and broken skin holds for him without always entering into that intimate relationship.

More firmly within the world of play is cutting for the sensation, for blood and/or the associated emotions, rather than to deliberately create scars and marks. Madeleine describes cutting as 'a much more intense journey' than other kinds of play, but she observes that the 'weirdest thing about it is that it's very fast ... The actual act itself, it's like "Okay, done".' She gets an 'incredible, incredible endorphin rush from seeing [her own] blood', and so she prefers to 'be cut somewhere I can see. I want to see the person, and I want to see them cutting me and I want to see what, where I'm being cut.' This is not only about the enjoyment of seeing the blood. As with Griff, she finds this to be an incredibly intimate act, saying that part of the emotion around allowing someone else to open her skin is the fear that 'they won't be there'

> I know that sounds strange, but don't go. Don't leave. They will have to become something else to do this, and [the fear is] that they will distance themselves from you and your body as they're doing it. So, for my part it's incumbent on me to not let them. I won't let them depart. If you're going to do this, you've got to be here.

Another of my research participants, Mistress Marina, says:

> I always suck the blood. So, it's like you're linked at that point by those things. And you couldn't get any closer than cutting someone and drinking their blood ... I think that's where the vampire thing comes in, that's so romanticised. Because I think that, at a very base level people know that doing that is the most intimate you can be.

The connection forged by this intimacy was brought home to her when her romantic partner was upset to discover that she had cut another submissive, even though he was happy for her to play with other people, 'because he said it was our thing and that I shouldn't have done it with other people'. Michael and Molly also achieve blood flow in their play, not through cutting but through impact and the use of vampire gloves. Michael describes how, when he has finished, he sends Molly to find a mirror, and 'that's an interesting version of when sub-space hits, because it hasn't happened until [she's] gotten there ... I've seen her do that with the blood, where I've made her bleed and she touches it or I touch it and show it to her and it's just [clicks fingers]'. Molly describes this as becoming 'shut down. It's just me, blood, fingers. It's all kind of [pause] yeah. So, I will be drifting off in the mirror for a while. Touching and looking, touching and looking'. The blood, as with other marks that Michael creates on Molly's body, are a visible sign of their relationship – 'he's painted his desire and his lust on me and it's this real visual mark of ... what I am to him, of our relationship, of his desire and lust and need for me'.

Probably the most common form of marks are those created by the various forms of impact play, which range from the distinctive lines of a cane stripe to a more generalised mottled bruising from flogging. Many bottoms delight in these marks, reacting as Bea describes: 'as soon as I have any marks ... I tend to jump up and down in front of the mirror going "I want to see", "I want to see", "I want to see!"'. Her partner Dee observes that 'unfortunately when we get to the point where it's likely to start marking we're also getting close to [Bea's] limit'. This physical marker of pushing limits may be partly why marks have value for some, as Rosie describes: 'I get off on being able to push myself, on being able to push my body to do something it's never done before, to go further than it's ever gone before ... It gives me a real kind of emotional buzz and satisfaction. That's why I love marks.'

Suchet understands the body as 'an ever-emerging, unfinished project whose meaning is acquired through symbolic gestures' (Suchet, 2009, p. 114). The literal creation of marks on flesh is perhaps not best described as symbolic, but such marks clearly have both meaning and value, in keeping with views of the body as a site for exploring subjectivity and creating identity. To Suchet's summary I add that the body is also a site for exploring intersubjectivity and relationality, an issue from which much academic work on the body is detached (Furey, 2012). As the accounts of my research participants show, BDSM play creates and relies upon a deep intimacy between players and the inherent relationality of bodies. Furey argues that it is necessary to find a way to connect both the 'inner' experience and the 'outer' environment within a relational context and an exploration of BDSM play offers an opportunity to do so.

Ruptures

> I think, you know your adrenaline starts pumping and that doesn't make you a rational creature ... adrenaline really does excise rational thought and it's one of the pleasures of this that it really does suspend your rational thought. It allows you to escape it.
>
> (Madeleine)

> It's like most of the time something's cut off, because it has to be so that you can do life-stuff – if you usually experienced things so intensely you'd

never get anything done! But when you're playing you can let yourself really touch what the world is like and how it interacts with your body.
(pussikin)

The limited social demography available on kinky people, arising mostly from researchers observations of the communities in which they conducted their research, suggests that the Scene is predominantly made up of white middle-aged members of the professional classes (Weiss, 2011) who have an affiliation with 'geekiness' (Newmahr, 2011b, p. 30). Kinky people also apparently tend to be 'rather intellectual' (MacKendrick, 1999, p. 153), and it is perhaps telling of the hypermodern dominance of mind over body that Mackendrick cautions against regarding this observation as a suggestion that people turn to kinky means of using the body because they are unable to use their brains. Indeed, several my research participants spoke of the power of kink to 'suspend your rational thought' (Madeleine) for a while. For someone who tends to 'live in my brain a lot' (Ivy), BDSM play can help them feel 'a lot more corporeal. It connects the two, I think' (Ivy).

The difficulty of speaking meaningfully about the experiences of play arises not from any lack of facility with language but because experience is created by (and understood in) the body, and the sometimes overwhelming nature of counterpleasures is able to rupture subjectivity. These pleasures are 'edgy and strange ... delight[ing] in the existence of boundaries, that they may be broken and overleapt [and] in the establishment of limits, that they may be surpassed' (MacKendrick, 1999, p. 17), queer understanding of terms like pleasure and pain and so rupture language even as they use it. Weiss however disagrees that subjectivity is ruptured by BDSM play, arguing that the 'bodily experiments' it involves have a reliance on knowledge and technique that suggests 'self-mastery and community production, rather than transcendence' (Weiss, 2011, p. 140). I suggest both stances are partially correct; body knowledge and technique are vital to successful play, but it is not just knowledge *of* a body, even of one's own body. Neither is it knowledge *about* the body. It is a somatic knowledge that is not stable, not static, not visual or linguistic but grounded in movements we make, which also make us (LaMothe, 2015). In this, MacKendrick (1999) is correct that there may well be no 'I' from whose perspective the experience might be described. Language is ruptured, because play is not primarily concerned with language, but with sensation, emotion and animate living bodies in which every cell and system is constantly moving.

This subsequently enables us to think the things we think; if we moved differently, we would think something else (LaMothe, 2015). Such dynamic happenings cannot be reduced to a word or a series of words, however complex and careful.

Gestalt in the flesh

Successful BDSM is a somatic, multi-sensory, kinaesthetic process, one in which an arc of embodied techniques is employed to forge an intimate relationship. To create this arc successfully the 'non-separation of thinking and doing' is essential (Sheets-Johnstone, 2009b, p. 30) and it is achieved through practice, which does not create the different world of more fluent play. However, once fluency is available, the possibility of 'thinking in movement [as] a way of being in the world ... taking it up moment by moment and living it directly in movement' (ibid., p. 35) arises. This is not a performance by a symbol-making body which mediates the world only through language but rather one made by an 'existentially resonant body' (ibid.), with the recognition that having meaning is not synonymous with having a verbal label. Sheets-Johnstone observes that an improvised dance might be read by an observer as 'standing for something', while from the perspective of the dancer it is the dynamic processes of the dance which matter: 'in *this evening's dance,* a particular movement is not 'about' something any more than a smile is about pleasure' (ibid., p. 33). This is an observation that translates easily and naturally to the process of BDSM play – what matters in any given performance of play is that play continues to flow. Whatever meaning that flow holds for the players in that moment is not readable in terms of symbols or captured in a breaking down of components. It is a gestalt, emerging from the performance as the experience is both grasped in the flesh and expressed through the flesh. This can only be approached from the perspective of the whole because it is an emergent property of the component parts, not another strand being woven in.

8

Exploring the edge

The hard act ... is that I learn to love the part of me that would make therapists visibly draw back in fear if I talked about it. I have had therapists react that way before. He doesn't ask that I try to change him – I am doomed to carry my Fenris nature to my grave ... – but simply that I love that part of me with the same love I have for the rest of me ... [That] means finding ways to feed him, finding people to feed him with, who desire what I desire, who can accept this with joy ... It's hands-on, up close, teeth and snarling and bruises that don't show off well after the fact. It's my own fear of me being rejected because of that part of me, a searing vulnerability in the midst of power.

(Kaldera, 2010, p. 106)

My weakness is precious. It is precious because it walks side by side with vulnerability; it is precious because it served as the baseline for my strength. It is counter measure, and that by which strength may be measured ... The desire to jump when you peer over the edge of a cliff or off the side of a bridge is human. We are curious creatures, and information about the point beyond death, beyond madness, is very scarce. No wonder we crave it. No wonder I push myself, again and again, to that edge, to that brink.

(Williams, 2010, p. 172)

Ideas of limit and boundary are important within the kink subculture and BDSM play. They form part of negotiating to play and how closely they are approached during play helps to shape the experience within the play-space. My focus in this chapter is to consider the role and nature of boundaries and, in doing so, to begin to lay a foundation for conceptualising BDSM play as a process of ritualising that is, perhaps, the most significant contributor to gestalt kink.

Many subcultures constitute themselves in comparison to what they understand as the mainstream or normal (Widdicombe and Wooffitt, 1990). Just as the concept of dirt can be understood to arise from classifications of cleanliness (Douglas, 1966) participants in the BDSM Scene self-define their activity as 'not vanilla', thus positioning BDSM as a process of transgressing particular boundaries of behaviour. Within this large-scale transgression, play both establishes and ruptures other, more specific, boundaries to create liminal spaces where social reality is both reflected and changed (Buenting, 2003). Experiences shared in spaces, where 'normal categorisations are abandoned ... there is willing suspension of disbelief, [and] the outcomes are uncertain' (Ezzy et al., 2009, p. 398) undoubtedly contribute to the sense of the kink Scene as a community (Xygalatas et al., 2013).

Liminality is a useful descriptor for any in-between state, place or moment, in which apparent certainties are challenged and new possibilities for relationship with self, with other and with the world are created (Ezzy, 2011, 2014). Liminal spaces are both powerful and unsettling, but when actively engaged with they are disturbing 'in a constructive way' (Ezzy, 2014, p. 41). They enable the individual to be immersed in an embodied performance which through which they can explore and respond to challenges (Ezzy, 2011). As it plays with boundaries and the emotions and risks associated with their transgression, BDSM creates such opportunity. Individual players understand and negotiate boundaries of many kinds: those that must be held at a distance; those that can be approached (or even touched) but must not be stepped over; and those that seem to exist outside play-space but dissolve within it. A scene involves a delicate dance among and perhaps along these edges, before returning safely with whatever experience has been created by the journey.

The experiences created by playing with the lines that separate 'normal' from 'deviant', 'acceptable' from 'unacceptable', 'sane' from 'insane' are diverse and multiplex. They can enable self-knowledge and self-creation (Holmes et al., 2006; Lyng, 2012), moments of 'experiential anarchy' (Holmes et al., 2006, p. 331) and a chance to touch the 'intoxicating tension *between* artistry and abandon' (Ferrell, 2005, p. 78). They create potential for transformation (Bromley, 2007), transcendence, and a recognition that the desire for such boundary exploration links people together (Lyng, 2005).

Because it creates access to what would be inaccessible to most people (Newmahr, 2011b), BDSM play is an intimate situation in which there is always a crossing or touching of 'boundaries of the self that one does not allow to be crossed mundanely' (Bauer, 2014, p. 111). This intimacy of mutually constructed and navigated edges adds another element to the already powerful potential of play-space: play includes an inherent risk that boundaries will be violated, and not only in ways that have been negotiated and agreed. Such a space of performed vulnerability allows for experience of access to another person that it is not possible to achieve elsewhere (Newmahr, 2011b). This kind of intimacy, created through immersion in potential violation, is a strong thread within the gestalt. The term intimacy itself was not commonly used in my research participants narratives, but alternatives such as connection, energy and intensity carried the same characterisation, because the narratives which use them focus on new ways of knowing others. Such narratives contributed strongly to the discussions about meaning and value I had with my research participants.

Transgressions

> There are things that are not people's edges ... things that people can make a compromise about, and say 'look, I don't really enjoy this, but I know that you do, and it certainly doesn't put me off and I like your excitement. So, I'll play along with that'. And then there's other things, activities that ... you *have* to enjoy. You have to have a *jouissance* for it. You have to have a hunger for it. And if you don't and you can't find that anywhere inside you it's an obscenity to do it. And you shouldn't do it because you're not going to enjoy the transgression.
>
> (Madeleine)

> Limits to me are ... important because they define who you are ... But limits are not, have never been, set in stone. Absolutely not. If it's not a physical thing that is stopping you from exploring something – like you can't unkill someone or if you are genuinely allergic to peanuts ... Taking those and putting them aside for a second I think that limits are the edges of your self-knowledge. You don't know yourself past your limits. And some people don't want to, which is absolutely their prerogative ... But I look at a limit that I have, and I can ... sort of see the shadow of the landscape behind it, but not quite. But I am curious.
>
> (Griff)

Limits cannot be conceptually isolated from the idea of their transgression – they are determined through recognition of what lies beyond them, and this creates meaning for both the line and the crossing of it (Jenks, 2003). Limit is meaningful in its fragility, and transgression in its 'imminent exhaustion', while both are given power and energy by the 'perpetual threat of constraint or destruction presented by the other' (ibid., p. 90). In the abstract, this complex, spiral relationship is amoral. But in practice, in the contemporary world, Jenks argues that transgression always relates 'to the mad, bad and dangerous' (ibid., p. 92), as defined by the codes, binaries, laws and oppositions that punctuate everyday discourses. As a result, some transgressive acts are criminalised, and so gain significance beyond the personal knowledge that a boundary is being transgressed. However, transgression is not synonymous with criminality. In a hypermodern society, where individuality is highly prized, the deliberate transgression of norms – and Jenks is clear that it must be both deliberate and actively intended to be a transgression – can be considered a 'hyperbolic announcement of identity and difference in a society where identity and difference are paramount yet difficult to achieve' (ibid., p. 3). This is not intended to imply any inherent moral quality in such transgressions but to position them as potentially purposive.

Most people engaging in BDSM understand that their practices violate perceived social and cultural norms to varying extents, and some undoubtedly enjoy the transgressive thrill of that. However, to reduce transgression to a concept concerned solely with the counter-reaction of hegemonic values supports the impression of absolute binaries separated by clear lines (Bauer, 2014). A more ambivalent relationship towards transgression in this political sense is demonstrated in responses to labels such as 'sadist' and 'masochist'. The root of these terms in nineteenth century medical discourse on psychopathology colours academic discourse on sadomasochistic behaviours (Greenberg, 2019; Langdridge, 2006; Langdridge and Barker, 2007; Moser, 1998; Moser and Kleinplatz, 2006; Weinberg, 2006; Weiss, 2011). Both also remain possible psychiatric diagnoses, according to the current iterations of the *Diagnostic and Statistical Manual of Mental Disorders* (DSM-V; American Psychiatric Association, 2013) and the International Classification of Disease (ICD-10; World Health Organization, 2016). ICD-10 states that these 'extreme or significant deviations' from the way in which the average person thinks, feels and perceives are not always associated with either distress or impaired social performance. This is in contrast to the DSM-V diagnostic criteria, which were changed in the latest iteration to specify that the 'paraphilia' must cause distress, impairment of function, harm to self or risk of harm to others before a diagnosis can be made (Boskey, 2013). The contradiction between two major sources suggests that the DSM-V alteration may well be insufficient to destigmatise consensual BDSM practised for mutual pleasure. It is also true that the diagnostic criteria retain a certain ambiguity with regard to what constitutes harm or risk of harm, and this ambiguity is generally shared by legal references to BDSM (Khan, 2014). It is generally perceived to be abnormal to deliberately seek pain or to enjoy giving it, so if this transgression were a political act of resistance, claiming those labels might be an expected choice. However, among my research participants, people were often reluctant to use terms which make negative connections with something they experience as positive and pleasurable.

The term sadism in particular is one which people are either wholly unwilling to claim or which they qualify as it applies to themselves. Oliver described a gradual realisation of its applicability and his resistance to it:

> When I started I played with a lot of people who were masochistic submissives. And so I thought that I was getting my enjoyment from getting them into sub-space and hurting them in the way that they wanted to be hurt. And then I played with a girl who wasn't a masochist at all – she enjoyed being spanked but she got the pleasure from the submission part rather than the actual being hit. And I realised that actually the part I really enjoyed was hitting her in a way that really made her flinch.

This was something he had think carefully about before deciding it was acceptable. By contrast, for Rocks, part of the enjoyment of topping comes from the fact that 'it's the dark side, it's the forbidden side'. Consensual play allows him to 'unleash the beast and [then] you can put it back in the bottle again'. However, Rocks is clear that the enjoyment is not in inflicting pain per se but is found in 'the reactions that come back ... there is enjoyment in the fact that here is somebody who has not merely given you explicit permission to hit them; they're getting off on it! ... It's that slight twisting of everything ... that I enjoy'.

This 'dark' association, which Rocks finds so powerful, can also lead people to discomfort with the 'sadist' label; Barry regards sadism as being 'more about inflicting something on the unwilling' although he recognises that he does have 'sadistic tendencies'. He concludes that 'it's a fairly fine dividing line' but feels there is definitely a distinction between 'dangerous sadism and, if you like, consensual sadism'. As Barry's sub, poppy's view is that Barry is not a sadist, because 'he's lovely'. For her the term is problematic because 'a [va]'nilla [would] say a sadistic person was somebody who purely wants to inflict pain. And that conjures up an image of somebody who doesn't care. So, a sadistic person will tear the head off a kitten, [but Barry] will give the kitten a saucer of milk.' She considers a sadist more likely to be abusive, while Barry is 'a gentleman' who would protect someone in distress:

> If you were in a club and you ran to Barry he would protect you, he would look after you. Whereas I think a sadist would say 'either get on with it or let me help' [pause] with a cane in his hand.

Yet, undoubtedly, Barry does create pain for poppy, and she enjoys that pain. But she does not consider herself a masochist. She offers two reasons for this: firstly, because she doesn't *only* want pain: 'I want the whole package, because I'm greedy'. The 'whole package' might describe BDSM activities that are not focussed on pain such as submission, or it might reference things like trust, pleasure and joy as important components of play. For Barry and poppy all of this is inherent in the D/s nature of their relationship. Her second reason was because 'I don't think I'm good enough to be a masochist, because I can't take enough pain to be classed as masochistic.' This idea was quite common: Kyndyl said 'I think I am [a masochist], then I look around at some of my friends and go "no I'm not!"'; while Madeleine, who sees herself as both as sadist and a masochist, talked of watching Michael using vampire gloves on Molly and thinking 'it's kind of hot. But oh man, she can, she can take pain in a way I can't!' For Bea there was a distinction between what she fantasised about enjoying, and what she was able to enjoy in reality – 'In my head I really, really like that [pain-play] side of things. In reality it gets a bit ouchy. So, a bit less so!'

Reflection on labels and what it means to accept or reject them is not uncommon for kinky people. Perhaps less common is the explicit declaration that 'I enjoy being slightly outside the norm' (Rocks). Bauer observes a division in pro-BDSM discourse between attempts to position BDSM within 'sexual citizenship' (Bauer, 2014, p. 8) on the one hand and a desire to construct a transgressive and oppositional identity around kink on the other. Most of my research participants seem to occupy a kind of middle ground between wanting to be sufficiently 'normal' to avoid medical diagnosis and/or criminal prosecution and wanting to be sufficiently different to demonstrate their commitment to individuality, autonomy and self-expression. Some individuals see themselves as contributing towards a new society through their kink, as Stoney-face describes: 'We are different. We get it. We don't belong in most normal societies. We are defining our culture and society until it's great'. Others are motivated by explicit political ends such as Ian's desire to challenge the 'enormous hypocrisy about sexuality' he sees manifest in contemporary culture. But many want to explore beyond the taboos created by society without rejecting or denying a desire to belong somewhere, as Rita describes:

> You have to try everything twice because the first time you might not have been in the right mood, or something might have gone wrong that weren't your fault ... So, if you try the second time and it doesn't work again, well two strikes and you're out ... [But] what if I skip by something and ... fail to recognise it and then die and it could have been the best thing in the world? [pause] But I [also] really want to fit in, and I really want to be normal. I want to feel normal. I want to see myself as normal. I want to be outrageous in the normal way ... I want people to point at me. I want to feel, I want to think normal ... So, I can ... outrage people ... in [pause] what's the word? [pause] like chavs or people who [pause] *Jerry Springer* [pause] you know what I mean? which is normal ... I can outrage them people and I can upset them with my abnormalities. However, I am normal because all the people that go to [the club] do things that I enjoy on a regular basis ... So, there's enough people to make me feel normal within myself and as long as I feel normal and as long as I feel part of something I'm happy ... I don't want to walk alone. But I don't want to follow the herd.

Bauer is clear that BDSM is deeply concerned with both 'boundary projects' (Bauer, 2014, p. 163) and social difference, and my own research supports this. But he also argues that it is important to distinguish transgressions that are focussed wholly on the generation of pleasures from those that might result in social transformation, rather than assuming that any and all BDSM is a political project simply because it is transgressive. This is a blurred distinction; a marginalised social position might well create opportunities for both subversive thought and boundary-breaking experiences, but it does not guarantee either. Experience gained in play-spaces might be initially motivated by pleasure-seeking but result ultimately in political action or interrogation of social systems (Bauer, 2014; Kraemer, 2014). It is also not impossible that opportunities for personal reflection and transformation result ultimately in gradual social change, without any explicit intention for them to do so.

Limits

Limits are limits, right? But then you've got the ... hard limits, and the soft limits and the stretchable ones. And pushing limits, people push limits, they don't know what the fuck they want, is what that is ... Again it falls into that trust – that trust, and that energy cycle. He trusts me explicitly to not break any of his boundaries.

(Aey)

[I like to find] that fine balance so that when they come out of it they're not sitting there going 'oh, you'll never touch me again! Don't you come near me!' They come out of it, and you can see them in essence feeling good about themselves – 'I've just done something that I didn't think I could do! I've felt that panic rise up but I controlled it and I went with it'.

(Damien)

In negotiating to play with a new partner, limits need to be explicitly discussed. There are two broad categories which are important – ethical and personal (Bauer, 2014). Ethical limits are widely agreed by most players to include refusal to inflict or submit to permanent damage, to be involved in real-world non-consent situations or to interact with people unable to give consent. These principles can apply beyond interactions with other kinky people as Madeleine describes:

I was teaching, at university level, and part of my job was pastoral care ... These young male students would come into my office and sit down and they'd fucked up marvellously on their academic record, and we'd talk about it and they'd ask the questions and if they started to cry it would turn me right on. And I could tell that I could push them to it. Remind them of their obligation to parents, I could ... whatever. [pause] Whatever. And it was like, 'Holy fuck, I am! I am!', and I can do this. But you know, it wasn't until I actually internalised it, that I was getting pleasure out of it ... that I realised that I have to acknowledge I'm a sadist because if I don't, that's more immoral. That's really, that's unethical. Because now I'm basically getting off on it and I'm not even admitting that I'm doing it. And I'm doing it to people who are not in the least bit the appropriate people to do this to. The situation is not appropriate, and it's non-consensual basically.

Personal limits are the things that an individual does not wish to do or have done to them. Griff says that these limits are 'not about how much you can take. It's when it stops being fun.' So things which are not enjoyable in even the ambivalent, complex ways that pain, shame and discomfort are enjoyed within kink settings constitute limits, beyond which play should not trespass. However, limits are often further divided into 'hard' and 'soft' to reflect their fluid nature and the multiple factors which create them in the first place. A hard limit is generally understood as a non-negotiable, no-go area during play while a soft limit describes something that may not be immediately desirable but which can be pushed over time, as Javelin describes:

> I knew a woman that was very afraid of electricity, and electrical play. And so I said, this was after we'd been playing for about four or five months on a fairly regular basis, I said 'I think it's time you started facing your fear of electricity. But we're not going to do it all in one jump, we're going to … build bridges to that'. And so, the first time we played I just set the violet wand in front of her for the entire scene. Not plugged in, not switched on. Just where she could see it. And we did our normal play. The next time I turned it on so it's humming in front of her, and so slowly I started reconditioning her to the whole idea of electrical play. And then, when we finally did play with it, I said 'let me do your hand first' and so I did her hand on a very low power setting and she goes 'wow that's not so bad', and I said 'okay let me do your body'. And I started doing all her erogenous zones, I'd already mapped them out and she was going 'oh this is nice'. And then I lifted up her hood and I gave her clit a good old jolt and she goes 'oh I like this'. And so, through the process she was not only able to face her fear but discover something new about herself. … And it can be so empowering when you can do that.

Through such deliberate exploration of limits, BDSM is able to create the same kind of experiences of constructive discomfort that Ezzy observes in rituals intended to enable connection with the unsettling, or disturbing aspects of life (Ezzy, 2014). Through these embodied performances people can directly address matters of deep concern or perceived threat; an opportunity to reflect on those matters, as they pertain to themselves is opened up. Ritual, for Ezzy, deploys both cognitive and cultural framings and BDSM does the same. This is not a wholly conscious or articulated process; limits and the processes of their exploration are at least as much somatic and emotional as they are cognitive. For limit-pushing play, as with Ezzy's discomfiting rituals, 'people do it because it feels right' (ibid., p. 5).

Edges

Edge-play I consider like ... art. Art is successful if it elicits an emotional response ... To me, edge-play is a specifically edge-play scene if it elicits an uneasy feeling from someone, anyone. If it made somebody uncomfortable you have succeeded ... The people going into edge-play know that it's weird. They know that it's at the edge of an accepted spectrum.

(Stoney-face)

I think everybody has an edge, no matter where it is. Some people, they'll do straps or whatever, but they won't do canes ... and to them that's too severe. Everybody has their limit to where they want to go, but I haven't quite found mine yet ... I mean I see things that look really severe to me ... People do blood, play with blood. That's a bit ... not my thing. That would be quite edgy for me, but it's not for other people. They're like 'yay, let's draw pictures!'

(cate)

Lyng's concept of edgework is concerned with people drawn to situations of voluntary risk where there is either no clear reward at all, or where the experience itself is classed by the individual as of higher value than any manifest result. People engaging in such risk-taking are exploring 'the edge' – a boundary, such as those 'between life and death, consciousness and unconsciousness ... sanity and insanity' or 'order and disorder, form and formlessness' (Lyng, 1990, pp. 855, 858). Edgework activities push as close to the edge as is possible without tipping over by consciously pushing both personal and/or technological limits.

The edge is a common kink term, used to carry the same sense of exploring boundaries. Edges and limits are perceived as somewhat different, although potentially overlapping concepts. Limits, in the personal sense, intersects with personal edges to describe play that directly confronts a personal boundary or fear. Being on the edge is the point at which that boundary is reached, so that in this form 'edge-play means pushing someone almost to their limits and then stopping before you go too far' (Kaz). There is a general sense that an edge is more acute than a limit, and carries some kind of existential risk, although not necessarily a physical one (Newmahr, 2011a). The other use for edge-play is as a descriptor for play that is 'at the edge of what's kind of acceptable, or safe' (Ivy). A general list of activities usually seen as 'extreme', and so within this category of edge-play, would include breath-play, fire- or needle-play, hook-suspensions, cutting, branding and electro-play.

Some edge-play is of both kinds and, for some, edge-play in the second sense carries much less anxiety or perceived risk than play with their personal limits. Newmahr (2011b) describes spanking as being a challenging and 'edgy' activity for her personally, but recognised that most practitioners would not call it edge-play; some would not regard it as BDSM at all (Plante, 2006). However, Newmahr was willing to engage in breath-play, commonly considered intrinsically edgy because of the physical risks involved (Wiseman, 1996). Many people who do these 'extreme' activities do not experience them as edgy in themselves, although they may have done so in the past. Stoney-face regards a recognition of extremity as the core of edge-play:

> If it makes somebody look twice, if somebody becomes uncomfortable, I would consider that edgy play ... You can still have edge-play with no witnesses because you know certain things are just going to do that. They would make people uncomfortable'.

He regards hook suspension as intrinsically edgy in this way because 'not everybody can handle the sight of somebody hanging up by their skin.

Activities commonly regarded as edge-play entail physical risk, but that risk may be less severe in reality than it is perceived to be. Similarly, 'mainstream' BDSM carries physical risks which often go unspoken. From a physiological perspective, a sterile surgical needle pushed through the surface of the skin carries very little risk, since it penetrates the skin cleanly, seals the opening with itself for as long as it is left in place, and is unlikely to cause bleeding. Wrongly placed needles can damage nerves but, contrasted with a misplaced cane stroke, the risk seems minor: a cane is fast moving, hard to control, and has the potential to split the skin wide open, with the concomitant risks of bleeding, infection and scarring. Yet caning is rarely described as edgy (although many people consider it to be at the more extreme end of sadomasochistic behaviour) whereas needles commonly are, suggesting that in BDSM conceptions of the edge as the emotional or felt edge of risk are at least as significant as the physical.

Some physical kinds of edge-play do carry harder-to-minimise levels of risk, including a risk of death. Breath-play can impact on and be affected by underlying medical conditions of which the players may be unaware and is therefore sometimes considered impossible to do safely. Colin equated edge-play with the physical edge between life and death and avoids play he considers edgy, because as a medical doctor he has 'confirmed too many dead bodies ... I've probably confirmed three or four bodies over the years of people in BDSM type things that have gone wrong ... and I am sure there are any number of very close calls'. Aey agrees with this conceptualisation of the edge, saying edge-play is 'where you can kill them by accident if you're not careful', and Mistress Marina also feels that 'edge-play is how far I can push things, before I have to stop. That's always been my definition. [We are literally talking about] the edge of life and death'.

Other forms of edge-play carry different kinds of risk, which may be combined with physical risk or may exist wholly in other realms. Role-play which recreates scenes of abuse, consensual non-consent, age- or incest-play all explore social taboos and carry a risk to emotional well-being. This can be understood as a psychological edge, requiring its own skill-set to traverse and return safely; cate recognises this in her description of the edge as 'the edge of sanity to be perfectly honest. Do you know what I mean? When you get to the point where you think "are you really going to ...?"' For her, this psychological edge is an opportunity to demonstrate and build on her submission and trust in her Master. Such edges are fluid for her so that, while needles would once have felt edgy, she no longer classes them as edge-play. This understanding of edges is important as, in the dynamic of her M/s relationship, she is determined that 'if it was his fetish then it wouldn't be my limit'.

Importantly, this approaching and deconstructing edges with her Master is not felt to be about the thrill of risk-taking but 'the trust':

> It's not a thrill that I might not have the use of my arm by the end of the day, you know ... Yes, I know what we do is risky. Yes, hanging me from the ceiling is risky. Yes, tying my hands behind my back, sticking a gag in my mouth and blindfold on is fairly risky at that point. But then ... it's a calculated risk. If he's doing that then he's constantly touching my hands, he's touching my face, he's touching my feet ... He's feeling for making sure my circulation is fine. Checking my lips, am I going blue? Are my fingers going blue?
>
> (cate)

The responsibility for managing that risk is shared: 'If we've been doing something and I've felt the rope here and it's pressing on a nerve, then I need to tell him. I have to be responsible, because he can't see the nerve being pushed' (cate). The risk and the negotiation of limit contributes to the creation of intimacy, a quality which 'is not only an outcome of collaborating the edge, but *central to its appeal*' (Newmahr, 2011b, p. 186).

Barry also understands the edge as being present less in specific forms of play, and more in qualities of experience. The edge is the point at which 'it is acceptable on this side of what you're doing and unacceptable on the other, whether it's psychological or physical' and to play on that edge is to ask if you can 'balance on that razor-edge'. Cee experiences the edge in similar terms, saying 'what you have to remember ... is knowing there's an edge, and you don't quite go over. You've just got your toes tipping over'. Unusually among my research participants, perhaps because of her professional involvement in play, she understood personal limits as being the far side of the edge, 'as a stone wall that you can't actually penetrate. You absolutely don't touch.'

Edge-play is clearly understood in different ways, and the relationship between edges and limits is both confused and highly personal. For example, for me the most terrifying edge is the psychological one of abandonment but, with carefully selected partners, it is not a limit; by contrast while I can take the pain of play which draws blood without significant difficulty that is a limit for me because of both the physical risk of long-term harm and the risk of psychological buttons being pushed by the remaining wound long after the scene is over. The fact that some of those buttons may well be identical to the ones that would be pushed by playing with my fear of abandonment complicates my explaining the distinction but doesn't shake my determination to maintain it.

Experiences of the edge as described by Lyng (2005) – including altered perceptions of self, situation, space and time, dissolution of the self-object boundary and/or a sense of hyper-reality – can result from most forms of BDSM (Easton and Hardy, 2004). This means that a BDSM activity could be considered edgework from an outside perspective even if those involved would not call it edge-play and care must be taken not to treat them as interchangeable terms. Newmahr, aware of this distinction, describes all BDSM as edgework. She argues that when placed against its broader social context BDSM clearly pushes normative, social, emotional and psychological boundaries, as it explores 'the edges of morality ... the liminal spaces between liberty and constraint, kindness and cruelty, and goodness and badness' (Newmahr, 2011a, p. 698). In these spaces, as viewed from the outside, players engage in a risk-trust cycle that appears to delight in risking, among other things, incompetence, betrayed trust, and physical or emotional harm. They also, assuming the play has been successful, emerge from it without these things having occurred. This cycle creates a unique sense of understanding and connection, existing only in that space of potential violation (Newmahr, 2011b). Intimacy then arises from the sense of boundaries being crossed together.

Together on the edge

> I think things become edge-play for me when I'm getting to the point where I can't see the way back to the world anymore. When I'm so close to losing my grip on, well, on here. So close that I can only cling to my Master and he is my only anchor. The only solid thing.
>
> (pussikin)

> I am always the one in control of it, so he is very submissive to me and he has given over all his control. And the thing is that he obviously trusts me ... But there's also ... almost like a fear of me. Because he knows how quickly I can switch from one thing to another, he also knows that I've got, to some people, very dangerous limits. So, when he gives himself over to me and allows me to make him powerless he's also got that little bit of fear about what actually I am going to do.
>
> (Mistress Marina)

Lyng (1990) originally defined the edge as lying between such apparent absolutes as life and death, consciousness and unconsciousness. Although he recognised that edges may come into being in relation to more problematic categories, like sanity and insanity, the edgeworkers he described were exploring fixed, corporeal and immutable edges. This emphasis 'ignores, marginalises or devalues phenomenological emotional experience' (Newmahr, 2011a, p. 690), but the concept of edgework itself need not do so. Boundaries between order/chaos, safety/danger, sanity/insanity or control/abandon create emotional or psychological edges that require as much skill to navigate as do physical edges. This broader skill set includes 'social-psychological and interpersonal [skills] ... such as trust, expressiveness, emotional management, perceptiveness, self-awareness, introspection and self-restraint' (ibid., p. 691).

Psychological edges should not simply be considered emotional aspects of physical edgework activities; they are edges in their own right. The deliberate creation of emotions at an intensity that most people would regard as overwhelming and/or uncontrollable constitutes a negotiation of emotional edges (Newmahr, 2011b). Madeleine describes negotiating this kind of edge in relation to risky forms of play, citing the need for both self-awareness and control as a source of the pleasure to be found in such play:

> I think needle-play and cutting and things like branding and you know anything like that, where the person who is the top has to be able to really push down passion. They can be feeling it internally, but they can't let themselves go. It's just too fucking dangerous to do that ... And there's a kind of, there's a really [pause] it's like the emotional and [pause] erotic version of corsetry. You know ... you're enjoying it because it's held in!

Bauer critiques the original edgework concept from a different perspective, describing Lyng's edgeworkers as appearing to 'operate in a social and ethical vacuum', which represents them as unaware of any non-physical ramifications of their risk-taking and reduces their edgework to a process of 'creating a spectacle demonstrating survival skills in a competitive context' (Bauer, 2014, p. 148). The edgework concept is thus rooted in 'a masculinist ideology' (Newmahr, 2011a, p. 689) which emphasises the individual and their independent negotiation of boundaries. By contrast both Bauer and Newmahr consider BDSM edgework as either 'interdependent, in which edgeworkers need one another in order to navigate the edge, or collaborative – that is, in which edgeworkers construct and constitute the boundaries for one another' (ibid., p. 692).

Ben describes such co-construction and exploration when he observes that BDSM is 'all about going into the areas that people will not go into in vanilla life'. This must entail exploring limits:

> A careful, no, a *responsible* Dom, and a good Dom, will push his or her subs limits. Not only for his or her own kicks or satisfaction but for [the sub's] as well. So, if there is activity that I would like that is not in a hard limit and she is not sure, or doesn't want to, but it's not a hard limit I would push. And I would push two or three times. At the third or the fourth time, if I feel that ... there isn't a joy for both of us, then that's out of the menu.

This process of exploration is at the heart of Ben's understanding of what BDSM really is – 'an exploratory journey to joy'.

To play like this requires something more than a calculation of the odds in relation to physical risk. Players take a 'leap-of-faith' (Bauer, 2014, p. 147), which allows their edgework to become a practice of taking care – of themselves, of others and of their relationships to others. Michael says 'oftentimes the edge that I have is the measure of my trust, and how much she trusts me. So oftentimes the edge that I tend to play with is [pause] can I convince her to trust me to do this thing? [pause] It's how can I push this boundary? Can I push this edge? Can I push this envelope in a way that, at the end of the time, she will find acceptable?'

The more established trust between play partners becomes, the harder it may be to play with these kinds of edge. For Griff:

> the best moments in a scene, any scene I've ever done that I thought afterwards 'whoa, that is one for the books', it has always been the moment where I saw the other party having to … forcefully reassess the situation. Having to go 'ooooookay'. Like a mental double-take. It's the moment [pause] the moment where they go 'oh, hang on, he isn't playing'.

In other words, the moment when there is a genuine realisation that the trust can be broken, that a violation is actually possible, is also the moment which creates the most intense pleasure for him. It is in these moments that he really experiences himself as in control, 'because up until that point they were allowing me to do things to them':

> Before, I am in control of the *situation*. I can make sure that this hits you, and that pinches you, and this happens there. But the moment you start thinking 'oh hang on, he's not kidding', that's the moment where I can do things to your brain.

This means that 'there are certain things that I really like doing that I cannot do with people I know too well'. A balance must be struck between there being enough trust to play together but not so much as to prevent those intense and real emotions:

> One of the things I like playing with is fear … but I'm not a dangerous person, which if you know me for more than say six months you do know. And the more in depth, the more I do know you the more difficult it is for me to actually convince you. It's not about fake fear, I don't want [pause] I don't get off on fake fear. It's the real fear and if you know me well it's more difficult for me to convince … you of the situation, to convince you that what I'm doing is genuine.
>
> (Griff)

This is playing with a number of edges for both players, not simply fear but also a confrontation with the 'beast in the bottle' described by Rocks. This self-recognition may be particularly acute in the type of play Griff describes but elements of it occur across the broader spectrum of BDSM play because of dominant socio-cultural attitudes to pain and distress ascribing negative association to finding enjoyment within those experiences. Awareness of this is evident in Griff's description of one of his favourite forms of fear-play: he calls it 'serial killer play – even though that is not a thing and it shouldn't be a thing even though it's really hot, but never mind'; as soon as it is named it becomes necessary to explicitly distance the idea from the reality of psychopathic murder.

Griff described one scene of this kind to me at some length, emphasising how real the experience became for his play-partner – 'she was convinced I was going to cut her up. She wouldn't safe-word, because she thought "if I'm going to safe-word he's going to kill me". She also didn't get up and run out of the front door'. Griff describes impact of this scene as being rooted in his successful creation of fear:

> I had absolutely convinced her that there was no way out. That she wasn't going to get up. That she wasn't going to grab things. Because it just doesn't happen. And you know I just slowly took away all the options, leaving her with the only logical conclusion, which is 'I'm going to die'. There is no way to [pause] describe that. And not in a good way, not only in a good way. Because that was the most intense scene I've ever done. Since and before. You know how some people say 'I don't think I could ever kill anyone', or 'I think I could'. Right, you don't actually know until you're in the situation. And, because I played it well, I was in that situation. She was on the floor with various cuts of meat written out on her in marker, with a saw and a chisel and a knife. All there – the bathtub was lined with plastic – it was all there. I could have done it.

Griff's account reveals how edges are mutually constructed through the process of play; if the bottom he was playing with had not responded in the right way, Griff could not have taken either of them as close to the edge as he did, neither could he reach or confront that edge alone. Both parties were necessary to make the edge, and then to walk it. This kind of play, where one player is led to feel the risk as real while the other knows it is not, is commonly called 'mind-fucking'. Bauer describes such play as having the potential to raise emotions that are disquieting, but which are accepted because of the intensity of experience created at the same time. He considers such an experience as necessarily intimate, describing it as an 'exuberant intimacy' which rejects 'reason, moderation, mediocrity, harmony and equality as well as reproduction and usefulness' in order to celebrate and engage with 'difference, tension, intensity, risk, excess, ecstasy, wastefulness, perversity, campy extravagance, fluidity and insanity, as well as becoming something beyond the human' (Bauer, 2014, p. 4).

Both Newmahr and Bauer agree that BDSM offers an opportunity to challenge conventional understandings of intimacy as inherently romantic, healthy and positive. Instead, they recognise that intimacy is inextricably entangled with ideas about boundaries, and that it can be experienced negatively – rape is, at least partly, a horrific experience of forced intimacy. Understanding intimacy as 'the revelation of that which is innermost to another actor' (Newmahr, 2011b, p. 168) allows for the recognition that intimacy is ambivalent. BDSM enables intimate encounter by creating experiences that access what would usually be inaccessible. Within those spaces people are deeply connected – as Cee observes 'at that moment in time with edge-play, I am theirs and they are mine' – but these are spaces where emotions are intense and contradictory feelings might be experienced simultaneously, a space where 'he doesn't ever want to hurt me, but he does want to hurt me' (Rita).

Spiritual edgework

> I think that BDSM and spirituality, even if you think they are separate paths, everyday you're going to learn something new and grow and change.
> (Kyndyl)

Lyng recognised the potential of edgework experiences to call the nature of reality into question and to enable individuals to transcend 'the giveness' (Lyng, 2012, p. 411) of the prevailing cultural constructions surrounding that concept. The 'potential for human actualisation' (Ferrell, 2005, p. 78) exists within these moments on the edge, where it is possible to discover and rediscover new ways of being, knowing and relating. However, 'spiritual edgework' is a more explicit demonstration of the connection between practitioners and 'a source of transcendent power' (Bromley, 2007, p. 289). Bromley does not equate this transcendent power with any concept of God or religion, but it nonetheless remains a concept most of my research participants did not use. They spoke of their intense play as being more concerned with enabling self-exploration, and connecting them to their partners, than with contacting something external. Yet when the terms in which people conceived of spirituality are considered alongside the nature and purpose Bromley ascribes to the activities of spiritual edgeworkers, the absence of an explicit belief in a transcendent power is not an impediment to framing BDSM as spiritual edgework.

Bromley argues that religion is a social form which is used by human beings to create a sense of empowerment via the construction of a 'mythically relevant edge' (Bromley, 2007, p. 287) which offers both certainty and contingency. People construct their own understanding of the transcendent, and his interest is in it as 'an autonomous source of power' (ibid., p. 287). Ritualised edgework forges connections to this power by creating and/or enhancing the edgeworkers sense of control and empowerment. Through this process edgeworkers are able to transcend the power-relations of the everyday world and thus 'gain control by ceding control' (ibid., p. 300). This paradox was well understood by Stoney-face who says was he was 'not fully realised as shaman in my own skull until I just said [to the Great Spirit] "yeah okay I get it. I get it. I give up, you win. I'm yours. Use me as you see fit"':

> It was an acceptance that I had to give in, I was not going to be the greatest evolution of myself without giving in. And once I submitted all of a sudden I had that confidence that 'yes, this is me'. So, I had to submit to fully realise the truly dominant aspect, because the dominant part is the confidence that I'm doing what I'm supposed to be doing.

Stoney-face's participation in hooksuspension rituals clearly resonates with Bromley's understanding of spiritual edgework practices that create situations of danger and mythic weight, into which tension is built through ritual sequence. Ultimately, the participants in these rituals confront that danger directly, and the tension is resolved by their survival through a transformational moment of direct connection with transcendent power. If the transcendent is socially constructed this description need not necessarily relate to any non-human other, or anything beyond the edgeworkers themselves. If transcendence is understood in its broadest possible sense of going beyond or outside the everyday experience of physicality to create or encounter something new, then it becomes clear that BDSM can create it, and that experiences of BDSM can be characterised by profound and transformational connection with it.

There are some clear similarities between Bromley's chosen exemplars of fire-walking and snake-handling and BDSM. None of these are practices that '"mainstream" comfortably' (Bromley, 2007, p. 288), so all are commonly dismissed as anomalous and/or pathological. All three activities involve notions of personal power that are distinct from everyday roles and understandings, which have the potential to create intense experiences of connection and transformation. More specifically, they create events and/or sensations which may be perceived initially as being beyond limits, together with opportunity to transcend those limits. People who attempt the activity in ignorance of the necessary skills or preparations are regarded as foolish; in all three contexts the central scene is built up to and prepared for, participants actively choose to 'step outside of safe space' (ibid., p. 296) and into a newly created liminal space. On a more conceptual level, fire and serpents are symbolically associated with life and death, creation and destruction; they also have the power to awaken primal fears. BDSM likewise uses symbolically weighty and fear-inducing tools – needles, knives, electricity – and plays with existential anxieties of engulfment, petrification and implosion (Langdridge, 2005). The risks involved in all these activities are real. But, in common with other edgework activities, it is not as great a risk as the casual observer may imagine, owing to the range of skills developed and deployed by the participants.

Going beyond these overt similarities it is possible to see how BDSM can push edgeworkers to challenge their own limits and potential in the way Bromley describes firewalkers doing. The stepping outside of safe space (as he describes it) is an expression of trust in a transcendent Other, while for BDSM players that trust is invested in one another. But the results can be similar moments of empowerment, connection and realisation. Griff describes a profound moment of self-discovery resulting from the powerful 'serial-killer' scene described above:

> Here's the thing, here's the thing. At that [pause] because I've never been in that frame of mind before [pause] ... you have to be convincing, you have to be convincing. And I could have done it, as in physically. I mean everything was there. But I couldn't. I discovered that there is [pause] an absolutely huge brick wall at that point in my brain that stops me from taking that further. There is absolutely no way I would ever kill anyone ... but you know what, I realised that I didn't know that wall was there before. Now I do.

In a similar vein, Mistress Marina describes edge-play scenes in terms of realisation and control. Edge-play 'highlights everything':

Everything is on edge – your nerves are on edge, your eyes are focussed, your hearing. You're concentrating totally because that's how close you are to that limit ... For me it's almost like thinking ... 'you can do this if you want, you can do this if you want' ... it's almost like taking control of myself. Because it is in my control what I do. I could do something really damaging that could then wreck everybody's lives or I could, just one second before it becomes that, say 'Okay you can breathe now'.

This kind of exploration is not the sole prerogative of tops; Molly also defines edges in this way, seeing them as distinct from 'things where I just go "no, they're not my things"', even though some of the things she rejects might be considered edge-play in the wider kink community. Instead, edge-play for Molly is constituted by 'those fuzzy boundaries that actually I want him to explore, that I get off on exploring'. This is because those are the places 'where I discover things about myself that I didn't know, where I had an inkling – I guess that's the kind of rape-play, consensual non-consent ... knife-play, cutting, blood-play and branding'.

This process is not the exploration of an isolated self, but what Cee describes as 'the interaction of two like-minded souls ... wanting to experience something on mutual ground'. She says it is 'not just spiritual' but all-encompassing, because 'it's all the different layers. You're targeting lots and lots different places – it's physical, it's emotional. Lots of different areas.' Neither is it a pure acquisition of abstract knowledge as it has the potential to change feelings and attitudes associated with that knowledge, as Penny says, 'I think now I've always realised that I was submissive but before it was always ... a very, very negative thing ... And now I've realised that is a good [pause] it's something that I allow to happen, it's not something that someone else takes from me.'

These new perspectives and understandings of self, relationship and reality are not grounded wholly in achievement, in learning that you can 'take it' or in triumphing over adversity. BDSM can offer those things, but it also requires the experience of things as they are. BDSM enables the exploration of weakness, of role reversal, of pain and humiliation or degradation as experiences in themselves rather than things to be overcome. These are areas of deep concern and engaging with them helps individuals to make sense of their worlds. More than this, by seeking to experience these things as they are practitioners can begin to move past some of the unhelpful binaries and absolutes which categorise much modern thinking about these areas.

Blurring boundaries

Some of my participants spoke about the ability of BDSM to embrace contradiction, ambiguity and paradox – to be, as Ivy put it, 'simultaneously meaningful and completely ridiculous!', as well as challenging concepts of pain, power and other such apparent absolutes that are not really absolute at all. For Kraemer these 'ecstatic, boundary-blurring experiences raise one's tolerance for the ungraspable and uncategorisable and so potentially permit us to re-examine our assumptions [about the world]' (Kraemer, 2014, p. 98). In this way, BDSM makes an abstract knowledge of the complexity of things, and the inadequacy of the labels we choose to describe them, into a lived reality. This kind of boundary blurring is made possible by the entrance into another world that is enabled through the process of play. Play offers a means of marking out time and place in a way which creates a 'special kind of expectancy' (Douglas, 1966, p. 78) about the experiences within this new place. Play offers a frame within which attention can be focussed to 'shut in desired themes or shut out intruding ones' (ibid.), and without this framing the intense and contradictory experiences would not be possible.

These experiences, the somatic grasping of them and the ways they change the world and later reflections upon them are all elements of the religioning process as it results from BDSM play. Through them worlds are created, explored and adjusted, new meanings and understandings discovered, and old ones challenged and adapted.

9

Kink ritualising

> I didn't realise that the work I was doing was spiritual, that the tools I was using ... were the same ones that people had used for thousands of years to induce transformative experiences. Rhythmic pain, trials of endurance, physical ordeals, confession, breath-work, energy work in the form of guided imagery – these were all things I did instinctively ... without knowing what doors I was opening.
>
> (Krittika, 2011, p. 182)

> The words 'spiritual' and 'sacred' mean different things to each of us. Some of us put religious value and context to these words, but I do not. I look at these words as classifying the intent of our rituals to strengthen our relationships and our commitment to them. I believe that for most Masters and slaves, the relationship that they forge using ritual, mythology and metaphor are considered sacred to the parties in the relationship.
>
> (Master K Ron, 2011, p. 66)

BDSM is process-oriented, challenging and subversive (Kraemer, 2014). Practicing it enables people to explore emotional and physical limits within settings which can heighten awareness of vulnerability or create a sense of great power, with the concomitant awareness that this is power wielded with consent, and the knowledge that one is both safe and greatly valued. The process of play which creates these experiences has many facets, which combine to enable the creation of an '"as if" or "could be" universe' (Seligman et al., 2008, p. 7) – an other-where, experienced as fully real and authentic, within which different potentialities can be shaped and explored. This 'standing ... consciously outside 'ordinary' life' (Huizinga, 1950, p. 13) is a feature of academic understandings of play: it allows people to 'play the game seriously, but [they] understand that [they] are playing' (Droogers, 2014, p. 23) and in this as-if space they can react to things as-if they are so. It also offers a basis for connecting play and ritual, where ritual is understood as 'the temporary emergence and playful enactment, in its own right, of a shadow reality' (Droogers, 2004, p. 138). Playfulness and seriousness are not intrinsically opposite; the process of ritualising involves experimentation with another reality, so ritual actors can be understood to be playing seriously with 'variations, inversions, contradictions, double play, irony, incongruity, and counterrealities' (ibid., p. 139) – all potential elements in the construction of a BDSM scene. That BDSM play is serious is evident in the effort expended to acquire skills and knowledge, in the durable personal and/or social/psychological benefits that result from it, in its subcultural unity and the ethos of its community, and in the extent of personal identification with the practice (Newmahr, 2010).

Ritual, too, is a dynamic process of activity and enactment (Grimes, 2002, 2013; Houseman, 2008; Kapferer, 2005; Schechner, 1993; Seligman et al., 2008). Through movement, and the responses of bodies to one another, ritual actions combine to create new spaces (LaMothe, 2015). Whether these are described as 'shared "as if"' subjunctive worlds (Seligman et al., 2008, p. 8), virtualities of 'self-contained imaginal space' (Kapferer, 2005, p. 47) or 'counterrealities' (Droogers, 2004, p. 139) is less important than the experience of them as real other-wheres, in which particular qualities of experience can be found. In this aspect at least, ritual-space and play-space are hard to distinguish.

I suggest that when the people in such a space begin to feel it, and/or the actions taking place within it, to be gestalt then understanding serious play as a process of ritualising becomes a potentially useful analytic approach to the phenomenon. Making this connection avoids presenting ritual as a simple acting-out of beliefs or symbolic representation of worldview and instead sees it as fluid, dynamic and active processes of creative construction by agents for whom 'the medium is very much the message' (Seligman et al., 2008, p. 113). The impact of the experiences so created, and their perceived difference from the everyday, enables the conceptual framing of the process which produced it as a self-contained event, distinct from its surrounding milieu. The qualities and potentials of such a process are the same whether we name it playing or ritualising and, at such fuzzy boundaries, a full understanding surely requires consideration of both sides.

In previous chapters, I have shown how BDSM play creates an other-where in which self and body are experienced differently, and relationship is created, communicated and performed. Such other-wheres have experiential qualities that are hard to put into words; elements contributing to the gestalt whole can be identified in the nature of the space itself, and the practice which creates and holds it for the people inside. Play-spaces are spaces of potentiality, where different possibilities can be brought into existence and such spaces are dangerous, because of the openness to chaos inherent in abandonment of norms (Douglas, 1966; Ezzy et al., 2009). Through a shared desire to explore such uncertainties, both personal connection and a broader sense of communitas can be forged (Lyng, 2005), as occurs in intensely emotional rituals (Whitehouse and Lanman, 2014). Edgework BDSM enables exploration of limits, and reflection on what lies beyond them, which contributes to people's discovery of ways to live and be in the world (Ezzy, 2014).

I have separated these elements, but in the performance of kinks they combine and interact to create the strength and power of the play experience and, perhaps, enable the emergence of a sense of kink as gestalt. Bringing all these elements together creates a strong impression of similarity between the practice of BDSM and religious ritual, but I wish to do more than argue that BDSM simply *looks* like ritual. Rather, I contend that gestalt play is a form of ritualising because it contributes to the religioning processes of the individuals involved. The ritual process of the play allows the gestalt to be foregrounded, made tangible and explored.

Given the nature of BDSM experience, and the fact that at least some elements of BDSM closely resemble ascetic practices, it may not be wholly surprising that the deliberate use of BDSM practices in named ritual contexts does occur within the Scene (Greenberg, 2019). But it is interesting to note that few, if any, of the people who do this confine their BDSM to contexts identified as ritual ones – kink ritualists are also kink players. This offers an unusual opportunity to explore the concept of ritual by looking at a collection of activities engaged in by the same people, using the same skills and knowledge but named differently on different occasions. It allows me to ask whether the naming creates a difference in the qualities and significances of the resulting experience and, if not, whether it is meaningful to separate the practice into fixed and discrete categories. This chapter will therefore consider kink practices named by the practitioners as ritual before using the perspective offered by an understanding of ritual to examine kink not so-named.

Kink named as ritual

I look at being a Dom as a kind of shaman; I'm taking them on a journey inside their headspace ... I think every Dom does, in a sense. Taking them on some type of journey, whether spiritual or not ... It's still a journey.

(Javelin)

I can't really separate who I am as a person and who I live with every day as a person from my kink identity ... I can't be a separate kinky version of myself, and go home to be a shaman version of myself.

(Stoney-face)

I just call it BDSM. Because it covers everything ... lifestyle is probably the other short term I use because for me it is that. It is part of everything I do, mundane or otherwise.

(Kyndyl)

Of the forty-four people with whom I conducted research interviews, three spoke of performing deliberately constructed ritual which used kink as an aspect of practicing their religious identity. In common with most of my research participants, the term 'religion' was not a positive one for these individuals, and all of them chose to describe themselves as spiritual in preference to religious, even though all identified with named traditions.

Kyndyl describes themself as a pagan and was, at the time we spoke, a practising reiki Master and 'training to be Wiccan clergy'.[1] Kyndyl describes their path as 'a mixture of Northern tradition, Buddhism and shamanism'. For Kyndyl, religion describes 'a doctrine based system for people to ... basically find their way to deity', while spirituality is the term to describe people finding their own way to the divine. In the context of their kink identification, Kyndyl identifies primarily as sub, but said they have 'tried it all', including lifestyle relationships from both the Dominant and submissive side. When discussing ritual Kyndyl spoke of incorporating kink into various rituals for 'raising energy or getting rid of something or sacrifice' and also 'honouring one of the deities I'm working with ... specifically for the primary deities I work with, I would consider myself their property'. However, this does not preclude Kyndyl taking the top role in a ritual context.

---

1. The use of 'they' and 'them' as personal pronouns was requested by Kyndyl.

Stoney-face is a shaman within Sioux traditions. He is 'readily accepted as a shaman by tribe members' and is 'living it' although he is not yet 'tribally affiliated officially because it's very murky with people like me who are not pure bloods'. He described his shamanic path as evolving but, at the time we spoke, he was walking the Heyoka path of the 'sacred clowns ... the contrary ones ... the weirdest of the weird'. The task of this path is to make 'people look at themselves but in humorous ways ... make fun and poke'. He described this path as 'sacred but not stoic' because 'if you're not laughing something is wrong'. Stoney-face prefers to describe himself as a 'spiritual being' but feels that 'religion doesn't necessarily have to be a negative'. What he dislikes about religious institutions is 'when you're trying to say that it works for me so it should work for everyone else or else, that's when I have a problem'. He feels that contemporary humanity has 'evolved to the place where we want much more self-journey, self-discovery, self-improvement. We want a personal relationship with our higher power', and this is what characterises his own spiritual path. In the context of kink, Stoney-face described himself as a 'collared Switch', living in a lifestyle relationship with his Mistress but happy to play either role with other people. His shaman aspect is very dominant but is also a 'paradox of duality' because he is 'submitting to the will of the Great Spirit'. This duality was evident in the form of ritual he spoke about in most depth – hook suspension. At the age of 11 he had a vision of 'the traditional Lakota Sioux ritual called the Sundance ... that is being hung up by hooks in your flesh', and years later 'I made it happen ... I manifested my reality to be with the right people at the right time'. He says that ritual hook suspension is not a kinky experience per se, but 'a transcendental spiritual experience that had elements of kinky knowledge and play'. These experiences shape his conception of spiritual kink as applied to himself: it is a process of 'incorporating what I can use in ritual and spiritual realms as a shaman, and incorporate them into my kink play to make people's raw kink play a lot more fun and more connected'.

Javelin started playing as a sub but is 'now a switch'. In both top and bottom roles, BDSM is an aspect of Javelin's 'calling in life', which is 'being a sacred harlot, being a sacred prostitute priestess ... [to help in] bringing about a more sex-positive culture'. Javelin became aware of this calling at the age of 15, a time when 'I felt so lost, I didn't feel like I had a purpose or anywhere I fit in. One of the things that the energies told me was that you will have a place but you have to be patient. And then they gave me a glimpse of it.' Following this calling takes various forms, including running workshops and organising both sex and kink related rituals, generally at pagan events. As well as facilitating ritual for others, Javelin has engaged in BDSM rituals for personal transformation, describing one 'reclaiming ritual' in which 'I had a reverse PA piercing, done very slowly ... to reclaim my female side.[2] I had a symbolic hole in my genitals to reclaim my femininity. And ... they also used a sound [a medical probe] to fuck my dick, so that I could be the receiver.' This ritual helped Javelin to claim 'my true gender, as being both [male and female]' and demonstrates how for Javelin BDSM is the means through which 'I was able to pull at every aspect of my life and have it make sense as a whole'. Javelin is an 'eclectic pagan':

> I take a little bit from the Taoists, a little bit [pause] well, a lot from the ancient sex temples, I take a little bit from Wicca, a little bit somewhere else. But I take what I want, that applies to me, and I don't want the whole toolbox, I just want this tool or that tool.

Javelin does not see paganism as a religion, because religion is 'an institution' which 'takes some kind of head and makes them the responsible person for your spiritual development'. By contrast 'spiritual is when you are responsible for your own spiritual development'. BDSM is part of this process for Javelin because it offers 'certain tools that I can open doors I couldn't open without them'.

None of the three said that all the ritual they participate in has kink elements, nor did they say that all their kink play has ritual elements. But each of them is 'using kink knowledge in a ritual way' (Stoney-face) sometimes, in the context of their personal religious practice. In addition, although all of them mentioned the role of intention when deliberately performing ritual and creating a ritual-space, they also each spoke of the possibility of play-space becoming ritual-space at times when there had been no prior intention for this. For Kyndyl, this kind of 'spontaneous' ritual had given them 'some of the more intense and basically helpful rituals I've been in'. Stoney-face agreed that play-space and ritual-space are 'neighbours of each other' but they are distinct in a way he described in terms of frequency: 'They're sort of inside the same frequency envelope. If you think of them as either oscillating or frequencies of a similar amplitude ... they're similar wave patterns of frequency'. This frequency shift

---

2. A reverse Prince Albert piercing enters through the urethra and exits through a hole pierced in the top of the glans.

exists largely because in ritual 'you are much more aware that you are creating the reality that's happening'. However, he agreed that it is possible for a ritual-type connection to be created during non-ritual play when a 'frequency adjustment' occurs. Sometimes this is a conscious decision made by the top during the play, and sometimes it is more spontaneous:

> If we're both just super-connected that day … and then all of a sudden we just click … everything just sort of fits right, and it just explodes. So, it can happen, and I'm not opposed to it happening, it's not like I dial it down and say 'No, you can't come out and play today'.

Javelin felt the main difference between play-space and ritual-space was that Javelin needs to 'be conscious of what's happening … all around me' when running a group ritual, which means that 'I can't go as deep into sub-space … [or] if I'm in Dom-space I can't ride as deeply as I would like with the submissive'. However, Javelin also felt 'the spiritual side of things' was always potentially present, because a Dominant is 'a kind of shaman', taking the bottom on a personal journey within a space that is 'a safe environment … Although we don't cast a circle, it's kind of implied that it is there.'

Tupper, writing from within the kink Scene, casts BDSM practice in the same mould as liminoid rituals, 'in which people step outside the normal social context and experience liminality, but then return to their former social status' (Tupper, 2018, p. 253), a contrast to liminal rites of passage which mark a permanent transition. He distinguishes kink from religion on the basis that it lacks 'a dogma, eschatology or other grand narrative of the world' but agrees it performs many of the functions of religion, including 'community, identity, transformation of the self' (ibid., p. 255). If essentialist views of religion are rejected and a polythetic approach to taxonomy adopted instead it is clear that such elements are sufficient to enable BDSM practice to be examined through the analytic lens of the religious. Certainly, it is clear that the tools offered by BDSM and the spaces it creates can operate as ritual, or be used for ritual purposes, and that boundaries drawn between ritual kink and kink play are permeable.

Both involve the creation of an other-where, both utilise the same skill set, tools and sensations and the enacting of relationship between parties. Non-ritual kink can also create the transcendence of sub-space, or the flow and hyper-awareness of Dom-space, which might be associated with concepts of spiritual experience. Indeed, using Javelin's experience, it is perhaps more likely to take this form than ritual kink, although Stoney-face developed his frequencies analogy to describe deliberate shamanic journeying as distinct from the more spontaneous experience of sub-space: 'It's a different kind of frequency. A different kind of wave altogether. They're really close to each other, but they are different'.

Where play-space and ritual-space are experienced as different, the clearest area of difference is intention, so that where the intention to create a ritual exists there is a degree of experiential difference within the space. Stoney-face did not experience his first hook suspension as a kinky experience, although it drew on kink skills, but he did connect this difference to being in space named as ritual-space rather than as play-space. He said that he is 'using an extreme edgy method to achieve a spiritual state of mind that I'm looking for', while other people undertake the same physical challenge 'in a non-ritual mindset':

> The body-mod people, brilliant people like CoRE [Constructs of Ritual Evolution], who do hook suspensions that are artistic and beautiful and moving and entirely invigorating to see but they're not rituals, its more theatre. And there's people who go into it with the mindset of that, almost sideshow element of 'oh, my god, I'm hanging by my skin by hooks'. And there's those adrenaline junkies ... who go into it just for the high, just to experience what it feels like.

Interestingly, CoRE does connect its work with ritual, describing it as 'blending the practice of performance art with extreme rituals both modern and ancient ... [through having] suspended our own concept of physical limitation, pierced the heart of our fears, and transcended the boundaries of social convention' (www.wearecore.com, accessed 10 March 2016). Other qualities of the ritual experience – including changes to bodily sensations, relationship with time, connection to others in the space and so on – closely parallel intense play experience.

I do not claim there is no difference between ritual and play, but the difference is not an absolute one and it is not tied to any single element present in one but not the other. Engagement in processes of play builds space through practice, as does a ritual process. The space in which play takes place does not become play-space until the loop of sensation, reaction and response is fully realised, while ritual-space can be named and identified before the play process begins. However, the creation of that space is still enacted and its establishment as an other-where is necessary for full immersion into the ritual. Similarly, the space does not snap out of existence in either setting once the action is over; those involved must return from where they have been. Play often takes place without a specific aim or end in mind but this does not place it beyond the realm of ritual, as 'causal opacity' (Whitehouse and Lanman, 2014, p. 675) is not uncommon in events understood by participants to be ritual. When a boundary from this world into another is crossed, that crossing is known (Seligman et al., 2008), and with both BDSM play and ritual that boundary and the space it encloses are consciously created.

What happens in play-space appears to be a process of ritualising, both in form and in effect, but it is not universally named as such. The kinds of process which occur in BDSM play are what Grimes (2002, p. 28) describes as tacit ritualisation: an 'activity that is not culturally defined as ritual but that someone could interpret as if it were'. This is the stance taken by Tupper (2018) when he identifies Turner's (2008) three steps of ritual – separation, liminality and aggregation – in the construction of a kink scene. Tupper also appears to concur with Grimes contrasting of such tacit rituals with the fully formed 'rites' which occur when 'a group enhances or emphasises the qualities to the point at which a definitional threshold is crossed' (Grimes, 2002, p. 28). Looking at the accounts given by my participants it seems that BDSM can be understood in both ways: sometimes it is explicitly named and constructed as ritual; on other occasions, while the activity may not be so identified, the significance, intensity or transformative potential of the play remains evident.

The primary difference between a 'ritual' and a 'scene' for the person engaging in one or the other is thus one of naming. Naming may incorporate a prior intention, or it may be claimed afterwards. It may refer to a set of actions intended to achieve a particular end, such as the ritual reclaiming of Javelin's birth body, or the realisation of a vision like Stoney-face's hook suspension; there may be an intention to raise energy and direct it to a purpose, or it may simply be a performed expression of identity as a spiritual kinkster. But these same things can happen, and do happen, without such naming because in play any denotive meaning is subordinate to the performative nature of the act (Seligman et al., 2008). In both play and ritual this creates a sense of meaningfulness that is always, to some degree, self-referential and self-validating (Handelman, 2005; Houseman, 2008).

It is important to remember that not all play is the same. It will not always achieve the creation of an other-where, or create the kind of 'distinctive evocative qualities ... and ... inherent conceptual uncertainty' (Houseman, 2008, p. 420) that are so much part of ritual acts. But it can, and it might, even when not named as ritual. Most of my research participants felt something more than simply enjoyment in their play, a feeling I identify as gestalt. I suggest that when people do feel this, and begin to value their practice as an 'end unto itself' (Newmahr, 2011b, p. 68), one way to understand what it is that they do is as a process of ritualising which contributes to their personal religioning.

Unnamed ritual

> I do feel the energy that's around, I feel very much in that sort of vibe of what's happening ... but then part of me says 'this is complete bullshit'.
>
> (Nomad)

> I think 'play' for a lot of people is the comfortable word, especially for those who go 'ick, I'm not going to mix healing or spirituality or anything else other than getting my dick hard, or myself wet' ... [Calling it play] lets them think they are keeping the boundaries. Language is a lot, unfortunately, about people's comfort levels.
>
> (Kyndyl)

The term and concept of religion was rejected absolutely and sometimes aggressively by many of my research participants. Few, other than Kyndyl, Stoney-face and Javelin, named what they do as ritual. Given the close association between religion and ritual it seems worth briefly visiting why this term may not have occurred. The generally unfavourable view of religion that prevailed among my research participants was even more strongly negative among those who did not identify with any named tradition (regardless of whether they considered that tradition religion/religious); for example Cee said that the very word 'just makes me feel sick'. If the idea of religion is felt so strongly to be negative, and experience of organised religion is either negative or absent, then it is unsurprising that terms with perceived connections to this undesirable concept are also understood in negative terms, if indeed they are considered at all once the over-arching concept has been rejected.

Contemporary cultural discourse commonly places science and religion in opposition, with the former on the side of reason and proof, and the latter being the domain of the unreasonable or the foolish. Such perceptions may well underlie the fact that many of my research participants were keen to emphasise their scientific interest, the value they placed on evidence and, often, their rejection of deity. Although I did not ask specifically about these things, many people felt it important to tell me that they knew the sensations and shifts in perception, experienced during play were caused by body chemicals like endorphins or adrenalin. This knowledge was usually presented immediately after descriptions incorporating intangible, immeasurable and otherwise hard to describe elements of experiences; to me this gave the impression of a recognition that such things as transcendence have associations with the domain of the foolish or unreasonable and a corresponding desire to distance the speaker from those labels. It is perhaps unconscious, but a concern that admitting to the 'non-rational and vaguer aspects' (Blum, 2012, p. 209) of an experience was somehow diminishing (unless 'real' knowledge was also demonstrated) seemed prevalent whenever conversation strayed into these areas. As well as explicit declarations of scientific knowledge, there were apologies for using terms like 'energy' to describe things which do not, in scientific terms, fit such a category. Some, like Nomad, explicitly distinguished types of understanding, saying 'one part of me says "ooh that's some hippy shit, or some altered plane", while the other part says "well it's just your brain doing what your brain does"'. But he also said that 'actually I don't care what it is', and this sense that the experience is worth having, regardless of causes it might be attributed to, was widely shared.

In the contemporary world, the biological, the economic, and/or the functional explanation is often seen as the only reasonable or admissible way to understand things. Ritual may be seen as simply out-dated or, perhaps more judgementally, as a means through which people seek 'psychological compensation' (McWhorter, 2004, p. 72) for realities of life they find themselves unable to cope with. Neither interpretation seems likely to lend itself to people reclaiming the term ritual when they consider themselves to have rejected the orientation which gave rise to it. None of this would remove a need for ritual, but it does affect the places in which people are prepared to recognise it, and the activities to which they are prepared to apply the term. If we think of ourselves as modern, and of modernity as progress, then 'because we think of ritual as primitive, irrational, or otherwise bad ... we refuse to see it in our lives' (ibid., p. 73).

The positioning of reason as an opposite to religion can be placed alongside the issue of belief, specifically of belief in deity. Scholars may be challenging the idea of any absolute connection between religion and belief

(Vásquez, 2011) but the association remains firmly entrenched in concepts of religion prevalent outside the academy (Nongbri, 2013), as seen in the personal understandings of the term my research conversations uncovered. The assumption that religion and belief are synonymous often formed the basis for a rejection of the term religion in any way applying to themselves –the association was so strong that the initial response to my question 'what does the term "religion" mean to you?' often took the form of 'well, I'm an atheist'. The thinking which characterises the modern person as 'someone who believes that others believe' (Latour, 2010, p. 2) in things which have no reality, while considering themselves by contrast to be endowed with critical reason that is based on solid facts, infuses how many people are prepared to see their own actions and speak of themselves. For such a modern person, religion is rendered unreal or superstition, because they lack the belief that is perceived in others, and perhaps this contributes to the scarcity of the term ritual in contexts outside the traditional institutions of religion. It also implies that if religion is belief in deity, then religious practice, including ritual, is a (symbolic) expression of that belief; a view which renders the concept of ritual meaningless in the absence of firm belief in deity. BDSM could not then be understood as ritual unless it is being engaged in as an explicit practice within a named religion, and with the aim of (in some way) expressing the beliefs associated with that religion.

Religioning and ritualising

> I had a symbolic hole in my genitals to reclaim my femininity ... It's highly symbolic, but it's a little more than just symbolic ... It was a very powerful and bodily empowering ritual that really helped me [pause] I can't think of the word, it's not so much 'accept' as kind of 'bring all my nature back together'. As a whole ... Rarely am I seen as my true gender, as being both. And it was a good way to express that.
>
> (Javelin)

It is my view that a focus on belief is too limited a view of what religion is, and therefore it also offers a limited a perspective on ritual. Viewing ritual wholly as an external marker of internal processes is distorting of the reality that people can engage in ritual activity without being concerned with meaning or symbolism, just as religion can be found outside religious institutions. The manifestation of both concepts within real individual lives is better represented via a shift from noun to verb that signals them as process or practice rather than thing, and allows attention to focus on the ways practice and performance create religious identities, power relations and manifestations (Nye, 2000). Religion is not an object, existing independently and impacting on people, but activity performed by people within the 'ever-evolving relational community' (Harvey, 2013, p. 95). Such activity becomes ritualising, not because of anything inherent in the actions themselves, but because of the way the actions are framed (or named) and oriented. Actions which take place within ritual can always be performed in non-ritualised contexts (Seligman et al., 2008) because, among the other things it does, ritual continually renegotiates boundaries by building and rebuilding the everyday world as-if it were one of many possible worlds.

Such negotiations and constructions are one means by which people participate in the 'ongoing experiment of reality' (Harvey, 2013, p. 82). These experiments require fluidity and creativity in order to create an as-if world as a shared could-be; they require the capacity to empathise, so that experiences which would otherwise be an individual 'is' can be shared 'in the potential space of what could be' (Seligman et al., 2008, p. 23). As this shared, as-if world is produced through ritual actions, those actions must fully engage the lived reality of the people who participate. Only if they do so will ritualists be marked 'in the heart, in the memory, in the mind, in texts, in photographs, in descriptions, in social values and in the marrow, the source of our lifeblood' as opposed to the 'skin-deep' impression of rites which do not effectively perform such experimentation (Grimes, 2002, pp. 7, 5). For the many people who dislike the concept of organised religion and reject any external authority figure able to pronounce on personal spiritual development, the rituals most likely to be effective in this way will be the unnamed emergent experiences that occur outside the structures of traditional organised religion.

The ways in which my research participants spoke of the role and importance of their play indicates experiments inscribed deeply into the marrow of those engaging in them. If ritual is a means of 'negotiating our very existence in the world' (Seligman et al., 2008, p. 8), this can be seen in Damien's description of BDSM as 'that sort of expanding people's horizons ... sometimes people are miserable without necessarily knowing why, and people are restricted without necessarily knowing that they are. And that's making them more miserable than they would otherwise be.

So that expanding their horizons thing, you could think of it as a service to humanity.' Alternatively, if ritual is a means of finding actions that 'are also bridges – reliable doings carrying people across dangerous waters' (Schechner, 1993, p. 230), then Mistress Marina's experience of BDSM as something which enabled her to become comfortable with 'the feeling of power, which I don't think for women especially we are comfortable with' constitutes such a bridge. Or if ritual offers a kind of 'spice[ing] up daily existence with flavours so exquisite that we are unable to forget the banquet ... revealing what is most deeply desirable, most cosmically orienting, and most fully human' (Grimes, 2002, p. 346), BDSM fits here too, as Ben describes it: 'a looking into ... the deep-down needs' that takes one on 'an exploratory journey to joy'.

Shaping a ritual – preparation and anticipation

> Every single pre-ramp-up is different, because all my situations are different. Nothing is consistent, there is constant change ... But I do have to mentally prepare myself and it will normally be the day before; so if there's props, clothes, whatever, I get that ready. And that ... you're sort of programming your mind as to what's going on ... And then just before, I have to just give myself five or ten minutes to tell myself what it is we're doing.
>
> (Cee)

> If it's meant to be a ritual I'm going to do everything beforehand. Call borders, invite whatever deities I want and ... most of my friends are also actively part of my BDSM spirituality group, so we all know what the heck's going on!
>
> (Kyndyl)

Anticipation of a ritual has been identified as a contributing factor to the power of that ritual to create liminal space and so to the potential impact and transformative power of the ritual (Bromley, 2007; Ezzy, 2014). Liminality is characterised by alterity and the dissolution of normality; anticipation of this state contributes to the framing of the space within which it will be experienced and heightens awareness of what is to come. This awareness can be read in the significance given to intention as a means of identifying named ritual, but this same kind of anticipation contributes to the experience of play and the creating of the play-space.

The importance of negotiation and informed consent prior to engaging in play is one part of this anticipation. Before playing together, new partners discuss likes, dislikes, interest and limits with a (hopefully) full recognition of the complexities and ambiguities involved. The knowledge of one another gained here makes a vital contribution to the eventual creation of an effective play-space, although it is unlikely to be sufficient in and of itself to create intense and immersive play. The lifestyle couples among my participants had carried out such negotiations at a much earlier stage in their current relationship, but they remained aware of it. Molly and Michael spoke of maintaining a spreadsheet in which their likes, dislikes, hard and soft limits and varying levels of interest in specific activities were recorded. Cate had a written contract with her Master, setting out the parameters of their relationship, including her responsibility to always be open and honest with him. Similarly, poppy said she had an obligation to always tell the truth, which extends to a sharing of limits and concerns. For these couples, play might occur spontaneously, but it might also be signalled by a specific instruction from the top or by an intention to attend a play-party – events which might also trigger anticipation in other players. Michael likes to play with anticipation itself, by delivering the anticipated in an unexpected way:

> [Molly] will have mentioned something to me … and I really pay attention to that and … so it will crop up. So, she might say … 'I'd like you to use the knife on me tonight, I'm in the mood for that'. So I'll think about it, and go 'yeah okay' and then what I'll do is I'll spank her with the knife.

For people not in lifestyle relationships or with multiple play-partners, occasions of play are more likely to be planned in advance and so more specifically anticipated. Ian spoke of 'a phase of preparation' which occurs before play; since he rarely plays at home this usually involves packing a bag: 'I'm going to take some toys along or ropes or whatever and I'm going to pack those … and then there's always a journey'. Nomad likes to 'work through some of my kung fu forms' before he engages in shibari. This is a process of 'clearing my mind of sort of everything that's around, and so it is really like meditation'. He says that he wants to do a 'sort of clearing out anything that may have happened, anybody else that may have interacted [with me] … sort of … wiping the slate of anybody else I may have worked with so I'm completely focussed on what I'm doing now'.

For Ivy, anticipating a play-date is like 'a slightly ramped up version of the preparation that I would do for any date'; Rosie agrees with this, because it is important to 'make sure you shave and put nice underwear on!'. But this is not the entirety of anticipation – the knowledge that play will definitely occur is a factor (and different to the thought that it might) as are expressed limits or interests. Griff emphasises the role of expectation, noting that 'really … what you're trying to do is, you're not negotiating what happens in the scene. What you're trying to do is get an idea of what the other person is like, likes, doesn't like.' For this reason, he doesn't ask people what they like:

> I always open with 'how do you want to feel? Do you want to feel scared, do you want to feel safe, do you want to feel exposed, do you want to feel under pressure, do you want to feel useless, do you want to feel … adored?'

Framing negotiations in this way contributes to the anticipation by leaving a greater degree of uncertainty about specifics; my response to this description during our conversation indicates as much – I said that, even in the abstract context of general conversation, that question 'opened doors in my head that maybe wouldn't have opened if you'd said you ask "what do you like in terms of sensation?"'.

Preparation might also take more concrete forms: Ivy says that she has 'had situations where in the run up to a play-date that I've been given instructions or things that I'm supposed to do during the day'. Unusually, Madeleine described some of her play, and in particular cutting, as being 'very ritual', and when she spoke most about preparation and anticipation it was in relation to this form of play. She said:

> You do have to know what's going to happen because there's, you know … structural … there's medical stuff to be taken care of. And you need sterilising equipment and you need gloves and you need alcohol and you need … butterfly band-aids … You know you're going to do it for a long time; you talk about it before you do it a long time before, and you're preparing for it a long time before and you do this thing like 'I'm not going to turn up. I'm not going to turn up.'

This level of anticipation makes submitting to being cut 'surrender on a level like nothing else'.

The quality of anticipation for tops is different in some ways, as they are the ones who will shape the play as it unfolds. Mistress Marina describes her process of getting ready to play as 'getting my Domme-head on'.

Although she is clear that she is always a Domme, she explained that this aspect needs to be more fully realised and explicit if she is going to play. An element of planning is part of the anticipation for some tops. For Barry this is minimal, as poppy's reactions and responses are crucial to the unfolding of a scene; he finds that 'after the first two minutes any plans I've had are gone'. Similarly, Damien says that he will just 'close my eyes for a couple of seconds, let my imagination run rampant and then, move on from there'. By contrast, for Griff, the level of planning and preparation required depends on how he is intending to play: 'if I'm playing with fear, or playing with someone's mind, someone's head, that takes a lot of thinking and planning in my head. Because that's something I really don't want to fuck up'. It should be emphasised that this kind of planning is not about scripting everything that will happen, but rather about determining the overall flavour or tone. His description of the process is worth quoting at length:

> I never plan with including [specific] things. What I would plan with is how would I get someone to be ... say we're going for scared. How do I get someone to be really scared that I have done something to their body that they didn't want, without actually doing it? Because that's the difference between playing and not playing right? ... So, this person, what do I know about this person? Alright, she works in healthcare so I can't really scare her with medical things, okay. She is quite vain, she likes the way she looks, as I can see by the number of selfies she takes [pause] so alright. Apparently she appreciates the way she looks, so I'm going to play with the way she looks. Right, okay. So how about ... I burn her hair off. But don't actually burn her hair off. So I call my hairdresser friend and say 'can you collect me some hair cuttings please?' I spend an hour tying hair in little bunches, trying to find a way to keep them hidden between my fingers ... But things like punching, things like rough body play [pause] that could happen at the drop of a hat ... with minimal negotiating. Because during a scene like that there is a lot more communication that happens as you do it.

The process of packing toys to go to an event, or setting up a play-space, is a form of planning, in that you cannot use what you do not have about you. Most tops would take a range of different things if playing away from home, as this enables them to respond to atmosphere or available equipment. Planning and anticipation do not always happen in isolation either, as pussikin describes:

> My Master always goes quiet for a while before we have a play-date. We do do spontaneous things; you know messing around spanking with a spatula in the kitchen or whatever. But if we're really going to play he spends time considering things. Then he goes to the dungeon and moves stuff about ... then he calls me. Or if we're at a club he likes to do a walkabout, with me on my lead, looking at what's there and what's going on.

Similarly, cate spoke of her Masters 'plotting face' and the sense of excitement this created in her: 'You get butterflies and, well I get fruit bats! ... It's you just know that it ... you know you're going to be, your head's going to go to a certain place and it's going to be really lovely.'

Anticipation of all kinds contributes to the ultimate creation of liminality in the play-space; Ezzy (2014) notes that the impact of rituals which occurred during a festival was greater for those participants who had anticipated the event well in advance, while individuals who had forgotten they were attending until the last minute found the rituals to be less transformative. The anticipation signals the start of a shift from one kind of space to another kind of space and helps to make the cognitive understanding of what is going to happen 'come alive in the physical acts' (ibid., p. 45).

Shaping a ritual – pattern and repetition

> Our relationship is fluid. It's constantly exploring, developing. Evolving. It evolves through every experience we share; it evolves through our wider life, through life experiences, through what is happening to us at any given time.
>
> (Molly)

> I'm not a fan of planning. Now, that being said, I plan. But not, you know, '9 to 9.15 there will be a flogging with this flogger, followed by this, to facilitate this end goal.' My favourite thing in play, and mostly in life, is to subvert expectations. To go to say something and mean something but mean it in a different way to the way it has been taken. And that brings me such great joy whenever I can do that ...
>
> (Michael)

Ritual is often understood as repetitive action. It is this perspective which characterises use of the concept within fields such as medicine, where it describes repetitive/obsessive behaviours associated with dysfunction

(Favazza, 1996), and biology, where it describes animal courtship behaviours (Bouissac, 2014). The underlying implication of this characterisation is that ritual action is mechanistic and prescribed, with no room for improvisation, accident or fluidity. However, ritual is also a quality of action and an action is potentially different every time for the person performing it. Aey describes this potential variety in a piece of writing she shared with me about the enduring appeal of flogging:

> It's like dancing. It has movement & rhythm. Big motor movement and fine. Loud and hard. Soft and sweeping. Steady and continuous – like a symphony – melodically moving through an area, intensity increasing, reaching crescendo, then fading into gentleness again. Steady and clear, definitive and focussed, movement around, dance forward and back on your feet, touch gently with falls and hands and nails.

The possible variety in application creates a similar possibility of variety for the receiver, all arising from what looks like the same action. But, within the variety, there is still pattern:

> Every time you make a strike, and the arse goes away from you and then comes back ... there's a very immediate pattern to that. Because there's acceptance of 'yeah go on, give me another one'. Whereas if it stays away too long you hit it too hard, because they're not wanting the next one. It's that line where they're coming back because they have to not because they want to.
>
> (Piers)

These patterns of sensation and response create the possibility of increased intensity. The first time someone plays may be enjoyable, and sufficiently interesting to keep them coming back, but it is only through practice that the skills involved in both topping and bottoming are able to develop and allow the play to flow. Play is a dynamic event involving multi-directional patterns of sensation and response layered onto one another. Each movement that is made also makes us (LaMothe, 2015); to move differently results in thinking differently, even if the movement occurs in isolation. But during play each movement is intermingled with the movements of others, contributing to the matrix of natural forces within which we all live. This is part of 'shaping a sense of self as the one who did' (ibid., p. 103) but this self-who-did is thoroughly relational and the matrix of sensation, response and movement extends beyond the individual. Such a matrix necessitates elements of unpredictability, and any dynamic event must have the flexibility to encounter and absorb change, even if it does not deliberately create it.

Much BDSM play takes the form of action, reaction and adjustment. Scenes do not follow a set pattern; even an established couple engaging in favourite activities will have different experiences of those activities over time, and will vary the order and intensity of what they do. The deliberate recreation of an earlier scene is generally understood to be unachievable, as responses vary 'from person to person and from time to time, and that duration of time can be seconds or days' (Barry). As a result of the top receiving and responding to the reactions they create, any intended pattern must be altered. Nevertheless, among the qualities which contribute to all different sessions of play are 'patterns of bodily movement' (LaMothe, 2015, p. 156). In the distinction LaMothe implies between these patterns and ordered sequences of specific actions is the difference between the learning of a skill and the ultimate achievement of 'an arc of embodied techniques' (O'Connor, 2007, p. 130), which obviates the need to think consciously about the actions being performed; this state, where action follows action without any awareness of conscious intervention, is a flow-state (Csikszentmihalyi, 2002). It is evident in individual descriptions of Dom-Space, but it is also a part of the matrix of connections between individuals. Freed from isolation within the individual, the flow-state becomes a '*social* process through which an event is experienced as taking on a life of its own for which the actors are merely channels – the play transforms them rather than they transforming the play' (Ezzy et al., 2009, p. 399). Griff uses the analogy of becoming fluent in a language to describe the shift from everyday awareness to flow:

> When you watch someone do something who is really good at it, it becomes entrancing. I think that also happens from the other point of view; if you do something that flows naturally it becomes meditative ... [you] don't consciously think about it anymore, in the same way that I don't have to consciously think about translating things into English, because I don't translate things into English any more ... There was a point when I was learning English ... I was watching someone on stage doing a speech, and I knew exactly what he was saying but I wasn't sure what language he was saying it in.

Ritual is an active interrelating of liminal points which construct a felt-necessity to complete a pattern shaped and demanded by the flow through the process (Ezzy et al., 2009). Each point flows to the next, reacting to circumstance and result. The process is fluid but shaping itself towards a satisfaction or sense of completion. The intuitive loop of action, reaction and response described by Oliver illustrates such a flow:

> I get into where [pause] it's very careful listening to the other person's body, in terms of what feels good and what you're doing. And you get out of your head ... You don't think 'oh I've been spanking her this much, it's probably time I do something else now' – which is how I used to start, very much in my head – whereas actually I go now to what feels good to me ... it's doing what feels right ... it's about listening to your intuition ... Your feelings are almost never wrong, you just have to listen to them and listen to them in the right way.

Moving through such a felt pattern allows both interior transformation, as individuals express 'their own individual human bodily potential for becoming themselves and their worlds' (LaMothe, 2008, p. 588), and the social dynamic of a ritual event constructed by a felt necessity to complete the pattern demanded by the flow (Ezzy et al., 2009).

LaMothe (2015) describes ritual as being characterised by a patterned arc of movement that travels through warm-up, peak and cool-down. The warm-up consists of movement that both activates and orients the sensory awareness of an individual and guides them to recognise whatever they currently feel as something that their ritual has the power to transform. In BDSM play, this is the opening sequence of actions decided on by the top and the initial response to them by the bottom, which may be continued with increasing intensity or abandoned for a new action that seeks to build on the sensory awareness created by the first. The patterns thus established are repeated and/or developed to reach the next stage – 'a time of play' (ibid., p. 161). This is the stage where movement flows into movement, and ritual participants allow themselves to be 'moved by powers that their culturally informed movements have stirred in them and bent them to perceive' (ibid., p. 160). It is the peak moment of the scene, when a point of sensation and/or emotion has been reached which cannot, at that time, be surpassed. Following this the intensity is reduced, a cool-down phase offering a time when the performers are able to 'abide in their own renewed sense of resilience and resourcefulness' (ibid.).

It is this overall shape which is repeated and repeatable, by combining different embodied actions in different ways to create an 'overall pattern of behaviour' within the space of the ritual (Houseman, 2008, p. 414). Each scene is distinct and must be so as many different elements feed into its creation, but it is also created from patterns of learned and embodied actions and responses.

Shaping a ritual – performing and exploring boundaries

> Everybody has an idea of how far they think they can go. Speak to most rational people they won't punch someone in the face unless circumstances [like] somebody threatened someone they love [pause], and then they will ... Somebody saying 'oh no, I could never do XYZ', well how do you know you could never do it until you've tried it?
>
> (Damien)

The relationship between BDSM and boundary exploration deserves consideration in the context of ritual, because the transformative potential entailed in such exploration is a part of the reason why 'before and after are not the same' (Houseman, 2005, p. 76). This is not necessarily transformation in the sense of changes to cognitive understandings of self, other and world, although such change is a possibility. As with the Faunalia rituals described by Ezzy (2014), which work deliberately with fear, anxiety and uncertainty, the transformations accomplished by BDSM ritualising are somatic, emotional and relational in nature, bringing players deliberately face-to-face with challenging or ambiguous aspects of the self and of others.

Langdridge describes kink activities like mummification as offering a means to psychologically confront 'ontical insecurity and existential anxiety' (Langdridge, 2005, p. 202). To play is to engage in a creative experiment which allows us to understand our existence has limits, and to meet them with courage. His analysis does not use the term ritual, but his description of processes deliberately creating genuine fear, within a situation that is also known to be temporary, is remarkably like the complex and ambiguous experiences of disquieting and/or threatening pagan ritual that Ezzy (2011, 2014) describes. In these rituals it becomes evident that fear and anxiety can become enriching and empowering experiences, and also that it is possible to 'simultaneously feel attraction and revulsion, fear and excitement and pleasure and pain' (Langdridge, 2005). For Langdridge the activities creating such paradoxical experiences are experiments in living; for Ezzy they are 'liminal ritual events [which] make space and time for transformations of soul' (Ezzy, 2014, p. 16). In my view, an active attempt to address existential angst is a practice of personal religioning and, given that ritualising requires more of a performative suspension of disbelief than it does an explicit set of beliefs, I see no reason why both these descriptions cannot equally apply to play that allows or enables ways of 'performing, thereby becoming identified with, our most troubling questions' (Grimes, 2002, p. 257).

The element of performance is important. BDSM is not experienced as role-play since what happens in the play-space is really felt, both somatically and emotionally. In describing 'rites of terror' Whitehouse and Lanman (2014) express surprise that these rituals are really painful, and truly terrifying. As they see it 'the costs of participation seem to be out of all proportion to the imputed symbolic value' (ibid., p. 679). It might similarly be said that the levels of pain, fear, humiliation etc. experienced within a play-space are disproportionate to the role being played. The confusion in both cases would be the same: these ritual events are not symbolic or conceptual, they are real; players are not acting, but living an alternate reality. The reality of the experience gives it power, even when a symbolic meaning is ascribed afterwards. This account by pussikin illustrates how different realities become embodied for her during play:

> This is something I've only done with my Master; I think I would only do it with my Master. This thing ... it's like a bag you get in, and there's pockets inside for your arms and when its zipped up it fits pretty much skin-tight all over. There's straps on the outside to tighten it up anywhere its loose. I couldn't even [pause] I couldn't even move my fingers ... I've never been so still [pause]. So still. And with a blindfold as well, stuff always freaks me out more if I can't see. Some people like it ... but for me it's scary. It was the closest to being totally immobile I've ever been and it was [pause] a serious head-fuck. Serious. Total. I don't know how long I was in it for ... I mean I was whimpering within minutes. Maybe seconds. I ended up screaming. There's just something about not being able to move ... something like [long pause] melting, maybe. Fading away. I can take a lot of pain. I mean I've been beaten until my skin starts to lift and been happy to carry on but this [pause] I think, maybe, pain kind of [pause] solidifies me. It says ... that I'm here. I'm real. And [pause] I guess that I matter enough ... that someone would take the time to hurt me, put the energy into it. But that immobility was the opposite to that ... Am I really real? [laughs] And that tells you all my hang-ups, right there!

Although this experience genuinely distressed pussikin she also found it affirming as she felt she learnt 'something about how I ... touch the world'.

The vulnerability needed to achieve that required a level of trust pussikin cannot imagine giving anyone other than her Master, and thus the experience is not simply one of facing fear but also one of trust given and justified. When Cee says that she 'took somebody out cross-dressed and I made them post a letter' the qualitative nature of the edge being encountered is different, but this can still be 'the edgiest play they've ever had ... to him that was "oh my God, that was too much. But I did it."' Regardless of what elements go into building the edge the dynamic of fear and trust is the same, resulting in a peak (or depth) of dysphoria which is permitted and made acceptable via the relationship between the players. Cee says this is 'almost like going to a priest, isn't it, for confessions ... You've gone through this huge emotional "I've done this, Father", and then you've dumped it, and it's done with.'

This kind of play is likely to require aftercare of some kind, ranging from time spent cuddling to extended periods of reflection and/or discussion. Aftercare was important and enjoyable for most people I spoke with, at least as an extended expression of the intimacy created by their play. One exception was Demon, who plays primarily with pain and says he is 'attracted to masochists'. He responded to the idea of aftercare with 'Oh arse, stick 'em in a corner!' and said that 'luckily' he had never played with anyone who needed aftercare. His descriptions of his own play were simpler and more specific than other tops I spoke with – for example, 'I tied her to a cross, and I went through my toys from soft to hard. I played with a toy until she said 'pause' ... but she knew if she stopped me the next toy was worse' – and he made no reference to limits in any context other than pain levels. He was also the person who gave the fewest indicators that kink was a gestalt in his life, saying 'it's only fucking with a variation'. This could be taken as an indication that a sense of kink as gestalt is more likely with certain kinds of play, but it is certainly evidence that no universal claims can be made regarding these matters.

But despite this exception, many people deliberately play with boundaries in ways that confront matters of ultimate concern, and that this in turn contributes to processes of meaning- and world-making. The experiences created enable transformation that is somatic in nature, but likely to be reflected on later. Because they are shared, such experiences forge a sense of kinship and connection, not restricted to personal relationships but contributing to the recognition of a kink community, and to the fusion of kink with other aspects of personal self-concept (Whitehouse and Lanman, 2014).

Shaping a ritual – performing and exploring relationship

> You can marry someone in vanilla life, and you can get divorced. You might be Catholic and you might say you never will, but you know you can and you just stop being a Catholic. But if someone has their hands around your throat, and they make a mistake ... You can't undo that. So, the level of trust is very different, I think.
>
> (Aey)

> [Play] is part of an interchange ... It's very important to me. It's beyond the 'meet somebody on line, go out and enact something'. For some people that's all they want. It wouldn't work for me. It's that depth which really defines whether it is BDSM or not.
>
> (Barry)

The fluid unfolding of play is formed through the enactment of relationship within the play-space. As the actions which shape the space are performed, they draw elements from pre-existing disparate domains into the totality of the new world being made. For Houseman and Severi this process is the key structuring element for ritual, creating a characteristic *'relational* field' (1998, p. 167) which gives a ritual its particular form. They view ritual as a descriptor for a particular mode of action, rather than a typology of acts. It is not only the creation of relationship which characterises this mode, but a 'particular type of relational configuration' (ibid., p. 262), constructed by and through performed actions and interactions. Within a ritual space, people live 'exceptional' (Houseman, 2008, p. 416) relationships that are polysemous and/or multiplex and which entail a 'condensation of nominally contrary modes of relationship ... recognised as distinct from those normally occurring outside the ritual frame' (Houseman and Severi, 1998, p. 262).

One such exceptional form of relationship is enacted within play-spaces. During play apparent opposites such as praise and mockery, care and hurting, power and powerlessness, wanting cessation and wanting escalation, are 'dramatically fused' (Houseman, 2008, p. 417), as the reality of the play-space exists in tension with the ordinary world. The relationships enacted here may spill over the edges of the space containing them, in the same way the qualities of the experience overflow and become gestalt. The connection between BDSM players is intimate; play is a process of weaving that bond 'tighter and brighter' (Aey), or a thing that 'communicates the ineffable between us' (Michael), as the experience of the relationship is 'driven deeply, by repeated practice and performance, into the marrow' (Grimes, 2002, p. 5).

This 'particular process of recontextualisation' (Houseman and Severi, 1998, p. 423) does not orient participants to any particular understanding of the relationships they enact, nor does it directly offer answers to problems or tensions from the world beyond the ritual. Instead it provides 'experiential grounds' (ibid., p. 424) for the commitment of the participants to the reality of their enacted relationships. It is the fact of the performance and the experience of the enactment that grounds the 'irrefutable yet difficult-to-define 'truths' they are held to enact' (ibid., p. 421).

Gestalt practice as rituals of religioning

Not all religious practice is ritual but, if people seek a sense of the religious in their lives, ritual practice may form a part of that religioning process. BDSM can be understood as a form of practice which makes manifest personal religiosity in the way that it contributes to the processes of 'making the invisible visible, ... concretising the order of the universe, the nature of human life ... and the various dimensions and possibilities of human interiority itself ... in order to render them visible and tangible' (Orsi, 2005, pp. 73–74).

Ritual can be framed in a variety of ways, and BDSM play can be described in terms which fit at least some of those framings. But, as previously stated, I wish to do more than say that kink sometimes looks like ritual. Ritualising is a pervasive human activity (Grimes, 2013) and as such it is a part of personalised processes of religioning. The multivalence of the concept speaks to its utility in these processes. Serious play becomes ritualising when the latent potential of the activity to transform, to enlighten, to confront and to explore become fully realised in the liminal as-if world of the play-space.

The experience created by play has qualities that ritual has, and can be understood as a ritual in an experiential way : because the 'before and after are not the same' (Houseman, 2005, p. 76); because the nature of the experience that creates that before and after is self-validating and difficult to conceptualise in terms other than the enactment of the ritual itself (Houseman, 2008); because play is not merely a set of repeated actions, or a simple telling of stories but a process of enacting 'particular realities' (ibid., p. 414), with participants being fully aware of this; and because, during and through this enactment of reality, spaces are created which are distinct from the everyday but also 'really real, a complete and filled out existential reality – but in its own terms' (Kapferer, 2005, p. 47).

Gestalt offers a means of considering the ideas of value or specialness in relation to specific occasions or activities without necessarily relying on either a transcendent Other or an established cultural tradition to provide it. A person for whom kink is gestalt feels that these extraordinary, somatic and emotional experiences are enriching contributions to self- and world-making, even where this contribution is not and cannot be fully articulated. BDSM can infuse the everyday, but BDSM play is outside the everyday by its very nature, as ritual is distinct from everyday religion. I suggest that when play becomes gestalt, it can be viewed as process of unnamed ritualising, a personal unnamed religioning.

10

Conclusion

Gestalt kink, gestalt religion

> Look into our eyes. When we return with those bruises, do we walk taller and stronger? When we touch our cuts, are we more serene? When we give up our power, do we grow more sure of ourselves? When we accept power over another, do we learn more compassion? Do we return from the Underworld better for the journey? That's how you know, those of you who are worried, whether we're doing it right.
> (Kaldera, 2006, pp. 7–8)

> Do not be fooled: though it may come in forms of play, or sensual exploration, or bliss, this is the work of our souls. This journey has the potential for turning the flax, the straw, of our beings into the gold of potential.
> (Harrington, 2009, p. 7)

The central argument of this book is that sometimes a person's kink can be, for them, other than the sum of its constituent parts. Through the experiences created by their practice kink becomes a gestalt, a whole to which each of the themes explored in the preceding chapters contributes. Such a gestalt is a contributor to the constant, dynamic process of exploration and creation of world and self that is religioning. Each of the themes I have identified can be understood and explored separately in relation to BDSM, while also being one strand among the many which contribute to the whole of the gestalt. They do not constitute an exhaustive list of all possible strands which could be woven into personal gestalt kink, but they are the themes which emerged most strongly from my research conversations.

By connecting the felt sense of gestalt to the concept of religioning as an active process I have sought to engage with the fuzzy complexities that seem to me a more accurate reflection of human lives than impermeable lines drawn around human behaviours to corral them into clearly delineated categories. Human activity and related phenomena are fluid in nature, with categories offering different perspectives from which to make contributions to overall understanding rather than a means of describing a fixed and essentialised reality. BDSM experience could be placed within many such categories, including but not restricted to those I have identified here and it is equally true that considering such experiences within a wholly different frame to any of those I have utilised would offer different insights into the activities themselves and/or experiences resulting from them.

Using religioning as my framework has allowed all experiences of BDSM play to carry equal weight when considering their value and role in individual lives. Based on my conversations, I argue that experiences of play as described by my research participants, in all their variation, contribute to an individual's sense that their kink as a whole is powerful, potentially transformative and productive of important and worthwhile experience. Play experience contributes to identity and community making, and self- and world-understanding in ways which cannot be clearly expressed but which are strongly felt. The sense of kink as a gestalt, with the associated sense of its meaning and value in individual lives thus develops from experience.

Placing experiences within a framework of religioning allows for the recognition that discrete experiences may contribute to the creation of a gestalt, but that simply having an experience is not the whole story. There is no intrinsic quality which must, through its presence, turn any experience into a 'Religious Experience'. It is possible to engage in the most sacred rites of a named religious tradition as a rote exercise in conformity, as the expression of an aspect of personal identity, as a deeply felt connection with an Other, or as a fluid and flexible combination of these (and other) qualities. Similarly, there is no essential component which divides the kinky from the non-kinky. Engaging with blurred boundaries and experiential qualities allows kink to be considered within the category of the religious, but I do not seek to create a kink-as-sacred category that would *require* the activity (or experiences created through it) to mean more, or to be more, than a mutually pleasurable interlude. My argument is that sometimes kink practice and experience *is* more than that, and that by understanding those times as contributions to dynamic processes of personal religioning understandings of the role, significance and value people ascribe to their kink is broadened.

A criticism sometimes levelled at this kind of approach to religion is that it makes the category so broad as to include everything; I would qualify this only slightly – it does not include everything, but it could include anything. People constantly and creatively find and develop personal practices which bring some aspect of their world into new focus for them, and such practices can build into a process of first constructing and then exploring that activity as gestalt – as more or other than the sum of its constituent parts. Lyng's edgeworking sky-divers (2005), Snyder's nature-loving fly fishers (2007), Taylor's Soul-Surfers (2007) and Sanford's whitewater kayakers (2007) all seem to me to be taking hold of something emerging from their practice – a practice that began as a leisure activity but has become filled up to the point where something new spills over the boundaries to be gathered. The experiences are felt, reflected on, and valued, and the experience is then sought out again so that the continued practice can enable the gestalt to become once more explicit and/or tangible.

To identify when religioning is in process is not a matter of identifying locations, events, behaviours or mysterious essences. There is no more necessity that a Muslim reciting the Shahada be actively weaving that experience into their lives in a purposeful or meaningful way than there is such necessity for a person being tied to a bondage wheel. People can, and do, go through the motions; they can find comfort in habit or feel rooted by tradition; they can seek to conform, or to please other people in their lives. So, to understand what is going on during a given time, and what is done with it afterwards, it is necessary to ask the doer. When the experience is overwhelming, substantially somatic (or otherwise non-linguistic), boundary blurring or subject shattering, it is also necessary to accept that such questioning will not produce clear and unambiguous responses. The questions I chose to ask concerned the nature of experience, and associated thoughts, feelings, relationships and practices. This is not the same as asking someone whether or not they identify as a religious person, whether they have a religion or whether they consider the term to apply to themselves because identity claims are not the same as analytic categories; my research has focussed on the uses to which kink are put and whether understanding such use as religioning can contribute to understanding the behaviour rather than on how kinky people self-identify in relation to religion. The reported qualities of experiences that contribute to religioning are not changed by the choice to use participants preferred term of play, the critical category of ritual or the broader term of religioning to name the process which creates them, but understandings of how such experiences fit into broader pictures may well be enhanced by explicit consideration of such different labels.

An emergent sense

> It's so difficult to put it into words. I mean even if you can remember an exact sequence of events, which isn't always the case [pause] you can't necessarily articulate how it felt, or what your headspace was like, or what the connection was like or just [pause] ... I think 'how was that for you?' immediately afterwards would be a bit like 'my brain is made of mush, and ... I can't remember what my name is and [pause] I don't know'.
>
> (Ivy)

Gestalt is an emergent sense arising from the complex and dynamic combination of many different elements, and as such it is not possible to directly perceive it separately from the totality of the phenomena from which it emerges. The chapters of this book identify elements which can contribute, but a sense of the whole is still necessary. Living religion is a 'multi-faceted, often messy or even contradictory amalgam' (McGuire, 2008, p. 208) which has a practical (rather than a logical) coherence, making sense to the individual and so 'working' within their life. This means the lustre of gestalt might be read as being present in descriptions of kink as: being intensely meaningful with explicit recognition that such meaning defies easy description; a means of making abstract knowledge of the complexity of things and the inadequacy of the labels given them into a lived reality; contributing to the ways in which the self is understood or part of a process of connecting individuals to the world and to each other; a core aspect of identity; a vehicle for exploring experiential living bodies; facing the edge between life and death; a creator of intense, profound and/or boundary blurring experiences that can 'raise one's tolerance for the ungraspable and uncategorisable' (Kraemer, 2014, p. 98), thus challenging assumptions about the world.

Gestalt kink

> Yeah, [BDSM] it really is [pause] It's definitely part of things. It definitely helped me push past that next, impossibly, inflexible barrier, that part of me ... that part of you that thinks I'll never do that, I can't.
>
> (Rita)

> To me it [my kink] means my life. It is who I am … I am just a person within the Scene that, over the years, has tried so many different things … I've tried to go vanilla after discovering it and I couldn't.
>
> (Kaz)

> Basically, when you go flying in sub-space you are going on inward journey. You're flying, and you can fly very high out there … When I go into sub-space I come out of it fully energised. I'm getting something from [pause] I'm getting a calm, a focus, a whole different perspective on life.
>
> (Javelin)

While my participants encompassed the full range of attitudes to the terms religion and spirituality – from accepting both to accepting neither – almost all agreed that BDSM, for them, is more or other than sex, than physical pleasure, than performed identity or than any other simple, single-focus explanation. They felt that it added a dimension of fulfilment to their life which could not be easily explained, a feeling this book has presented as a sense of gestalt.

The different ways in which this was expressed makes it appropriate to give them some last words on this hard-to-say, strongly felt matter:

- Simon/Effie explains that kink is 'meaningful for me' because 'it gives me sensations and it gives me thoughts … to re-examine life through this experience', and this examination is fulfilling and life-enhancing.
- Mistress Marina observes that 'when you put the right people in it, the right circumstances, the right things [pause] you get something more … There is definitely something in it over and above the ingredients'.
- Molly also describes play as 'a kind of bigger thing; it's this whole thing of doing this, of putting myself here, of giving in this way, of receiving in this way, to put myself here'. She sees BDSM as powerful – 'it's a hammer' – which can be positive, but doesn't have to be: 'It can be enlightening; it can be freeing; it can be abusive and it can be distressing and it can be damaging.' The hammer can smash things or it can 'create something absolutely beautiful'.
- Cee emphasised the need to take a holistic view, saying that 'within the BDSM world what you're exploring is not something with a label. It is so far, far diverse, in another dimension and another experience. It is almost like a sixth, seventh, eight sense

that we haven't a great understanding of yet.' She says that her involvement with kink 'has really made me complete. I feel very complete and very content as a person. Because I have obviously explored myself through meeting all these wonderful people, but I have also had a greater understanding of society and what their needs are.'

- Oliver emphasises connection, saying that BDSM 'creates a closeness that other things don't. It can be really beautiful ... you have that moment, or however long it takes when you feel so close to another human being ... You go deeper.'
- Griff described BDSM as one among many strands that he uses to fill 'the hole in my life [that] needs to be filled by me. By knowing who I am ... that knowledge of knowing who you are. BDSM is part of it. And if I hadn't had BDSM I don't think there is anything else I could have done that would have filled the same void.' Although he is clear that BDSM is one among many elements in developing this self-knowledge, he also says that 'it's one of the more meaningful things in my life'.
- Kaz goes a step further when she says 'to me [BDSM] means my life. It is who I am ... It makes me feel that I am whole. And without BDSM in my life I am not whole.'
- For Madeleine kink is 'extremely meaningful' in its relationship both to what it is to be human, and to 'a big Other' of some kind. She sees her kink as 'being completely and utterly intentional' and this 'matters a great deal to me because it is, I think, in a way, what makes me human. And, especially when it comes to enduring pain – the ability to do that, the ability to sublimate it, or to get on top of it and ride it is ... is to me an act of great human control.' She also sees a 'dynamic of sacrifice' where 'you are giving something up, you are allowing this ... I feel the same way when I'm topping in that I'm bringing this thing out for this other. For this Other. I am enabling the [pause] emergence of something into this ... It is a kind of [pause] well, it's magic, in that sense of primitive ideas of magic and the fact that they buy you trespass into a place you shouldn't be. They are the cost for stepping over the line of taboo.'

Gestalt religioning

An experience which has spilled over the boundaries of easy definition, as play-experience can, is a kind of experience very likely to be reflected upon later and refined through that reflection and/or through seeking further such experiences. The container of the play-space allows a bubble of experiencing to be perceived as isolated from the constant stream of experiencing that is the state of being alive. Such a marked-out 'Experience' constitutes a crucible within which particular fragments of sensation, emotion, cognition, proprioception, interoception, etc. are combined, concentrated and calcined. Some will be intensified, and others will be lost, so that a specific BDSM scene might come to be felt, for example, as wholly about pain even when other sensations were involved. This concentration of particular elements makes up the kind of vivid and enduring episodic memory on which people tend to reflect subsequently (Atkinson and Whitehouse, 2011). Both felt and thought components are refined, reflected on, and refined again in an iterative process that results in a personal sense of the significance of that experience for the individual, their life and their world. An experience of profound kink thus carries the potential for transformation, not only in a somatic and transient sense (created within the play-space and fading with it), but at other levels also. As the memory is refined – somatically, cognitively, emotionally – it contributes to the ways an individual relates to themselves, to others, to boundaries and to existential concerns.

I have argued that the process of creating play-space and the experiences therein constitutes ritual, in that they are a purposeful exercise in creating a crucible of experience. Grimes observes that anything can be seen as ritual, but he also suggests that there is a difference, of some kind, between a Catholic attending mass and a Catholic engaged in cleaning their house. This is not a difference of the religious versus the non-religious but instead the distinction between being ritual and being seen as ritual. I have identified kink experiences falling on both sides of this distinction, but where the qualities of experience involved were less disparate than such a separation might imply. My view of ritual as the practice of foregrounding a gestalt passes beyond the issue of who it is who does the seeing and the labelling of what they see and asks instead whether the container is filled to the point of spilling over; whether the experience of the practice becomes more than the practice itself can contain. Understanding Grimes's 'definitional threshold' (2002, p. 28) between rites and ritualising as experiential rather than linguistic allows practices that might otherwise be sited on either side to be understood as aspects of religioning, when they are being felt and used in such a way.

In sum if religion is a gestalt, then the religious for an individual can be constructed from any practices, experiences, ideas and social milieu in which they find that gestalt element. The practices that bring the gestalt into the foreground of their experience for a time, that make it explicit, are the practices that express and explore individual constitutions of the religious. Viewing experience as a crucible, refining personal outcomes from the concentrated stuff of which it is made, allows for a given form of experience to be part of religioning for one person and not for another. The traditional rites of established religions may likewise serve as a means of highlighting or foregrounding a sense of gestalt that already exists within a community or culture, creating a similar process. However, I do not propose this process to be either the essence of all religion, or essential for any religion; I offer it as one possible means of creating experiences which contribute to religioning. The 'specialness' of kink, or indeed any other practice, occurs in its movement beyond the sum of the elements from which it is made. In what is then constructed from and/or built upon that I locate the religious as it is for an individual and, while my work here has been on kink, there is in my view no restriction on the practices which can become gestalt in this way.

Appendix A

A kink glossary

Age-play: Assuming a persona of a different age (usually younger) in the context of role-play.
Bondage: Restraining or restricting movement.
Bottom: General term for the person on the receiving end during a scene; often used to signal situations where no power-exchange is felt to be taking place.
Consensual non-consent: Agreement to engage in play as if no consent has been given; usually involving agreement not to use safe-words. Since specifics are not generally discussed beforehand, and even the time may be unknown to the bottom, it is a strong expression of trust.
CP: 'corporal punishment'; play which involves spanking, flogging, caning and similar forms of impact play. Can be used to describe a specific community within the kink scene.
D/s: 'Dominance and submission'; often a descriptor for a lifestyle relationship where the power-exchange exists for the duration of the relationship.
Dominant: Person who takes control during a power-exchange. Often shortened to Dom/Domme.
Edge-play: Forms of play seen as more extreme or risky.
Electro-play: Forms of play involving electricity such as e-stim (TENs technology) and violet wands (glass electrodes which apply low current, high voltage, high-frequency electricity).
Figging: The insertion of peeled root ginger into the anus or vagina.
Fire-play: Forms of play involving fire; including brushing burning torches or sparklers across the skin and igniting fuel on the skin.
Flogging: Beating with a many-tailed implement; by contrast whipping is generally understood to refer to a single lash or tail.
Hard limit: An activity in which a player has declared they do not wish to participate, or come close to.
Hook pull: Hooks are inserted into the skin and then attached to fixed points, or to another person, enabling the pierced individual to pull the piercing against resistance.

Hook suspension: Suspending the body via hooks pierced through the skin.

Kinbaku: 'Tight binding'; another term for shibari, elaborate rope bondage based on Japanese tradition.

Kink: The opposite of vanilla (normal/conventional); often used interchangeably with BDSM to describe the overall scene. Also a designation of personal interests within the portfolio of kink activities – 'my kinks are ...'.

Knife-play/blade-play: Forms of play involving knives, run over the skin for sensation or used to create fear; most people who engage in cutting use scalpels or razor blades for a cleaner wound.

Lifestyle: Descriptor for a 24/7 D/s relationship, where the power exchange performed during play is understood to run throughout the relationship.

Little: an age-play identity; a person who identifies as a little has a play persona that is younger than their actual chronological age.

Mind-fucking: Creating dissonance between expectation/mental experience and physical reality, for example the top creates the belief that they will cut their submissive with a large sharp knife then runs a blunt metal knife across their skin where they cannot see it.

Mummification: Bondage intended to wholly immobilise and/or isolate; commonly done with cling-film or specially designed bags.

Needle-play: Inserting needles or surgical staples into skin, piercing without inserting jewellery.

Play: Active engagement in forms BDSM activity; not all kinks involve play, for e.g. wearing and/or enjoying the visual aesthetic of latex could be considered a kink.

Power exchange: A situation where one person has given power over themselves and their bodily integrity to another person.

Predicament bondage: Bondage in a position intended to cause discomfort and/or fatigue.

Primal: Can describe an identity or a form of play; focus on unfiltered raw emotion and reaction

Safe-word: Agreed word that can be spoken to stop or slow-down play, either temporarily or altogether; includes non-verbal signals.

Scene/session: Names given to BDSM encounter or periods of play.

Shibari: 'To tie'; another term for kinbaku, elaborate rope bondage based on Japanese tradition.

Soft limit: An activity in which a player has declared they do not wish to participate, but which they might be willing to approach in the right circumstances.

Spanko: Abbreviation of spankophile; a person interested in all aspects and forms of spanking.

Spiritual BDSM: Engaging in BDSM play for an explicit spiritual purpose, such as achieving an altered state.

Submissive: The person who gives up their power in a power exchange.
Suspension: Bondage which supports the weight of the body off the ground.
Top: A general term for the person on the giving end during a scene; often used to signal situations where no power-exchange is felt to be taking place.
Topping-from-the bottom: Where the partner taking the bottom role is directing what happens during the scene.
Vacuum bed: A latex bag or envelope from which the air can be sucked, fitting the container around the body inside it; a form of mummification bondage.
Vanilla: Anything that is felt not to be kink.

Appendix B

Research participants

Aey is happy to be described as a Dominant, a Mistress or a top. She considers herself spiritual, and sees her kink as being involved in her spirituality because 'it has that connectedness. As a spiritual person I think that everything is connected with energy'.

Barry is a lifestyle Dom in a committed relationship with poppy. He doesn't see himself as religious or spiritual, but considers his kink to be meaningful 'given it's a part of me it has to be ... . If you were to say it isn't you're almost questioning "do I deserve to be here?"'

Bea describes herself as a submissive and is in a committed relationship with Dee. She would not use either religious or spiritual to describe herself but says she can see kink and spirituality occupying 'that same kind of space ... I think there is a connection there. It's just one I'd never thought about before'.

Ben is a Dom. He is a Hindu; he describes religion as 'the pathway to spirituality' and spirituality as 'where there are no distinctions between you and other beings'. It is spirituality that 'is the material that makes me, the material that makes the diamond. BDSM is a part of that diamond'.

Cate identifies as a slave and lives in a committed lifestyle relationship. She is a pagan, but considers this spirituality rather than religion. Spirituality 'means that you're in touch with yourself' and BDSM is 'very spiritual' because 'it's all to do with where it takes you in your mind'.

Cee is a professional Fetish Practitioner who dislikes most of the conventional terminology associated with kink because of the associated stereotypes. Cee says that spirituality is 'my connection with the greater energy in the world and the energy within other human beings' and kink is a meaningful part of this 'because it's the interaction of two like-minded souls ... that are wanting to experience something on mutual ground'.

Colin is a switch and a cross-dresser within school role-play scenarios. He sees religion and spirituality as the same thing, and uses neither term about himself. His kink is 'terribly important', especially the 'powerful' experiences of cross-dressing. He says play 'takes me somewhere different ... [and] I feel so different' in play-space.

Damien identifies primarily as a top, but prefers to 'introduce myself by my name'. He describes religion as a 'desire to have something beyond the physical' and it is distinguished from spirituality only because of the 'rules and restrictions and dogma'. He is spiritual because he looks 'at the world beyond, I see things that I marvel at ... that interconnectivity'. Play contributes to this in the moments when 'it's just flowed and it's just felt [pause] good. Right. And I've had that same sort of feeling'.

Dee describes himself as a top or a Dom, and is in a committed relationship with Bea. He sees religion as a 'form of control' and spirituality as 'a sense of yourself and what is around you'. Dee says that his kink does not currently contribute to this 'but it does have that potential'.

Demon identifies as a sadist; he would accept the label Dom but he would not choose it. He is anti-religion, which he sees as 'weakness', and also anti-spirituality – 'girly rubbish'. He is the only one of my research participants who minimised the importance of his kink as being 'only fucking with a variation'. But he also described kink in terms which imply something more, saying play is performance of his identity as 'an outsider', and like poetry or art in that it is 'pure self-expression'.

Digi is a switch within his relationship with Twisted. Their exploration of kink has been a journey, which has become meaningful as they have travelled further: 'it's something that ours. No one else has this that we have'. Digi is not religious but thinks 'there are things that we don't understand'. Spirituality is found in 'connectedness ... [and] having an openness or to be aware of other people and your environment and what's going on around you' but Digi is 'too much of an engineer to be spiritual'.

Esteban is a practitioner of self-bondage. At the time we spoke he had not fully explored his kinks with anyone else, but felt he was best described as a switch. He dislikes the term religion but says 'I get spiritual satisfaction from doing what I do ... If it didn't do that then I wouldn't be doing it in the first place.'

Friedrich is a Dom in a committed relationship with Rita. He feels negatively about religion, which he describes as a 'man-made constraint' for controlling people's thoughts, but he considers himself spiritual. BDSM can be spiritual as people 'attain things during these moments, they learn things in these moments. It's very intuitive. It's knowledge about yourself that comes from nowhere, and if that's not a spiritual experience what is?'

Griff describes himself as a primal, which he says is the best fit for his kink interests but not a perfect one. Griff considers his kink to be meaningful because 'a meaningful thing is something you use to create, or adjust or check your own identity. And I think that me being kinky ... the skills I have learned, the traits of my personality that have had something to do with it, have had a profound effect on me as a person in other boxes of my life'.

Ian identifies as a top. He dislikes the concepts of both religion and spirituality and says his kink is important to him personally because it offers 'the freedom to ... manifest the ... the things I want to do in real life'. He also sees a political edge to it in the potential to challenge 'an enormous hypocrisy' around sexuality and monogamy. Ian is polyamorous and has a play relationship with Rita.

Ivy identifies as submissive. She is a witch, and does connect paganism with religion. She sees spirituality as a broader concept 'to include religion but also to include people who don't identify as religious ... But who have an aspect to their life that is about something more than the physical and mental'. Kink is a part of this because 'I don't think that my religion makes me able to inhabit my world any better ... whereas I think BDSM perhaps does'.

Javelin is a switch who identifies as a sacred harlot, following a clear spiritual path that requires Javelin to educate others about kink, sex, gender and sexuality as well as spirituality. Javelin is a practitioner of spiritual BDSM and identifies as a pagan. However, paganism is not a religion to Javelin, but a spirituality which 'gives you the tools to change yourself'.

Kaz says if she has to label herself she chooses 'Domme' but overall she avoids labels because they imply restrictions on what she enjoys. She associates religion with man-made systems of belief and says these are 'not pure'; spirituality is pure because 'we don't control it'. While she values her kink greatly she feels meaningful is 'too deep' a term to apply to something that is 'just part of who I am' but this part of her identity is extremely important 'and it will always be who I am'.

Kris identifies as a top. He is married to a submissive but says that they do not play together as she had a Master before he discovered his own kinks. He does not feel he is religious because 'it's been a long time since I've been to church', and he does not see himself as spiritual either although this is 'a grey area'. He says BDSM gives his life 'a richness' that would otherwise be lacking.

Kyndyl does not give themself a specific kink label, saying they seem to be primarily sub but are unsure as they have played all roles. Kyndyl is a pagan who considers that 'my spirituality and BDSM are pretty much mixed together'. As well as more casual play Kyndyl engages in deliberately created kink ritual and says that 'for the primary deities I work with I would consider myself their property'.

Madeleine describes herself as a sadomasochist, as she enjoys playing with both giving and receiving pain. She says 'if I have any religion it is extremely private and idiosyncratic', and considers her kink to be an aspect of that 'in terms of a practice that gives your life meaning'. She considers herself less spiritual 'because I am so language-bound' whereas spirituality is 'more intuitive, more emotional ... not mitigated by law. And I mean law in the big sense, of the organised, structured world sense.'

Marie describes herself as both a submissive and a masochist, although she is less likely to use the latter term unless asked about it explicitly. She identifies as a Christian, and says she can be 'spiritual without being religious'. Marie feels that BDSM 'fulfils a need' in her life, but has not thought about the nature of that need because 'I'm somebody that doesn't question reasons very much at all'.

Matt identifies as a slave, although he did not have a Mistress at the time we spoke. He views both religion and spirituality as being focussed on things outside the world, and does not see himself this way. He describes kink as more 'carnal', as it derives from 'that human nature, that primal desire ... that I would equate to eating or sex. It's something that I need to find, something that drives me'.

M-Cat identifies as a Domme, and has done some professional work in that capacity. Her kink 'makes me feel powerful'. M-Cat is a Christian and, although she recognised spiritual possibilities in kink, was clear that she did not need to explore these because she already has her religion.

Michael describes himself as Dom in terms of his relationship to Molly, but says that if he plays with other people he is a top or a 'stunt-arm'. Michael has 'rather strong opinions about religion. Mostly that it is very bad for society in general and people specifically, outside of a very certain framework.' He sees spirituality as 'a separate thing' which is 'whatever makes that indefinable part of you sing and be happy' and says that 'you could say that the way [Molly and I] practice BDSM is spiritual between us, because it communicates the ineffable between us'.

Mistress Marina identifies as a Domme; she lives with a full-time slave and plays with other submissives. She describes herself as spiritual, saying that 'spirituality is ... an innate need in everybody ... we're all searching for it and finding it in different ways. Spirituality is a connection. To the divine, whatever you see [that] as. It doesn't have to be a thing or a person, it could be nature ... its feeling connected'. She feels BDSM is an aspect of this for her 'because of the feeling of wholeness, because of the feeling of almost ... separation from the physicality. Because of the feeling of power.'

Molly is a submissive in a committed D/s relationship with Michael. Molly says of religion, 'sadly, it means judging people. Based on your very narrow-minded view.' She also wants 'to reject' spirituality as a loaded term, but says she does have 'a deep, for want of a better word, spiritual life ... Through our relationship, through discovering things about myself that I love ... [sometimes] there's a kind of intense moment, a spiritual moment where you just ... that inner part of you just goes this is peace. This is perfect. For no other reason than it just is.' She says this is 'absolutely, absolutely' a quality of experience play can create.

Ms Lucy is a Domme; she has a committed relationship with a single slave and considers play an expression of that relationship. She considers spirituality to be 'the state of mind that is self-aware of the entire being: mind, body and soul ... and how we're all inter-connected'. Kink contributes to this for her because 'it's a tool that touches our spirituality, sexuality, physical pleasures, pain ... it allows us to be creative ... It's a gateway to feel emotionally connected.'

Nomad describes himself as a top who switches very occasionally, he is also a Tantra practitioner and sees substantial overlaps between what he does as Tantra and what he does as kink. He does not consider himself religious but says that 'spirituality is more about people. It's more about ... being with oneself' and he can relate to that term although whether he would use it 'depends on who I'm with!'. He says that BDSM 'can very much push you down that journey' towards understanding.

Oliver is a Dom, who says that he can be sadistic but has struggled with choosing that as a label. He regards spiritual activity as something pursued as an end in itself, and he cannot be spiritual as he has goals for what he does. He says that BDSM can be 'transformative for some people ... [and it's] helping me learn much more about myself ... BDSM has made me reassess the bits of my life that I wasn't happy with and helped me change.'

Paolo said that, at the time we met, he was 'undecided' about his kink identity and felt he would have to describe himself as a switch and a hedonist. Paolo says 'if I've got a religion at all it's Buddhism', but he feels he is on a personal spiritual journey of which kink is a part. Such a journey is spiritual in nature because it contributes to 'getting in touch with the universe'.

Penny identifies as a sub. She is also a little, at least in terms of her relationship with Piers. She is a Catholic but 'I don't go to Mass regularly'. She was fairly new to the kink scene at the time we met, but feels finding it has 'made me more confident. More accepting ... of how I was'.

Piers describes himself as a daddy, at least in terms of his relationship with Penny; he says he is 'a mirror for what my partner needs. I can even be a bottom, but that's rare.' He is a Christian and doesn't distinguish religion and spirituality. He says that he finds play liberating because 'when you are playing with someone the rest of the world doesn't matter'.

poppy is a lifestyle submissive in a committed D/s relationship with Barry. She doesn't distinguish religion and spirituality and identifies as a Christian. For poppy her personal relationship with God is the heart of her religion because 'for me religion has to have a head, a top, a dominant ... Because there has to be something that you can channel your needs to and your questions to – should I do this, or should I do this?' She sees the expression of her kink through play is fundamental to her well-being, without it 'I think I'd probably just explode'.

pussikin describes herself as submissive, but 'not service focussed ... more of a pet'. She also considers herself a masochist. She is a witch, and regards religion and spirituality as effectively the same; she considers her kink to be spiritual because 'it is the thing that helps me see the world as it is, and travel between worlds and such. If it is powerful – and we've been talking like it is – it is spiritual power.'

Rita says that she is a switch, although at the time we spoke she has only taken the bottom role in play. She is polyamorous and in a primary relationship with Friedrich. She says that religion is 'interesting, because everybody says that its god. But it's not really, is it? It's the following of. So, football can be a religion. Obviously God and church and stuff, but there's all the different ones. But I sort of, follow each of my religions.' This includes BDSM which helps to fulfil 'the need to feel connected'.

Rocks is a switch who says he mostly tops 'for practical reasons', as his regular partners prefer to bottom. He says religion 'seems to be a good way of starting an argument these days!' and spirituality 'is one of those words that has been bandied about to cover a multitude of feelings'. He doesn't feel 'particularly spiritual' but he can see why people choose that word to describe BDSM 'when the energy is right, when the feelings are right'. His kink 'means quite important things ... It's strengthening the relationship. It's the feelings of intensity ... From the canes to the floggers to the cuddling up afterwards, to the look in her eyes of "yes, you are my partner, you are important to me".'

Rosie identifies as a submissive and says her kink is 'very much a part of my identity and its very much emotional satisfaction'. She is not religious and is unsure about whether anything she does is spiritual, which she considers to be 'very much a self-defined kind of thing'.

Rudge describes himself as a switch, who tops men and subs to women. He is not religious, and sees spirituality as 'like a light religion. A slimline one.' His kink is important to him because 'it is so different to my normal life' and it enables him to learn new things, such as his ability to endure (and even like) things 'I thought I'd never handle at all'.

Shaun identifies as a Dom. He sees religion as 'a bunch of hogwash', involving doctrine and rules and spirituality 'as more of an individual's ability to think for themselves regarding faith and religion'. He says that spirituality 'makes you certain of what you are, and hopefully comfortable in what you are', but while BDSM does do these things for him thinking of it as spiritual practice 'just doesn't resonate with me'.

Simon/Effie identifies as a TV sub; when dressed he becomes Effie. He says 'being Effie, it's transforming. It allows me to be a kind of pretend woman and to be things that I can't express as a man'. He does not think of himself in terms of religion or spirituality but can see how BDSM might be described in those terms as 'it's out of the mundane; it's out of the ordinary. It's not just 9 to 5. It's not just feeding your face it's ... it's almost an icon isn't it? It becomes something very special.'

Stoney-face identifies as a collared switch; he has a Mistress, but when he plays with other people he does not always take the bottom role. Stoney-face is a shaman, and describes this as spirituality. His kink and shamanic identities are fully integrated and having come to understand this 'I can now practice a form of kink spiritual BDSM, a spiritual kink. That's how I play when I'm playing right with energy play, the kind of thing that incorporates more spiritual elements than just knowing how to hit somebody with a crop.'

Twisted is a switch within her relationship with Digi and together they have explored various kinks that they did not initially expect to enjoy. She says she has 'always detested religion' and has 'not really thought' about spirituality in relation to herself, but describes 'spiritual love' within their kink community where 'you're all in the same boat, and you all have the same kind of interests'.

Will is a switch who plays with CP and impact play. He is not religious and says 'I don't know what [spirituality] means ... I just think it's a bit silly'. He does think of his kink as meaningful, and says he can't think of a better word to describe it; it is 'extremely important ... it's part of who I am', and he says 'I think if it wasn't [meaningful] I wouldn't be doing it.'

References

Alison, L., Santtila, P., Sandnabba, N. K. and Nordling, N. 2001. Sadomasochistically Oriented Behavior: Diversity in Practice and Meaning. *Archives of Sexual Behavior*, 30, 1.
American Psychiatric Association. 2013. *Diagnostic and Statistical Manual of Mental Disorders: DSM-5-TR*. Washington, DC: American Psychiatric Association.
Ammerman, N. T. 2013. Spiritual But Not Religious? Beyond Binary Choices in the Study of Religion. *Journal for the Scientific Study of Religion*, 52, 258–278.
Argue, B. 2009. Bondage for People, Not Parcels. *In:* Harrington, L. and Rudel, R. A. (eds) *Rope, Bondage and Power*. Las Vegas, NV: The Nazca Plains Corporation.
Asad, T. 2000. Agency and Pain: An Exploration. *Culture and Religion: An Interdisciplinary Journal*, 1, 29–60.
Atkinson, Q. D. and Whitehouse, H. 2011. The Cultural Morphospace of Ritual Form: Examining Modes of Religiosity Cross-Culturally. *Evolution and Human Behaviour*, 32, 50–62.
Barcan, R. 2004. *Nudity, A Cultural Anatomy*. Oxford: Berg.
Bauer, R. 2014. *Queer BDSM Intimacies*. Basingstoke: Palgrave Macmillan.
Baumeister, R. F. 1988. Masochism as Escape from Self. *Journal of Sex Research*, 25, 28.
Baumeister, R. F. 1991. *Escaping the Self*, Basicbooks.
Beckmann, A. 2009. *The Social Construction of Sexuality and Perversion: Deconstructing Sadomasochism*. Basingstoke: Palgrave Macmillan.
Blessed_Harlot 2011. Anarchic Christian Submission. *In:* Kaldera, R. (ed.) *Sacred Power, Holy Surrender*. Hubbardston, MA: Alfred Press.
Blum, J. 2012. Radical Empiricism and the Unremarkable Nature of Mystic Ineffability. *Method and Theory in the Study of Religion*, 24, 201–219.
Boskey, E. 2013. Sexuality in the DSM 5. *Contemporary Sexuality*, 47, 1–5.
Bouissac, P. 2014. *Circus as Multi-Modal Discourse: Performance, Meaning and Ritual*. London: Bloomsbury.
Bourke, J. 2014. *The Story of Pain*. Oxford: Oxford University Press.
Bromley, D. 2007. On Spiritual Edgework: The Logic of Extreme Ritual Performances. *Journal for the Scientific Study of Religion*, 46, 287–303.

Buenting, J. 2003. Rehearsing Vulnerability: BDSM as Transformative Ritual. *Chicago Theological Seminary Register*, 93, 39-49.

Califia, P. 1994. *Public Sex: The Culture of Radical Sex*. San Francisco, CA: Cleis Press.

Carrette, J. R. 2005. Intense Exchange: Sadomasochism, Theology and the Politics of Late Capitalism. *Theology and Sexuality: The Journal of the Institute for the Study of Christianity and Sexuality*, 11, 11-30.

Charles, S. 2009. For a Humanism Amid Hypermodernity: From a Society of Knowledge to a Critical Knowledge of Society. *Axiomathes*, 19, 389-400.

Christina, G. 2013. Are We having Sex Now or What? *In:* Power, N., Halwani, R. and Soble, A. (eds) *The Philosophy of Sex*. Lanham, MD: Rowman & Littlefield Publishers.

Crocker, S. F. 1999. *A Well-Lived Life: Essays in Gestalt Therapy*. Gestalt Press.

Csikszentmihalyi, M. 2002. *Flow*. London: Rider.

Cusack, C. M. 2013. Play, Narrative and the Creation of Religion: Extending the Theoretical Base of 'Invented Religions'. *Culture and Religion*, 14, 362-377.

Desjarlis, R. 2012. The Background of Experience. *In:* McCutcheon, R. T. (ed.) *Religious Experience: A Reader*. Sheffield: Equinox.

Dominguez JR, I. 2004. *Beneath the Skins: The New Spirit and Politics of the Kink Community*. Los Angeles, NV: Daedalus Publishing.

Douglas, M. 1966. *Purity and Danger*. London: Routledge.

Driver, C. 2011. Embodying Hardcore: Rethinking 'Subcultural' Authenticities. *Journal of Youth Studies*, 14, 975-990.

Droogers, A. 2004. *Enjoying an Emerging Alternative World: Ritual in Its Own Ludic Right*. Oxford: Berghahn Books.

Droogers, A. 2014. *Religion at Play: A Manifesto*. Eugene, OR: Cascade Books.

Easton, D. and Hardy, J. 2004. *Radical Ecstacy: SM Journeys to Transcendence*. Greenery Press.

Ezzy, D. 2011. An Underworld Rite: A Pagan Re-enactment of Persephone's Descent into the Underworld. *Journal of Contemporary Religion*, 26, 245-259.

Ezzy, D. 2014. *Sex, Death and Witchcraft*. London: Bloomsbury.

Ezzy, D., Easthope, G. and Morgan, V. 2009. Ritual Dynamics: Mayor Making in Early Modern Norwich. *Journal of Historical Sociology*, 22, 396-419.

Favazza, A. 1996. *Bodies Under Seige: Self Mutilation and Body Modification in Culture and Psychiatry*. Baltimore, MD: The Johns Hopkins University Press.

Federman, M. 2004. What is the Meaning of the Medium is the Message? Retrieved from www.individual.utoronto.ca/markfederman/article_mediumisthe message.htm (accessed 23 March 2016).

Ferrell, J. 2005. The Only Possible Adventure: Edgework and Anarchy. *In:* Lyng, S. (ed.) *Edgework: The Sociology of Risk-Taking*. New York: Routledge.

Fitzgerald, T. 2000. *The Ideology of Religious Studies*. Oxford: Oxford University Press.

Foucault, M. 1978. *The Will to Knowledge: The History of Sexuality: 1*. London: Penguin.

Furey, C. M. 2012. *Body, Society, and Subjectivity in Religious Studies*. New York: Oxford University Press.
Glucklich, A. 2001. *Sacred Pain: Hurting the Body for the Sake of the Soul*. New York: Oxford University Press.
Greenberg, S. E. 2019. Divine Kink: A Consideration of the Evidence for BDSM as Spiritual Ritual. *International Journal of Transpersonal Studies*, 38.
Gregory, R. L. (ed.) 1987. *The Oxford Companion to the Mind*. Oxford: Oxford University Press.
Grimes, R. L. 2002. *Deeply Into the Bone*. Berkeley, CA, University of California Press.
Grimes, R. L. 2013. *Beginnings in Ritual Studies*. Createspace Independent Publishing Platform.
Haenfler, R. 2014. *Subcultures*. New York: Routledge.
Hall, E. L. 2010. What are Bodies for? An Integrative Examination of Embodiment. *Christian Scholar's Review*, 39, 159–175.
Handelman, D. 2005. Introduction: Why Ritual in its Own Right? *In:* Handelman, D. and Lindquist, G. (eds) *Ritual in its Own Right*. Oxford: Berghahn Books.
Harrington, B. 2006. The Many Paths of Earthly Bondage: Bondage as a Tool Towards Spiritual Release. *In:* Kaldera, R. (ed.) *Dark Moon Rising: Pagan BDSM and the Ordeal Path*. Hubbardston, MA: Asphodel Press.
Harrington, L. 2009. *Sacred Kink*. Mystic Productions.
Hart, L. 1998. *Between the Body and the Flesh: Performing Sadomasochism*. New York: Columbia University Press.
Harvey, G. 2013. *Food, Sex and Strangers*. Durham: Acumen.
Holmes, D., O'Byrne, P. and Gastaldo, D. 2006. Raw Sex as Limit Experience: A Foucauldian Analysis of Unsafe Anal Sex Between Men. *Social theory and Health*, 4, 319–333.
Houseman, M. 2005. The Red and The Black: A Practical Experiment for Thinking about Ritual. *In:* Handelman, D. and Lindquist, G. (eds) *Ritual in its Own Right*. Oxford: Berghahn Books.
Houseman, M. 2008. Relationality. *In:* Kreinath, J., Snoek, J. and Stausberg, M. (eds) *Theorising Rituals*. Leiden: Brill.
Houseman, M. and Severi, C. 1998. *Naven or the Other Self: A Relational Approach to Ritual Action*. Leiden: Brill.
Huizinga, J. 1950. *Homo Ludens: A Study of the Play-Element in Culture*. Martin Publishing.
International Association for the Study of Pain. 1976–77. Taxonomy. Retrieved from www.iasp-pain.org/Education/Content.aspx?ItemNumber=1698#Pain (accessed 19 February 2016).
Jenks, C. 2003. *Transgression*. New York: Routledge.
Kaldera, R. 2006. *Dark Moon Rising: Pagan BDSM and the Ordeal Path*. Hubbardston, MA: Asphodel Press.

Kaldera, R. 2010. Blood Run Down. *In:* Harrington, L. (ed.) *Spirit of Desire: Personal Explorations of Sacred Kink.* Mystic Productions.

Kapferer, B. 2005. Ritual Dynamics and Virtual Practice. *In:* Handelman, D. and Lindquist, G. (eds) *Ritual in its Own Right.* Oxford: Berghahn Books.

Khan, U. 2014. *Vicarious Kinks: S/M in the Socio-Legal Imaginary.* Toronto: University of Toronto Press.

Kraemer, C. H. 2014. *Eros and Touch from a Pagan Perspective.* New York: Routledge.

Krittika 2011. Arc and Covenant. *In:* Kaldera, R. (ed.) *Sacred Power, Holy Surrender.* Hubbardston, MA: Alfred Press.

LaMothe, K. L. 2008. What Bodies Know About Religion and the Study of it. *Journal of the American Academy of Religion,* 76, 573–601.

LaMothe, K. L. 2015. *Why We Dance: A Philosophy of Bodily Becoming.* New York: Columbia University Press.

Langdridge, D. 2005. Actively Dividing Selves: SM and the Thrill of Disintegration. *Lesbian and Gay Psychology Review,* 6, 198–208.

Langdridge, D. 2006. Voices From the Margins: Sadomasochism and Sexual Citizenship. *Citizenship Studies,* 10, 373–389.

Langdridge, D. and Barker, M. 2007. *Safe, Sane and Consensual: Contemporary Perspectives on Sadomasochism.* New York: Palgrave Macmillan.

Latour, B. 2010. *On the Modern Cult of the Factish Gods.* Durham, NC: Duke University Press.

Lindquist, G. 2005. Bringing the Soul Back to the Self: Soul Retrieval in Neo-shamanism. *In:* Handelman, D. and Lindquist, G. (eds) *Ritual in its Own Right.* Oxford: Berghahn Books.

Lipovetsky, G. and Charles, S. 2005. *Hypermodern Times.* Cambridge: Polity Press.

Love, B. 1992. *The Encyclopaedia of Unusual Sexual Practices.* London: Abacus.

Lowrey, S. 2010. Soul Stitiching. *In:* Harrington, L. (ed.) *Spirit of Desire: Personal Explorations of Sacred Kink.* ?: Mystic Productions.

Lunning, F. 2013. *Fetish Style.* London: Bloomsbury Academic.

Lyng, S. 1990. Edgework: A Social Psychological Analysis of Voluntary Risk Taking. *American Journal of Sociology,* 95, 851–886.

Lyng, S. 2005. Edgework and the Risk-Taking Experience. *In:* Lyng, S. (ed.) *Edgework: The Sociology of Risk-Taking.* New York: Routledge.

Lyng, S. 2012. Existential Transcendence in Late Modernity: Edgework and Hermeneutic Reflexivity. *Human Studies,* 35, 401–411.

MacDonald, M. 2006. Empire and Communication: The Media Wars of Marshall McLuhan. *Media, Culture and Society,* 28, 505–520.

MacKendrick, K. 1999. *Counterpleasures.* Albany, NY: State University of New York Press.

Master Dennis. 2010. The Sacred Role of the Provoker: There's a Coyote Within the Dance. *In:* Harrington, L. (ed.) *Spirit of Desire: Personal Explorations of Sacred Kink.* Mystic Productions.

Master K Ron. 2011. On Becoming More ... *In:* Kaldera, R. (ed.) *Sacred Power, Holy Surrender.* Hubbardston, MA: Alfred Press.

McGuire, M. 2007. Embodied Practices: Negotiation and Resistance. *In:* Ammerman, N. (ed.) *Everyday Religion.* Oxford University Press.

McGuire, M. B. 2008. *Lived Religion: Faith and Practice in Everyday Life.* Oxford: Oxford University Press.

McLuhan, M. 1964. *Understanding Media: The Extensions of Man.* New York: McGraw-Hill.

McWhorter, L. 2004. Rites of Passing: Foucault, Power and Same-Sex Commitment Ceremonies. *In:* Schilbrack, K. (ed.) *Thinking Through Rituals.* New York: Routledge.

Midori. 2005. *Wild Side of Sex: the Book of Kink.* Los Angeles, CA: Daedalus Publishing.

Miller, P. and Devon, M. 1995. *Screw the Roses, Send Me the Thorns: The Romance and Sexual Sorcery of Sadomasochism.* Fairfield, CT: Mystic Rose Books.

Minax, E. 2010. Managing Psychic Waste: Transcendence Through Humiliation. *In:* Harrington, L. (ed.) *Spirit of Desire: Personal Explorations of Sacred Kink.* ?:Mystic Productions.

Moberg, M. and Ramstedt, T. 2016. Recontextualising the Framework of *Scene* for the Empirical Study of Post-Institutional Religious Spaces in Practice. *Fieldwork in Religion*, 10, 155–172.

Moser, C. 1998. S/M (Sadomasochistic) Interactions in Semi-Public Settings. *Journal of Homosexuality*, 36, 19–29.

Moser, C. and Kleinplatz, P. J. 2006. Introduction: The State of Our Knowledge on SM. *Journal of Homosexuality*, 50, 1–15.

Musafar, F. 1989. Fakir Musafar. *In:* Vale, V. and Juno, A. (eds) *Modern Primitives.* San Francisco, CA: V/Search Publications.

Nagy, P. 2005. Religious Weeping as Ritual in the Medieval West. *In:* Handelman, D. and Lindquist, G. (eds) *Ritual in its Own Right.* Oxford: Berghahn Books.

Newmahr, S. 2008. Becoming a Sadomasochist: Integrating Self and Other in Ethnographic Analysis. *Journal of Contemporary Ethnography*, 37, 619–643.

Newmahr, S. 2010. Rethinking Kink: Sadomasochism as Serious Leisure. *Qualitative Sociology*, 33, 313–331.

Newmahr, S. 2011a. Chaos, Order and Collaboration: Toward a Feminist Conceptualization of Edgework. *Journal of Contemporary Ethnography*, 40, 682–712.

Newmahr, S. 2011b. *Playing on the Edge: Sadomasochism, Risk and Intimacy.* Bloomington, IN: Indiana University Press.

Nongbri, B. 2013. *Before Religion: A History of a Modern Concept.* New Haven, CT: Yale University Press.

Nye, M. 2000. Religion, Post-Religionism and Religioning: Religious Studies and Contemporary Cultural Debates. *Method and Theory in the Study of Religion*, 12, 447–476.

O'Connor, E. 2007. Embodied Knowledge in Glassblowing: the Experience of Meaning and the Struggle Towards Proficiency. *The Sociological Review*, 55, 126–141.

Orsi, R. A. 1997. Everyday Miracles : The Study of Lived Religion. *In:* Hall, D. D. (ed.) *Lived Religion in America: Toward a History of Practice.* Princeton, NJ: Princeton University Press.

Orsi, R. A. 2005. *Between Heaven and Earth: The Religious Worlds People Make and the Scholars Who Study Them.* Princeton, NJ: Princeton University Press.

Paasonen, S. 2018. *Many Splendored Things.* London: Goldsmiths Press.

Plante, R. F. 2006. Sexual Spanking, the Self, and the Construction of Deviance. *Journal of Homosexuality*, 50, 59–79.

Plate, S. B. 2010. Religion is Playing Games: Playing Video Gods, Playing to Play. *Religious Studies and Theology*, 29, 215–230.

Plummer, K. 2015. Before 'Spanner': A Sociologist Tries to Make Sense of 'Sado-masochism' in the 1970s. *Remembering Operation Spanner: Culture, Law, History and Crime.* Colchester: University of Essex.

Réage, P. 1985. *The Story of O.* London: Corgi Books.

Robertson, A. and Wildcroft, T. 2016. Sacrifices at the Altar of Self-Knowledge. *Body and Religion*, 1, 88–109.

Rudel, R. A. and Fairfield, M. J. 2014. *BDSM Mastery.* Austin, TX: Red Eight Ball Press.

Sanford, A. W. 2007. Pinned on Karma Rock: Whitewater Kayaking as Religious Experience. *Journal of the American Academy of Religion*, 75, 875–895.

Scarry, E. 1985. *The Body in Pain: The Making and Unmaking of the World.* New York: Oxford University Press.

Schechner, R. 1993. *The Future of Ritual: Writings on Culture and Performance.* New York: Routledge.

Scott, C. 2015. *Thinking Kink: The Collision of BDSM, Feminism and Popular Culture.* Jefferson, NC: McFarland and Company.

Seligman, A. B., Weller, R. P., Puett, M. J. and Simon, B. 2008. *Ritual and its Consequences.* New York: Oxford University Press.

Sheets-Johnstone, M. 2009a. Animation: the Fundamental, Essential and Properly Descriptive Concept. *Continental Philosophy Review*, 42, 375–400.

Sheets-Johnstone, M. 2009b. *The Corporeal Turn.* Exeter: Imprint Academic.

Sheets-Johnstone, M. 2012. Movement and Mirror Neurons: A Challenging and Choice Conversation. *Phenomenology and the Cognitive Sciences*, 11, 385–401.

Sheff, E. and Hammers, C. 2011. The Privilege of Perversities: Race, Class and Education Among Polyamorists and Kinksters. *Psychology and Sexuality*, 2, 198–223.

Sills, C., Lapworth, P. and Desmond, B. 2012. *An introduction to Gestalt.* Los Angeles, CA: Sage.

slave Rick. 2009. M/s Relationships as Vehicles for Salvation. *In:* Kaldera, R. (ed.) *Sacred Power, Holy Surrender.* Hubbardston, MA: Alfred Press.

Smith, J. Z. 1982. *Imagining Religion: From Babylon to Jonestown*. Chicago, IL: Universty of Chicago Press.
Snyder, S. 2007. New Streams of Religion: Fly Fishing as a Lived, Religion of Nature. *Journal of the American Academy of Religion*, 75, 896–922.
Soja, E. W. 1996. *Thirdspace: Journeys to Los Angeles and Other Real-and-Imagined Places*. Oxford: Blackwell Publishing.
Stockwell, F. M. J., Walker, D. J. and Eshleman, J. W. 2010. Measures of Implicit and Explicit Attitudes Towards Mainstream and BDSM Sexual Terms Using the IRAP and Questionnaire with BDSM/Fetish and Student Participants. *Psychological Record*, 60, 307–324.
Suchet, M. 2009. The 21st Century Body: Introduction. *Studies in Gender and Sexuality*, 10, 113–118.
Tanos. 2003. BDSM. Retrieved from www.urbandictionary.com/define.php?term=BDSM (accessed 4 June 2016).
Taves, A. 2009. *Religious Experience Reconsidered*. Princeton, NJ: Princeton University Press.
Taves, A. and Bender, C. 2012. Introduction: Things of Value. *In:* Taves, A. and Bender, C. (eds) *What Matters? Ethnographies of Value in a Not So Secular Age*. New York: Columbia University Press.
Taylor, B. 2007. Surfing into Spirituality and a New, Aquatic Nature Religion. *Journal of the American Academy of Religion*, 75, 923–951.
Taylor, C. 2003. *Varieties of Religion Today: William James Revisited*. Cambridge, MA: Harvard University Press.
Taylor, G. W. and Ussher, J. M. 2001. Making Sense of S&M: A Discourse Analytic Account. *Sexualities*, 4, 293.
Thompson, M. (ed.) 1991. *Leatherfolk: Radical Sex, people, Politics and Practice*. Los Angeles, CA: Daedalus Publishing.
Tupper, P. 2018. *A Lover's Pinch: A Cultural History of Sadomasochism*. Lanham, MD: Rowman and Littlefield.
Turner, V. 2008. *The Ritual Process*. New Brunswick, NJ: Aldine Transaction.
Varga, I. 2005. The Body: The New Sacred? The Body in Hypermodernity. *Current Sociology*, 53, 209–235.
Vásquez, M. A. 2011. *More Than Belief: A Materialist Theory of Religion*. Oxford: Oxford University Press.
Weille, K. L. H. 2002. The Psychodynamics of Consensual Sadomasochistic and Dominant-Submissive Sexual Games. *Studies in Gender and Sexuality*, 3, 131–160.
Weinberg, M. S., Williams, C. J. and Moser, C. 1984. The Social Constituents of Sadomasochism. *Social Problems*, 31, 379–389.
Weinberg, T. 2006. Sadomasochism and the Social Sciences: A Review of the Sociological and Social Psychological Literature. *In:* Kleinplatz, P. J. and Moser, C. (eds) *Sadomasochism: Powerful Pleasures*. New York: Harrington Park Press.

Weiss, M. 2011. *Techniques of Pleasure: BDSM and the Circuits of Sexuality*. Durham, NC: Duke University Press.

Westerfelhaus, R. G. 2007. The Spirituality of Sex and the Sexuality of the Spirit: BDSM Erotic Play as Soulwork and Social Critique. *In:* Lovaas, K. E. and Jenkins, M. M. (eds) *Sexualities and Communication in Everyday Life*. Thousand Oaks, CA: Sage Publications.

Whitehouse, H. and Lanman, J. A. 2014. The Ties That Bind Us: Ritual, Fusion and Identification. *Current Anthropology*, 55, 674–695.

Widdicombe, S. and Wooffitt, R. 1990. 'Being' versus 'Doing' Punk: On Acheiving Authenticity as a Member. *Journal of Language and Social Psychology*, 9, 257–277.

Williams, D. J., Thomas, J. N., Prior, E. E. and Christensen, M. C. 2014. From 'SSC' and 'RACK' to the '4Cs': Introducing a New Framework for Negotiating BDSM Participation. *Electronic Journal of Human Sexuality*, 17.

Williams, M. 2010. Another Dead Nigger. *In:* Harrington, L. (ed.) *Spirit of Desire: Personal Explorations of Sacred Kink*. Mystic Productions.

Winge, T., M. 2012. *Body Style*. London: Berg.

Wiseman, J. 1996. *SM 101: A Realistic Introduction*. Greenery Press.

World Health Organization. 2016. International Statistical Classification of Diseases and Related Health Problems, 10th Revision (ICD-10). Retrieved from http://apps.who.int/classifications/icd10/browse/2016/en (accessed 25 April 2015).

Xygalatas, D., Mitkidis, P., Fischer, R., Reddish, P., Skewes, J., Geertz, A. W., Roepstorff, A. and Bulbulia, J. 2013. Extreme Rituals Promote Prosociality. *Psychological Science (Sage Publications Inc.)*, 24, 1602–1605.

Index

ABH 102
abusive 52, 135, 183
adult 43, 60
aesthetics 85–88, 90, 97, 104, 125
aftercare 24, 52, 71, 117, 175
age-play 20, 33, 141
altered consciousness 7, 35, 41, 55, 72, 73, 94, 142,
ambiguity 6, 112, 115, 134, 151
Ammerman, N. 8
analogy 57, 64, 67, 75, 159, 171
arousal 5, 6, 21, 27, 28
Asad 121
as-if world 152, 164, 177
assault 20
authenticity 12, 51, 84, 85, 88, 96, 104, 106, 107, 152

Barcan, R. 100, 101
Bauer, R. 9, 132, 133, 135–37, 144, 146, 147
BDSM
  as commodity 96-97, 100
  as edgework 138, 140 141, 144,
  as gestalt 6,7, 59, 107, 113, 177, 178, 179, 182–84
  as ritual 154, 157, 158, 160, 163
  as sex 23-28, 56
  as transgression 131, 133,134,136
  concept of 14-17, 20-22, 31, 32, 42, 43

community 18
experience 61-62, 80, 94, 96,106, 128, 129, 150, 174, 180
intimacy 127, 147
lifestyle 48, 49
relationship 31, 56,
as transcendent 63, 73
beauty 80, 87, 88, 98, 102, 118, 159. 183, 184
Beckmann, A. 16, 41, 63, 65, 66, 73, 74
belief 3, 148, 153, 162–163, 174
belonging 96, 98, 125
betrayal 53, 57, 142
blood 75, 102, 107, 108, 116, 125, 126, 139, 142, 150
bodies 12, 17, 28, 62, 100, 102
  body image 87, 88, 101, 118
  body modification 18, 125
  marked bodies 81, 102, 103, 127
  relational bodies 33, 80, 81, 82, 99, 103, 126
bondage 2, 15, 26, 32, 33, 47182, 55, 92, 94, 110
bottom 30, 31, 46, 50, 51, 53, 55, 56, 59, 96, 98, 108, 110, 114, 121, 146, 156, 158, 172
boundaries 25, 41, 45, 52, 53, 61, 81, 94, 105, 128, 130, 133, 136, 139, 142–44, 147, 150, 153, 160, 164, 173, 180, 185

boundary blurring 151, 181–182
boundary-breaking 136
brain 75, 118, 120, 123, 128, 145, 149, 162, 182
Bromley, D. 131, 147–49, 165
bruising 47, 102, 116, 121, 124, 127, 130, 179
bubble 54, 55, 57, 61–63, 66, 68, 185

Califia, P. 84, 85
Carrette, J. 97
category 3–5, 8, 11, 16, 17, 19, 23, 45, 73, 137, 139, 143, 154, 162, 180, 181
capitalist commodity exchange 97
choice 8, 11, 15–17, 29, 33, 41, 42, 44, 77, 81, 82, 84, 85, 88, 96, 104, 134, 181
co-constructed 33, 55, 59
collar 82, 100, 102–4
   collared 103, 156
   collaring 104
communication 43, 53, 62, 84, 168
community 9, 12, 16–19, 22, 30, 79, 84, 97, 128, 150, 153, 158, 164, 175, 180, 186
   of consumption 95, 96
conform 82, 89, 181
conscious 55, 69, 70, 73, 89, 113, 118, 138, 158, 171
consensual 20, 21, 134, 141, 150
   consensual non-consent 141
   consent 2, 51, 52, 61, 137, 152, 166
construction 21, 55, 59, 63, 80, 148, 153, 160, 164
corporal punishment 14, 18, 19, 33, 87
   belts 34, 51, 120
   canes 23, 34, 47, 78, 82, 108, 110, 112, 114, 116-18, 123, 127, 135, 140
   caning 61, 116, 117, 122, 140

crop 34
flogging 33, 34, 45–47, 55, 61, 98, 108, 114, 119, 121, 127, 169, 170
paddles 47, 121
spanking 6, 38, 45, 54, 55, 64, 89, 134, 140, 166, 169, 172
whipping 24, 34, 82, 95, 106
corset 36, 85, 86, 90–92, 94, 96
costume 51, 81, 96, 97
counterpleasures 128
counterrealities 153
criminal 21, 41, 52, 135
   criminalised 82, 133
   criminality 102, 133
cultural imaginary 89
cutting 35, 37, 61, 102, 107, 125, 126, 139, 144, 146, 150, 167

dance 43, 45, 63, 113, 117, 129, 131
danger 52, 143, 148
dangerous 85, 133, 134, 143–45, 154, 165
deviant 20, 101, 131
discipline 14, 20, 39, 48, 49
discomfort 110, 138
doing
   and being 56, 88, 104–6
   and loving 25
   BDSM 17, 19, 40, 42, 49, 52, 80, 107
Dom 14, 29, 47, 56, 64, 78, 102, 144, 155
dominance 14, 16, 26, 78, 128
dominant 20, 29, 31, 49, 52, 102, 103, 148, 155, 156, 158
Dominatrix 89
Domme 14, 29, 168
Dom-space 73, 74, 77, 78, 158, 171
dress code 86, 89, 95, 101
D/s 14, 16, 17, 20, 24, 31, 40, 49, 50, 104, 135,
DSM-V 133, 134

edge-play 33, 139–43, 147, 149, 150
edges 53, 130-151, 175-176, 182
   emotional 143
   physical 139, 142, 143
   psychological 141, 143
   of morality 142
edgework 139, 142–44, 147–49, 154
edgeworkers 143, 144, 148, 149
edgy 86, 90, 128, 139–41, 159
electricity 57, 138, 149
   e-stim 37
   electro-play 37, 139
   violet wand 46, 57, 102, 108, 138
emotion 22, 25, 29, 32, 44, 46, 55, 81, 100, 113, 120, 122, 125–26, 128, 131, 143, 145–47, 172, 178, 185
   emotional rituals 154
   emotional satisfaction 44
empowerment 138, 148, 149, 163, 173
enactment 21, 153, 176–78
endorphins 36, 64, 123, 126, 162
energy 63, 71, 72, 78, 106, 107, 111, 132, 137, 155, 160–62
enjoyment 18, 32, 36, 39, 43–44, 46, 51, 55–56, 68, 72, 74, 78, 89–90, 107, 121, 123, 126, 132–135, 137, 144, 146, 161, 170, 175
erotic 14, 26, 86, 87, 144
euphoria 78
expense 90, 95, 97, 98, 100
experience
   altered consciousness, transcendence 66, 73, 74, 75, 77, 78, 156, 158, 159
   description 62, 115-118
   gestalt 5, 6, 70, 129, 176, 180, 186
   indescribability 7, 33, 63, 64, 114, 119, 128
   intimate, relational, shared 93, 99, 132, 147, 169
   multi-sensory 12, 88, 89, 90–92, 94, 106–08, 110, 111, 113, 129

   of pain 120, 121, 123, 124
   reality 146, 165
   value of 43, 50, 97, 98, 136, 139, 153, 162, 165, 174, 180, 181, 183, 185
Ezzy, D. 7, 94, 131, 138, 154, 165, 169, 171–73

fantasy 21, 41, 50, 51, 135
fashion 81, 82, 84–86, 88, 90, 91, 101
fear 46, 117, 126, 138, 139, 142, 143, 145, 146, 168, 173–75
fetish 17, 30, 92–96, 98, 100, 141
   fashion, look 84–86, 89, 90, 101
Fetlife 9, 29
fire 139, 149
floating 34, 66, 73–75
flow-state 64, 171, 172
Foucault, M. 26, 28, 81
fun 5, 34, 44, 48, 137, 156

gag 141
games 37, 44, 50, 61, 152
genitals 14, 24, 25, 47, 157, 163
gestalt 40, 41, 44, 59, 79–81, 104, 105, 107, 112, 119, 129, 130, 132, 153, 154, 161, 175–83, 185, 186
   concept of 4–8, 10, 107,
Glucklich, A. 124
god 23, 147
Grimes, R. 43, 44, 153, 160, 164–65, 174, 177, 185

harm 20, 46, 134, 142
headspace 68, 122, 155, 182
hit 29, 70, 72, 78, 134, 170
hooks 108, 123, 139–40, 156, 159–60
hook-suspension 148
human 5, 26, 27, 41, 43, 99, 101, 111, 113, 117, 124, 147, 148, 156, 165, 172, 177, 180, 184
humiliation 14, 34, 122, 150, 174
hurt 38, 75, 119, 134, 147, 174

hyper-awareness 66–67, 69 158
hypermodernity 12, 81–82, 96–97, 104, 106, 128
hyper-reality 142

ICD-10 133
identity 3–4, 6, 8–10, 17, 19, 26, 43, 44, 79, 125, 127, 133, 135, 155, 158, 160, 164, 180–83
  performance of 43, 79, 81–82, 160, 180, 183
image 46, 65, 87, 88, 94, 96, 99
imaginal 153
immersion 12, 41, 66, 68, 73, 80, 98, 110–11, 131–32, 160, 166
immobility 75, 110, 174
impact 34, 46, 47, 108, 114, 116, 117, 126, 127
individualism 81, 96
individuality 81, 133, 135
ineffability 7, 73, 176
injury 102, 116
insanity 101, 131, 139, 143
intimacy 11, 21, 25, 38, 59, 61, 94, 99, 101, 102, 108, 112, 125–26, 127, 129, 131–32, 141, 143, 146, 147, 175–76

Jenks, C. 133
journey 78, 126, 131, 144, 155, 158, 165, 166, 183
joy 55, 71, 100, 117, 121, 135, 144, 165, 169
judgements, the Spanner case 21, 26

kinaesthetic 2, 92, 108, 111, 129
kink 16, 17, 128, 135, 136, 138
  concept 19, 24–28
  consumer 97–99
  gestalt 6–7, 8, 119, 154, 178–86
  identity 43, 51, 79, 85, 100, 104, 105, 135, 155

  Scene, community, world 18, 50, 84, 85, 105, 121, 130, 131, 150
kinks 16, 17, 22, 23, 32–34, 80, 81, 154
kinksters 29, 40, 42, 52, 104, 106, 160
kink style 81, 84, 91, 104
  aesthetic 85
  bondage trousers 88
  catsuit 92, 93
  clothing 89–91, 94, 103
  corsetry 84, 103, 144
  PVC 87, 89
kinky 82, 85, 86, 104, 105, 180
  people 4, 15, 27, 34, 84, 96, 98, 106, 120, 128, 135, 137, 181
  sex 24, 56

labels 3, 4, 8, 17, 18, 29–30, 42, 61, 98, 114, 120, 121, 129, 133–35, 151, 162, 183
LaMothe, K. 111–14, 116, 128, 129, 153, 170–72
Langdridge, D. 23, 27, 149, 173
  and Barker, M. 26, 133
latex 84, 86, 88, 90, 92–94, 96, 103
Latour, B. 163
law 11, 52
law lords 21
legal 20, 26, 53, 103, 134
leisure 5, 97, 181
lifestyle 9, 11, 20, 29, 47–50, 52, 82, 85, 99, 102, 103, 155, 156, 166
liminality 94, 142, 158, 160, 177
liminal spaces 40, 131, 149, 165
limits 9, 12, 25, 26, 34, 42, 45, 47, 52, 53, 61, 94, 108, 127, 128, 130, 132, 133, 137–44, 149–50, 152, 154, 166, 167, 173, 175
  ethical 137
  physical 42, 152, 159
  pushing 127, 138
lived experience 3, 114, 115, 124
lived religion 5, 7, 44, 201–3

love   17, 23, 26, 39, 56, 97, 122, 127
Lyng, S.   131, 139, 142, 143, 147, 154

Mackendrick, K.   84, 117, 128
mainstream   33, 39, 80, 84, 85, 104, 131, 140, 149
marks   46, 81, 82, 101, 102, 103, 108, 116, 120–21, 123, 125–27
masochism   2, 14, 16, 119, 120
masochists   121, 123, 124, 133–35, 175
Master   14, 16, 29, 37, 48, 49, 77, 100, 141, 143, 166, 169, 174, 175
McGuire, M.   5, 44, 182
McLuhan, M.   12
meaning   4, 6, 8, 79, 97, 100, 102, 104, 127, 129, 132, 133, 163, 174, 180, 182
meaningfulness   6, 7, 8, 81, 121, 133, 151, 160, 182
meaning-making   41, 81, 105, 124
medical   21, 26, 120, 133, 135, 140, 157, 167, 168
medium as the message   12, 107, 153
memory   62, 63, 115, 164, 185
mind-fucking   146
mirror   68, 86, 87, 88, 126, 127
Mistress   16, 156
modernity   12, 81, 99, 162
Moser, C.   116, 133
    and Kleinplatz, P.   133
movement   15, 91, 92, 96, 108, 111–13, 115, 119, 129, 153, 170–72, 186
mutual pleasure   21, 33, 44, 134
mutual trust   52, 53

nakedness   24, 80, 96, 100, 101
naming   4, 33, 61, 154, 160
needle-play   33, 61, 139, 144
needles   36, 82, 140, 141, 149
negative   25, 121, 134, 146, 150, 156, 161
negotiating   130, 137, 143, 164, 168

negotiation   45, 61, 141, 143, 144, 164, 166, 167
Newmahr, S.   6, 9, 16, 21–28, 43, 51, 56, 88, 96–98, 106, 128, 131, 132, 139–44, 147, 153, 161
non-consensual violence   20
non-consent   137
non-sexual   26, 27
norms   12, 18, 53, 81, 82, 84, 98, 100, 105, 112, 133, 135, 154
nudity   25, 82, 97, 101
Nye, M.   4, 164

obscenity   132
Offences Against the Person Act   102
orgasm   25, 116
Orsi, R.   5, 44, 177
other-where   55, 152, 153, 158–60

paganism   155, 157, 173
pain   2, 14, 21, 22, 26, 30, 32, 34, 36, 37, 46–48, 69, 70, 74, 75, 90, 107, 116–17, 119–25, 128, 134, 135, 138, 142, 146, 150–52, 173–75, 184, 185
paradox   148, 151, 156, 173
pathology   24, 26, 120, 149
peak   11, 41, 60, 72–74, 77, 78, 79 116, 124, 172, 175
penetration   24, 25, 142
penis   25, 36, 57, 107
performance   17, 55, 97, 125, 129, 132, 154, 155, 157, 160, 171, 174, 177
    art   159
    embodied   131, 138
    of identity   11, 43, 51, 81, 82, 88, 104, 160, 164, 183
    of relationship   11, 49, 59, 125, 153, 164, 176
    social   133
persona   50, 86, 104

perversity 147
pervertables 98, 99
physicality 87, 88, 148
physical risk 140–42, 144
physical sensation 25, 32, 33, 46, 112, 114, 123
piercing 85, 157
planning 113, 166, 168, 169
play
   as religioning 42, 61, 128, 147, 151, 181
   co-constructed, relational 19, 55, 56, 57, 59, 71, 72, 94, 99, 125, 127, 145, 146, 149, 166, 169, 171, 172, 175, 176
   gestalt 40, 41, 79, 107, 129, 154, 161, 178, 180, 183
   nature of 17, 20, 24–29, 33, 43, 44, 48, 49
   negotiations 45, 52, 130, 137, 138, 166
   play-date 166, 167, 169
   play-party 166
   processes 11, 55, 57, 59, 60, 65, 107, 112–114, 129, 152, 159, 165
   public 68, 86, 96, 101, 110
   serious, non-trivial 2, 41, 43, 50, 152, 153, 154, 161, 164, 173, 176, 177, 183
   transition into 48, 49, 54, 103, 104, 166
   transition out of 76–77, 142
playfulness 42, 50, 153
Playspace 101
play-spaces 11, 40, 41, 43, 45, 47, 49, 50–56 57, 59–69, 63, 65, 67, 69, 71–75, 77–80, 91, 94, 100, 101, 102, 103, 105, 110, 111, 130–32, 136, 153, 154, 157–60, 165, 166, 168, 169, 174, 176, 177, 185
pleasure 20, 21, 22, 24, 25, 28, 33, 44, 45, 71, 74, 97, 98, 100, 120–23, 127, 128, 129, 134, 135, 136, 137, 144, 145, 173, 180, 183
pleasure-pain 47, 117, 120, 121
popular culture 84, 85
power 22,
   resistance 26
   power-exchange 14, 16, 20, 21, 29, 30, 48, 49, 101
   powerlessness 176
   unequal distribution 21, 29, 52, 53, 152, 176
powerful 7, 12, 32, 47, 59, 71, 82, 95, 100, 101, 119, 124, 131, 132, 134, 163, 180
prosecution 41, 135
psychological damage 24
psychopathology 26, 52, 133
punishment 34, 39, 48

rape 147, 150
rational 60, 125, 127, 128, 173
real-and-imagined 62, 80, 117, 118
realities 33, 41, 61, 162, 174
real-world 9, 40, 137
relationality 11, 22, 33, 81, 93, 94, 96, 97 106, 111, 124, 127, 164, 170, 173, 176
relationship 2, 3, 6, 9, 10, 11, 12, 16, 17, 18, 20, 25, 29–31, 40, 43, 45, 48–50, 53, 56, 57, 59, 61, 62, 71, 79, 80, 81, 91, 94, 101–4, 107, 112, 125–27, 129, 131, 135, 141, 144, 150, 152, 155, 156, 158, 166, 169, 175, 176, 177, 181
release 5, 37, 44, 71
religion 2–5, 7–9, 14, 20, 22, 23, 28, 41, 44, 49, 50, 61, 147, 148, 154–58, 161–64, 178, 179, 181–83, 185, 186
religioning 1, 3–5, 7–9, 11–13, 41, 42, 44, 61, 72, 79, 81, 112, 116, 151, 161, 163, 174, 177–81, 186

religiosity 8, 177
religious 2–4, 8, 9, 13, 49, 60, 72, 73, 152, 154–57, 163, 164, 177, 180, 181, 185, 186
  religious experience 73, 180
resistance 26, 91, 94, 97, 98, 108, 134
rhythm 34, 46, 116, 170
risk 20, 21, 24, 25, 41, 42, 50, 66, 67, 96, 110, 116, 131, 132, 134, 139–42, 144, 146, 147, 149
  emotional harm 142
  risk-taking 139, 141, 144
  risk-trust cycle 142
rites 27, 158, 160, 164, 174, 180, 186
ritual 12, 27, 53, 54, 60, 61, 91, 94, 103, 138, 148, 181, 185
  ritual-space 153, 157–59
ritualisation 100, 160
ritualising 12, 44, 130, 152–78, 186
role-play 14, 44, 50, 51, 141, 174
rupture 127, 128, 131

sacred 32, 152, 156, 180
sacrifice 123, 124, 155, 184
sadism 2, 14, 16, 22, 119, 134
sadist 30, 37, 121, 133–35, 137
sadomasochism 16, 18, 25, 26, 27, 30, 48, 119
sadomasochist 26, 30
safe 26, 32, 46, 66–68, 70, 139, 149, 152, 158, 167
safe-word 37, 45, 48, 52, 53, 66, 75, 108, 146
sane 26, 101, 131, 139, 141, 143
Scarry, E. 124
Scene, the 35, 80, 84, 85, 95, 96, 97, 98, 102, 105, 119, 123, 128, 131, 154, 158
scene, a (session)
  construction of 45–47, 50, 55, 160, 168, 171–73,
  experience of 51, 108, 113, 114, 149, 185
Schechner, R. 41, 60, 61, 153, 165
school 38, 39, 51, 87, 88
self
  awareness 143, 144
  bondage 33
  discovery 149, 156
  exploration 42 147
  knowledge 55, 131, 132, 184
  self-world- and story- making 81, 105, 178, 179
  sense of 6, 65, 78, 112, 142, 170
  and other 3, 53, 60, 78, 120, 131, 134, 173
  self-voyeur 68
  understanding 3, 5, 12 17, 81, 173, 180, 182
sensation 22, 25, 29, 30, 32, 33, 34,45–47, 51, 64, 65, 70, 71, 94, 96, 97, 98, 108, 116, 119, 120, 121, 122–25, 128, 149, 158, 162, 167, 172, 183, 185
  and response 11, 112, 113, 114, 159, 170
  intrusive 110, 114
serial-killer 37, 38, 66, 146, 149
serious leisure 43, 97, 98
serious play 50, 152, 153, 177
sex 11, 16, 23–28, 56, 97, 111, 157, 183
sexual 5, 6, 10, 16, 21, 23, 24, 25–28, 33, 42, 48, 56, 57, 81, 84, 97, 123, 135
  sexuality 26–28
shaman 148, 155, 156, 158
Shamanic journeying 159
Sheets-Johnstone, M. 89, 107, 111, 112, 114, 115, 119, 129
skill 43, 68, 91, 95, 97, 98, 114, 116, 141143, 144, 153, 154, 158, 159, 170, 171

skin 46, 47, 49, 81, 82, 85, 89, 90, 93, 94, 102, 108–10, 116, 117, 120, 121, 125, 126, 140, 159, 174
  skin-tight 92, 94, 174
slave 14, 16, 22, 29, 48, 96, 106, 152
society 12, 81, 84, 85, 96, 100, 111, 133, 136
somatic 88, 106, 115, 124, 128, 129, 138, 151, 173, 175, 178, 181, 185
soul 44, 71, 150, 173, 179
space 9, 11, 17, 24, 40, 53–55, 60, 61, 62, 70, 80, 82, 89, 90, 94, 98, 101, 107, 112, 115, 123, 131, 142, 147, 149, 152–54, 160, 164, 165, 169, 172, 173, 178
spacing 34, 36, 72, 73, 74, 75, 77, 79, 114
Spanner case 20, 26, 102
specialness 8, 178, 186
spiritual 8, 11, 17, 44, 60, 73, 79, 81, 96, 124, 147, 148, 150, 152, 155–60, 164
spirituality 7–9, 14, 28, 147, 155, 161, 165, 183
stimulation 14, 21, 25, 49, 98
story-making 3, 6, 7, 10, 105
style 12, 81, 82, 84, 91, 92, 95, 98, 104
subculture 12, 107, 124, 13, 153
submission 14, 16, 26, 33, 35, 36, 49, 52, 123, 134, 135, 141
submissive 14, 20, 29, 31, 47, 48, 49, 52, 57, 64, 78, 102–4, 115, 118, 126, 134, 143, 150, 155, 156 158
submitting 36, 37, 52, 122, 137, 148, 156, 167
sub-space 72–79, 113, 116, 126, 134, 158, 159, 183
suspension 50, 94, 108
switch 4, 29, 70, 75, 121, 143, 156
symbolism 6, 12, 21, 107, 127, 149, 153, 157, 163, 174
symbol-making 119, 129

Taves, A. 5, 8, 60
technique 20, 35, 57, 78, 114, 128 129, 171
Thirdspace 62, 115
tied 24, 29, 33, 35, 37, 175, 181
top 30, 31, 50, 51, 53, 55, 59, 66, 67, 70, 75, 77, 79, 89, 97, 101, 103, 113 114, 116, 134, 150, 167, 168, 171, 172, 175
topping 65, 66, 70, 78, 134, 170, 184
topping-from-the-bottom 30, 52
top-space 78
touch 37, 39, 57, 93, 94, 102, 126, 128, 132, 137, 141, 142, 170, 174
transcendence 11, 41, 73, 128, 131, 148, 158, 162
transcendental states 63, 65, 73
transcendent power 147–49, 178
transgression 12, 25, 27, 33, 41, 61, 81, 82, 105, 131–34, 135, 136
trust 12, 25, 52, 53, 57, 59–61, 75, 135, 137, 141–45, 149, 175, 176

uniform 84, 87–89

value 4–6, 8, 81, 82, 97, 100, 107, 119, 127, 132, 139, 152, 161, 162, 174, 178, 180
values 81, 82, 84, 105, 120, 121, 133, 164
vanilla 29, 102, 131, 144, 176, 183
violation 100, 104, 132, 143, 145
violence 20, 21, 45
violet wand 46, 57, 102, 108, 138
vulnerability 20, 22, 75, 101, 130, 132, 152, 175

Weille, K. 16, 21, 53
Weiss, M. 16, 18, 20, 21, 26, 84, 85, 96–98, 128, 133
WIIWD 19

Winge, T. 81, 82, 84
world
    different, other 12, 144, 53, 54, 57, 62-67, 82, 94, 110, 129, 151, 160, 164, 176

everyday, ordinary 40, 42, 53, 72, 94, 105, 11, 148
real 9, 40, 137
world-making 3, 6, 7, 41 ,72, 81, 105, 131 154, 173, 175, 178, 179

www.ingramcontent.com/pod-product-compliance
Lightning Source LLC
Chambersburg PA
CBHW062027220426
43662CB00010B/1503